Tyranny of the Textbook

Tyranny of the Textbook

An Insider Exposes
How Educational Materials
Undermine Reforms

Beverlee Jobrack

ROWMAN & LITTLEFIELD PUBLISHERS, INC.
Lanham • Boulder • New York • Toronto • Plymouth, UK

Published by Rowman & Littlefield Publishers, Inc.
A wholly owned subsidiary of The Rowman & Littlefield Publishing Group, Inc.
4501 Forbes Boulevard, Suite 200, Lanham, Maryland 20706
www.rowmanlittlefield.com

Estover Road, Plymouth PL6 7PY, United Kingdom

British Library Cataloguing in Publication Information Available

Library of Congress Cataloging-in-Publication Data
Jobrack, Beverlee.
 Tyranny of the textbook : an insider exposes how educational materials undermine reforms / Beverlee Jobrack.
   p. cm.
 Includes bibliographical references and index.
 ISBN 978-1-4422-1141-4 (hardback) — ISBN 978-1-4422-1143-8 (electronic)
 1. Textbooks—United States. 2. Textbooks—Publishing—United States. 3. Textbook bias—United States. 4. Curriculum planning—United States. 5. Educational change—United States. 6. Education and state—United States. I. Title.
 LB3047.J64 2011
 371.3'2—dc23
                                                                    2011039071

∞™ The paper used in this publication meets the minimum requirements of American National Standard for Information Sciences—Permanence of Paper for Printed Library Materials, ANSI/NISO Z39.48-1992.

Printed in the United States of America

*To all my teachers, including my parents,
my siblings, my children, and
most of all my husband, Stewart,
with whom I've learned about
enduring loyalty, love, and
realizing your dreams*

Contents

Acknowledgments

I owe thanks to the many people who informed my understanding of education, including my teachers, administrators, students, and colleagues in educational publishing.

I am deeply indebted to my editor, Patti Belcher, and the following people who carefully reviewed my manuscript from their different points of view and provided intelligent and constructive criticism, which helped me correct mistakes, address unanswered questions, and develop my arguments.

Tamera Bryant
Diana Butts
Ruth Cochrane
Alice Dixon
John Geiger
Grant Kearns
Stuart Lazarus
Fran Lehr
Thomas McCain
Lynda Pearce
William D. Pflaum
Carol V. Rubin
Shane Spicer
Sally Whiting
Stephen S. Willoughby

My deepest thanks goes to my husband, Stewart Jobrack, who continually encouraged my efforts to produce this work. His love and support have always given me the courage and freedom to pursue my dreams.

Introduction

Newspapers and the media are full of information about educational reform and improvement: adequate yearly progress for schools, teacher performance, professional development, higher educational standards, parental involvement, school funding, and meeting individual needs. Improving education and student achievement is not an easy task. It involves teachers, administrators, educational research, publishers, the free market, and business principles.

Notably, and disturbingly, with all the attention paid to educational reform, there has been little, if any, focus on curriculum as part of the problem and how it might impact educational reform. Curriculum, for the purposes of this book, is defined as the teaching, learning, and assessment activities and materials that are organized and available to teach a given subject area. In other words, curriculum is the substance of what is taught. Curriculum involves educational, instructional materials, whether they be printed textbooks, workbooks, hands-on experiences, practice exercises, or electronic activities that teachers use to provide daily lessons in the different subject areas from prekindergarten through high school.

I have been intimately involved in education for fifty years, as a student, a teacher, a parent, and as a curriculum developer for an educational publisher. In 2007, I officially retired from publishing after my position was eliminated and started a small business working with publishers and educational product developers. Over the years I have gained an integral knowledge of how educational materials are produced, marketed, sold, and used throughout the country. I have seen how the different elements of the educational system relate to each other and have spent a lot of time thinking about why student achievement remains static, no matter what standards, technologies, or reforms are implemented. It has become clear to me that student achievement will at best remain static unless educational reform includes reevaluating and improving how curriculum is developed, assessed, and selected. My experience over the years confirms my conviction that educational publishing must play a much greater role in improving education.

This introduction describes the experiences that led me to the arguments I develop in this book.

MY EXPERIENCE AS A STUDENT

I come from a long line of educators. My great, great uncle Albert Metzger and great aunt Joanna Nettelhorst taught in one-room schoolhouses in Ohio. Great uncle Pat Ulery was a high school principal as school districts in Ohio became consolidated. My grandmother Charlotte Orland taught high school math and history. My mother taught high school math, and as a graduate student, my father taught introductory college courses.

Throughout school, I idolized my teachers. At Woodburn Elementary School in Falls Church, Virginia, I firmly believed my teachers lived at school, and I was always excited to learn facts about them such as their first names. Teachers were all-knowing, all-powerful beings, whom I desperately wanted to please. Miss Labato, Mrs. Green, Mrs. Ferguson, Mrs. Fraleigh, Miss Rynex, and Mr. Trennis were my first grade through sixth grade teachers. At the age of fifty-five, there is still no need for me to look up their names. I remember them so clearly.

I also remember projects I did in elementary school: a sawdust relief map of Virginia . . . a report on sponges . . . a report on Uruguay.

Shortly after Virginia schools became integrated I attended Luther Jackson Junior High, which had formerly been the African American high school. What I mainly remember from these days is all about trying to fit in and find and keep friends, and school dances, and parties. Teachers represented the necessary work of school but now I realize I learned some lifelong skills. For example, I learned about the structure of the English language from Miss Copeland, my seventh grade English teacher. In eighth grade, Mr. Woodzell and his wife took me and two of my friends on a trip to Gettysburg. I didn't have Mr. Woodzell, but my older sisters had, and he thought the three friends would be interested in learning more about history. I still am.

In high school my English teachers were most memorable, especially Mr. Dowell, who really taught me how to write, and Mrs. Fitzgerald, who saw that I was capable of much more and was disappointed that I hadn't taken advanced classes.

In college, at Clark University in Worcester, Massachusetts, I majored in English and took courses in education to earn a grade 6 through 12 teaching certificate. In addition to my English classes, I took educational philosophy and several theory classes. None of these prepared me for entering the classroom.

LEARNING ABOUT EDUCATION
THROUGH TEACHING

My student teaching was a semester at Chandler Junior High in Worcester, Massachusetts, in seventh and eighth grade English classes. I started with all the wide-eyed naïveté for which new teachers are mocked. Luckily my co-operating teachers, the teachers in whose classrooms I was a student teacher, liked me and gave me much needed support. My advisor, who was working on his master's degree following a stint at teaching middle school English, was particularly helpful. He would observe my classes from the back of the room and point out to me that none of the kids in the back were paying attention. He taught me basic but vital classroom management strategies like walking around the room and calling on different students to hold their attention.

I also got a glimpse of the teachers' world, and it was nothing I had expected. Teachers were people with lives outside the school that included spouses and parents and children and health problems. Instead of finding a teachers' lounge with inspiring discussions about new information, trends in education, or effective practices, the lounge was often a venting place that included complaints about students, parents, the community, the school administration, or something else.

I quickly learned that teaching was more about discipline and control than education. Without organization and discipline no lesson plan could stand a chance. Especially as a new teacher, strategies including seating arrangements and routines for starting class, passing in assignments, and cleaning up were often more important than conjugating verbs or analyzing *Treasure Island*.

The very best teachers were efficient and worked hard. They had good discipline, a bank of lesson plans they reused from previous years to minimize prep time, and efficient and effective assessment processes. They covered the required standards, challenged students with an adequate amount of work, and had a good bell curve of final grades that reflected student achievement. Students in their classes knew what was expected and most of them met expectations. They were "fair" in grading and in disciplining students. Inspiring students to develop interest in the subject matter was a plus.

Many teachers who were considered adequate maintained discipline and learned to survive by giving short shrift to lesson preparation and grading so they wouldn't have to take home extra work. They had figured out how to set things up in their first couple of years of teaching and coasted from then on regardless of how boring they were or what students did or did not learn.

Bad teachers, those who were not immoral or criminal, may have had great lesson plans and knowledge but had trouble controlling the class. They were inconsistent in discipline and incompetent in presenting material. They kept re-creating the curriculum or were inefficient in grading. They spent too much time on some things and not enough time on others. They were ridiculed by experienced teachers and taken advantage of by students. Unless they were very likable or were assigned mentors in the school, those teachers had a miserable existence in school life. Their best hope was that students and other teachers would feel sorry for them and help them out.

I saw the same patterns when I got my first teaching job in Ohio after graduation. I finished the year for an eighth grade English teacher, Mrs. Masters, who had been teaching for thirty years and who had suffered a heart attack over Christmas break. By the time I was hired, Mrs. Master's students had already gone through five other substitute teachers. I was so desperate for money that I hung in until the end of the year. I was shorter and looked younger than many of the students, so I tried to be extra tough. Some boys in one class absolutely hated me and when my grade book was found in the boys' toilet on the last day of school, I had a good idea who was responsible. I took comfort that I fared better than another long-term substitute whose students had climbed out the windows of her classroom.

Far and away the best education course I took was Developing Discipline over the summer in 1979. It was taught by Dr. William Wayson at The Ohio State University. The course taught me to establish a few rules and enforce them consistently. Our assignments included visiting at least two students in their homes to help break down the walls between teachers and students. Amazingly, after implementing the methods I learned, much of the classroom management fell into place. Over the next four years, I gained experience, learned about mastery learning techniques, and started my bank of lesson plans. One year I won the school's Teacher of the Year award for my efforts. Of course, there were always students and parents who did not like me for one reason or another, but to this day, former students who are now in their thirties with children of their own call me Miss Rubin.

Although maintaining discipline was my primary concern, motivating and teaching my students how to write and read critically was a huge preoccupation. I followed the recommendations in the instructional materials I used to develop my daily lesson plans. During my tenure I used the Plain English grammar workbooks, McGraw-Hill Kottmeyer Spelling, and a new Houghton Mifflin literature series. At the time I would not have been able to name the titles of the books or the publishers. It was only the blue or the green book.

These were materials that had been selected by a committee for the school. Mrs. Masters, who returned part-time in the spring, liked the Plain English grammar book but not the literature book. She had replaced several readings with selections from her bank of materials. When she retired at the end of the year, she passed her bank of materials on to me.

When I secured a full-time job in the district the following year, I used the texts the school district issued and adapted them as I wished. We reordered the latest editions of all the workbooks. That year we moved to an over-crowded school that had been designed for an open classroom environment. Because there were no walls, classes of thirty-five students each butted up against each other and for the first few weeks before the district invested in temporary walls, teachers had to shout over each other and try to keep their students focused on their classes and not on the others. Curriculum was the least of my problems. My main goal was to maintain control and discipline, especially since three other teachers could observe every move I made.

In my first full year of teaching, the principal secured a grant to implement a mastery reading program from the Exemplary Center for Reading Instruction. All teachers in all subjects were to be trained in mastery learning techniques for decoding, vocabulary, and comprehension. Being new and recognizing that a significant number of my seventh and eighth graders could not read very well, I embraced the program and appreciated the foundation it provided in reading instruction, a foundation that my secondary teaching degree in English did not address. All teachers were required and paid to participate in training sessions. There was a vehement mass rebellion and even though they were paid, only three of the thirty-two teachers completed the program. The three included another new teacher, the art teacher, and me. Everyone else, including other English teachers, concluded that it was a waste of time. All of these teachers claimed that it wasn't their job to teach reading, even the English teachers. They believed that teaching reading was the job of the elementary school teachers.

The following year, based on my limited knowledge of reading instruction, I was asked to tutor an eighth grade boy who read on a second grade level. During one session, one of the other English teachers overheard him reading aloud. Although the boy had been in the teacher's eighth grade literature class for six months, the teacher was shocked at how poor the boy's reading skills were. He taught literature, so he did not feel any responsibility to teach reading skills and had no idea how poorly some of his students read.

During my teaching career, I served on two textbook selection committees. In one, we were to select English texts. As a young teacher, I simply deferred to older colleagues. One of the teachers liked a Ginn text he had used previously so he promoted that publisher's English book. I felt that I would be able to adapt my lessons to any text, so I voted for it without ever reviewing any of the other choices.

The purpose of the second committee I served on was to reinstate the previous edition of the McGraw-Hill Kottmeyer spelling program. The English teachers hated the latest version because it was no longer organized into thirty-six lessons, but rather five units. The publisher had tried to do something innovative, but because it was so different it was not well accepted. I had already adapted the new edition to my mastery learning program, so I had no interest in changing, but the other English teachers had ignored the new edition and had been copying the lessons from the previous edition, so they reverted to it. Because there was no concern about curriculum consistency, I was able to stay with the newer program. Interestingly, Kottmeyer lost its dominance of the spelling market after publishing the program my colleagues did not like.

MY EDUCATION ABOUT EDUCATION IN EDUCATIONAL PUBLISHING

After four years of teaching, I began to look around for other opportunities. Over the summer I found a job in educational programming at QUBE. Launched in Columbus, Ohio, QUBE was a joint venture in interactive television between Warner Communications and American Express. I learned about television production, reviewed thousands of documentaries, and critiqued and selected televised instructional programming. It was a great environment and an introduction to the world of business. After four years, QUBE dissolved when American Express decided to terminate its relationship with the venture and I was out of a job.

With my experience in teaching and in educational programming, I secured a job at Charles E. Merrill Publishing in Columbus, Ohio, owned at that time by Bell and Howell. I was hired as an assistant editor trainee. My first project was to work as editor of seventh and eighth grade spelling books, a subject I thought I knew all about since I had taught it for four years with two different editions of the Kottmeyer spelling program. I was amazed by the amount of effort that went into developing a curriculum, as opposed to teaching a curriculum. Prior to the computer age, a project editor would have spent several months studying the competition and developing a card file of spelling words from different research-based word lists and would have organized them by spelling pattern and grade level. The four program authors worked on different grade levels. They took the assigned words and developed six units for each grade level, each with six lessons, including a review lesson. My job was to edit the authors' manuscripts. I had to make sure each word was used a specified number of times and that the activities followed the instructional guidelines. I also had to fill in any missing pieces, copyfit each page, and revise for readability. At times this meant a complete rewrite of the manuscript. My work was then reviewed by the project editor, reviewed by teachers, reedited, proofread, and then typeset. The process from manuscript to published book took a minimum of twelve months. I was astonished at how much was involved in creating a simple spelling book. It was definitely not a process of collecting words students misspelled and having the students memorize the spellings by writing them over and over. There is, I learned, a huge difference between teaching children how to spell and teaching them how to memorize the spelling of one word.

Since the previous edition of the program had not sold well, the company decided to invest in a new market research technique, the focus group. In a focus group the publisher representatives sat behind a one-way glass and observed teachers reviewing materials. The Merrill speller and several other competitor books had been laid out on a table. After an initial discussion, the focus group moderator told the teachers to select a book to review. The teachers had passed over the Merrill speller and only reviewed it when the moderator handed it to a participant. This was a critical lesson in the importance of cover design. When the teachers did open it, they claimed it did not have the features they had seen in the other programs. The features were included but they were not cleverly labeled, so in a "flip test," the features did not stand out. Because of the cover design, the teachers were predisposed to dislike the book. This was the second critical lesson: features do not exist unless they are labeled in language the teachers expect. Over the course of my twenty-four years in publishing, I learned these lessons again and again. For a host of reasons, I came to realize that hard-working teachers, who have the best interests of their students at heart, are rarely the most effective evaluators of curriculum effectiveness.

To support the sales of the spelling program, I was asked to develop a monograph on spelling research. I spent several weeks at The Ohio State University library reading about the history of spelling instruction, from the nineteenth-century blue-backed spellers to the early twentieth-century behaviorist techniques to help students memorize words, to the exciting work done at the University of Virginia in developmental spelling, identifying how children learn to spell, and how spelling relates to reading. None of this type of research was included in my teaching preparation. And little of it was considered in the textbook development. The textbooks were developed based on tradition and competing products. In textbook development, the primary factors were what the successful competition did, what would appeal to teachers, and how to design and label the work to highlight the appealing features. Using research-based strategies or demonstrating effectiveness was not a priority.

Over the next twenty years, Merrill was bought and sold to an investment group, then to Macmillan, and then to McGraw-Hill. The company acquired Optical Data, Open Court, the Tribune educational properties, along with several other companies. I advanced in my career from assistant editor to associate editor, editor, senior editor, executive editor, and finally to editorial director of SRA/McGraw-Hill having worked on reading/language arts, science, math, fine arts, and instructional technology projects. My products earned a host of awards for design, innovation, sales, and editorial excellence. They never earned any awards for effectiveness because to my knowledge awards for effectiveness do not exist.

In the late 1980s the standards movement began to take hold and added additional priorities. States had always had state guidelines, but during the 1990s states began to align with state tests. In addition to political considerations related to concerns about controversial topics such as the discussion of evolution or sex education, instructional materials were evaluated based on how effectively they met state standards. Publishers rose to the task by creating intricate lists of standards from different states and having editors make sure that each standard was "covered" the required number of times. Standards affected the inclusion of some content, but they rarely affected how content was organized or presented. The competition, design, and teacher appeal remained the key determiners of success.

As I built my career in publishing, my two daughters started and completed their journeys through preK–12 school and I got involved in their education, as well as Girl Scouts and Destination Imagination. I was amazed at how similar our student experiences were. The teaching strategies and materials were amazingly similar to those I had experienced as a student and used as a teacher.

Educational research also got more traction when the No Child Left Behind legislation was passed. As part of the legislation, the What Works Clearinghouse was established, and funding was available for research-based materials. To address this, publishers added authors who were involved in research, bought research-based curriculum to promote along with their core materials, and wrote monographs to demonstrate how their existing materials addressed current academic research. Most customers were convinced that the materials reflected research and adopted materials based on the same criteria as before: design, labeling, and teacher appeal. True research-based materials, such as SRA's Direct Instruction product line, Open Court Reading, or Real Math, required intensive training since they were very different from teachers' common practices. Although these programs could demonstrate legitimate results, while others could not, they rarely did well in focus groups nor sold very well outside of a committed base.

AFTER A LIFETIME IN EDUCATION

Over the past couple of years I've thought a lot about my experiences in education and how and why educational reforms fail. I'm old enough to have seen many reforms come and go. Phonics, whole word, whole language, mastery learning, open classroom, team teaching, constructivism, discovery learning, multiculturalism, learning modalities, multiple intelligences, and differentiated instruction have all had their days in the sun. The educational pendulum swings from teacher-directed to student-driven instruction, back and forth with the latest trends clearly labeled in instructional materials. I've seen experienced and cynical teachers bide their time, continuing to teach what they believe works regardless of the latest fads.

I have also realized with astonishment that education is the one industry that does not build on its foundation. Instead of incorporating the best practices and emerging with versions 2, 3, and 4 as software or cell phones do, educational reformers tend to throw out everything and start afresh with the latest fad. Reformers denounce other methods and vilify publishers and educators who advocate them. Followers try the new methods until the grant money runs out or until someone introduces a new fad. Even when districts implement reforms, practices drift back when the advocates in the administration change. Only in rare instances have I seen reforms translate into long-term higher student achievement.

The status quo in education is firmly entrenched. Teachers are reluctant to change their ways and throw out their banks of lessons to accommodate a fad that may go away. Publishers are incentivized to create materials that appeal to teachers who don't want to change, so curriculum materials that could have a significant impact on education reform are less profitable.

Instructional materials, including textbooks and electronic materials, by and large provide the curriculum that is used in American education. These materials are developed by privately owned publishers. The free market should inspire a competition among publishers to produce the best materials. One would think that best meant most effective materials that address content standards and incorporate the most effective strategies identified by research. But that is not the case. Unless the instructional materials selection process changes, the status quo in education will predominate for the foreseeable future.

Over my lifetime in education as a student, a teacher, and in educational publishing, I can attest that people who devote their lives to education, including teachers, administrators, authors, editors, and publishers, do so in pursuit of making the world a better place. A higher calling than making money or gaining power and influence is essentially what motivates them. People who have never experienced teaching English grammar to seventh graders have no idea the challenges teachers face in organizing their classrooms, maintaining discipline, and actually delivering productive lessons. By the same token, people who have never tried to develop a textbook series to meet the needs of teachers, parents, students, and administrators and improve the level of education are unqualified to comment on how easy it must be to do that. I have great respect for educators, whatever role they play.

What I do believe is that there is a system created by people with the best of intentions that is perpetuating mediocrity in instructional materials and in American education. This system involves everyone who has a part in the development, selection, and use of instructional materials.

This book reveals a system in which curriculum materials are inadequately reviewed, selected, and used. It lays out an argument for changing the way curriculum is reviewed and selected so that publishers are incentivized to create the most effective materials that will contribute to the improvement of education and student achievement.

Chapter 1 describes the current textbook/curriculum materials selection process and reveals how it is that a combination of factors limits the selection and use of the most effective materials.

Chapter 2 explains the business of publishing and how it affects the process of developing curricular materials that could but does not affect the quality of the materials.

Chapter 3 outlines how curriculum is developed and identifies the priorities of marketing versus effectiveness.

Chapters 4, 5, and 6 suggest why standards, achievement testing, technology, and professional development have had little effect on improving student achievement.

Chapter 7 suggests changes that can be made to select and maximize the potential of the most effective educational materials to promote student achievement.

Chapter One

The Most Effective Curriculum Materials Are Rarely Adopted

In August 2010, President Obama reasserted the well-accepted principle that education is an economic issue: "If we're serious about making sure America's workers, and America itself, succeed in the 21st century, the single most important step we can take is to make sure that every one of our young people . . . has the best education that the world has to offer. . . . Education is a prerequisite for prosperity."

Education is vitally important to our nation's and the world's prosperity and well-being. The American education system has historically been the best in the world and has been responsible in large part for American strength and prosperity. Yet in the last few decades other countries have caught up and even surpassed American dominance in the quality of K–12 education as well as high school and college attendance and graduation rates. The United States has reached a plateau in student achievement while other nations are moving ahead. In 2009 the United States ranked thirty-second out of sixty-five developed countries in mathematics, twenty-fourth in reading, and thirtieth in science (Organisation for Economic Co-operation and Development, OECD, 2010). Much attention is being focused on what can be done to improve our educational system and promote student achievement to secure a better future for our children and our nation.

This attention often focuses on individual elements of what constitutes a good education. These essential ingredients are good teachers, motivated students, safe schools, effective administrators, parental support, and quality curriculum materials. All of these elements must work together to deliver high-quality instruction that motivates students and prepares them for whatever the future may bring. One ingredient alone will not produce satisfactory results, no matter how powerful it may be. Schools that have wonderful facilities but are poorly managed, motivated teachers that have little parent support, or a quality curriculum poorly implemented are recipes for mediocrity or worse.

The one ingredient that is rarely part of public discourse is curriculum. The way in which curriculum is developed, selected, and used in American schools should be dramatically improved. Combined with other ingredients curriculum is a critical element in the advancement of American education. There are local, state, and federal initiatives to improve education, including school choice, closing failing schools, replacing ineffective teachers, incentivizing good teachers, and promoting parent involvement. Added to this list of reforms should be a reevaluation and improvement of curriculum and a change in the way materials are selected so that educational publishers are incentivized to create the most effective materials.

WHAT IS CURRICULUM?

Educational conferences often include sessions in which a teacher presents a lesson or strategy that was particularly effective in his or her classroom. But curriculum does not comprise individual lessons that were effective in specific circumstances. A curriculum represents a comprehensive, organized scope and sequence of lessons whose instructions can be communicated effectively so that other teachers can use them effectively. "A curriculum sets forth that body of knowledge and skill our children need to grow into economically productive and socially responsible citizens" (American Educator 2011).

Curriculum includes instructional activities, readings, and exercises designed to educate its users in a particular subject. Regardless of the form the curriculum takes, be it electronic, print, or hands-on, the curriculum is the body of organized lessons that are designed to build understanding. Publishers do not sell books or technology. They do not sell educational philosophy. They do not sell professional development. They sell curriculum.

A quality curriculum has these characteristics that involve content, organization, access, teaching support, and assessment:

- Age appropriate in content, readability, and skill expectations
- Up-to-date content and references
- Accurate content with appropriate balance of essential concepts
- Engaging and appropriate mix of activities that develop concepts
- Organization that promotes natural learning progressions and logical development of skills and concepts
- In-depth, comprehensive development of critical concepts
- Incorporation of best practices identified by educational research

- Mitigation of bias that focuses on exposition as opposed to persuasion
- Teaching strategies that build professional development
- Tools to conduct accurate assessments of student progress accompanied by strategies to reteach, maintain, and develop concepts and skills based on the assessments

With few exceptions most curricula fall short in many of these areas. Educational publications include most of these characteristics but sometimes in name only. It takes a number of trained evaluators to be able to recognize whether a curriculum includes these characteristics and then evaluate how effectively they are executed. Surprisingly, very few people have the knowledge and experience to evaluate a curriculum. As a result the critical aspects of quality curriculum are ignored, misinterpreted, and sometimes even denounced because the people reviewing materials don't know how to examine them. Because of this, instead of being based on quality, curricula are commonly adopted based on marketing strategies or superficial elements such as visual appeal or superfluous features or components.

An effective curriculum has the potential to build a solid skill, concept, and knowledge foundation in a particular subject for students and to instill a love of learning. An effective curriculum that teachers know how to employ has the potential not only to raise test scores, but also to promote student achievement, interest, critical thinking, and expertise—the ingredients for a promising future for individuals and for nations.

HOW CURRICULUM IS USED

As a foundation for the object of instruction, textbooks can provide the following support.

- **State and National Standards and Guidelines**—Every state has curriculum guidelines that teachers are expected to address in every subject area, including the Common Core standards in English language arts and mathematics. For those textbooks that are state specific, such as California and Texas math books, the guidelines are provided within the curriculum at point of use. The readings, exercises, and questions are all geared toward providing instruction and practice so that students learn what the state expects them to learn. Even if a textbook is not state specific, guidelines can be identified and emphasized within the program. For a teacher to write the entire curriculum for each subject complete with lesson objectives, exercises, practice, and assessment would be an overwhelming project.

- **Scope and Sequence**—A textbook's scope and sequence plots when concepts are introduced, practiced, related, developed, reviewed, and assessed so that logical developmental progressions can maximize learning.
- **Teaching Strategies**—An effective textbook provides strategies for activating students' prior knowledge, introducing concepts, connecting concepts, developing concepts as well as questioning, reflecting, and assessing concept understanding.
- **Student Activities and Exercises**—Textbooks provide appropriate readings, exercises, and activities to engage students in introduction, exploration, experience, and practice in lesson content.
- **Ideas**—A good textbook prompts teachers with ideas for activities and exercises to further develop concepts.
- **Differentiation**—Textbooks often provide strategies and resources to help teachers differentiate lessons for various student populations.
- **Assessment**—An effective textbook provides opportunities for formative and summative assessment to help teachers judge if students are grasping the concepts taught and to identify areas needing review.

Even if teachers do not use instructional materials as the object of instruction, textbooks can still provide the following.

- Student exercises and activities that support teacher instruction
- Ideas to extend concepts
- Extra practice to reinforce instruction
- Alternative lesson presentations

COMPLAINTS ABOUT TEXTBOOKS

Even the best textbooks are not a panacea for educators, and educators have many complaints about textbooks.

- **Not Challenging**—If instructional materials are too basic for the level of students, students will be bored and teachers will be frustrated.
- **Too Challenging**—If instructional materials are too challenging and students are failing, teachers need to find other resources to address the concepts to ensure student learning.
- **Design Not Age Appropriate**—Materials may seem too babyish for some ages. The illustrations or text size may embarrass students. On the other hand, materials with smaller type and fewer illustrations may make students and teachers feel that the material is too difficult.
- **Readability**—If the reading level is too high with too much new vocabulary, students and teachers will be frustrated that the material is not accessible.

- **Scripting**—Some programs provide a teacher script with exact words that a teacher may use in an effort to ensure fidelity to the program. This is often the case with research-based materials that are effective if they are used faithfully and could be ineffective if they are not. Some teachers complain about scripted teacher's editions because they find such controlled practices insulting. They perceive this approach to make teachers irrelevant.
- **Scope and Sequence**—Teachers often complain, particularly in mathematics, that the concepts are not presented in a logical order or that they skip around too much and students and teachers cannot follow them. This may also be a function of moving too quickly from a simple concept to a more difficult concept.
- **Not Enough Practice**—A common complaint among teachers is that there are not enough skill practice exercises. This is true whether the subject is math, vocabulary, spelling, or grammar, usage, and mechanics.
- **Errors**—Another common complaint is that a program has errors. This is often the result of mismatched printings in which an uncorrected first printing of one component is used in the same classroom as a corrected second printing. In some cases, publishers are under tight development schedules driven by late release of state requirements. Wrong answers in the teacher's edition and typos are other common complaints.

Rarely do teachers complain that there need to be more effective teaching strategies, thoughtful discussion questions, or project ideas. This leads publishers to assume that those features are less important.

INADEQUATE REVIEW OF CURRICULUM

The news is full of stories about education. Stories are written about the importance of professional development for teachers, adequate yearly progress for schools, state and national standards, teacher merit pay, the effect of teacher unions, educational trends, charter school movements, and more. Yet few articles address the ingredient that provides the content and substance of what students learn: curriculum delivered in instructional materials such as textbooks, workbooks, and electronic resources.

When instructional materials do make the mainstream news, it is almost always because of some controversy or errors. Errors range from typos to wrong historical dates or information, wrong answers, or disputed definitions. Controversies erupt over the need to replace outdated textbooks, or the inclusion or omission of evolution, sex education, or historic figures. Censorship or lack of censorship inspires energetic debate (Ravitch 2003).

Although some of these issues may concern one aspect of a quality curriculum, they do not provide a comprehensive evaluation and often distract evaluators from critical issues.

Educational publications do introduce new ideas and trends in education and may present arguments for or against certain methods or practices. For example, the phonics/whole language issue or the math wars of basic skills versus conceptual understanding may be debated. But rarely is the effectiveness of a textbook or instructional program or series a cause for comment. There are several reasons for this and they all contribute to maintaining the status quo in education.

Reluctance to Question the Expert

There is a certain reverence for resources such as dictionaries, encyclopedias, handbooks, and almanacs, and historically, textbooks have been included in this category. These materials do not present stories or arguments. Instead they present facts and figures, which appear to have been thoroughly researched and vetted by experts. These are the materials that are cited by writers who are developing arguments. Even the textbook critics Mel and Norma Gabler, who founded Educational Research Analysts to review and reject objectionable textbooks from school adoptions, at one time "trusted textbooks almost as much as they did the Bible" (Hefley 1976, 13). If the purpose of curriculum is to march students through incremental skill development, the careful development of lessons that build skills is tremendously appreciated. Otherwise the body of knowledge that needs to be covered is overwhelming. Curriculum, however, is more than dictionaries and almanacs. Curriculum review requires close scrutiny to ensure effective materials are being selected and used, but rarely does curriculum receive adequate evaluation.

Students are unlikely to question instructional materials. The letters that publishers receive from students mostly have to do with perceived errors students find in textbooks. Most often these are inconsistencies between different printings of a text.

Teachers and administrators are unlikely to question instructional materials. Many people believe the printed word, regardless of whether it appears in a book, a newspaper, or on the Internet. Textbooks are supposed to be written by experts in their respective fields. Teacher expertise is working with students, not expertise with content, especially at the elementary grades. Furthermore, textbooks are adopted by groups of people: a school, district, or state adoption committee, who supposedly have carefully reviewed available materials and selected the best ones. Teachers may complain about errors in textbooks or wrong answers or they may not like a particular feature, but they are used to adapting materials to suit their needs. They are unlikely to question the materials.

In addition, effectively reviewing a textbook is a lot of work. It requires a great deal of expertise and critical analysis.

- **Curriculum Design**—One must be knowledgeable about curriculum design to intelligently criticize the organization of a program.
- **Teaching Methods**—One must be knowledgeable about research-based teaching methods to criticize the strategies and teaching methods employed.
- **Children's Learning Trajectories**—One must be an expert in how children learn a particular subject or skill set to question the development of skills and concepts.
- **Content Expertise**—One must be an expert in science, history, geography, or math to criticize the inclusion, exclusion, or definitions of content.
- **Standards**—One must be an expert in grade level standards to question the inclusion of specific standards at specific grade levels.
- **Lesson Planning**—One must be knowledgeable about lesson planning to critique how effectively a program develops lesson objectives.

All of these areas of expertise take years of education and thought to develop. Teacher expertise is working with students and delivering curriculum. If something seems amiss, they are more likely to learn to live with it or assume there is a good reason for it than to question it.

The public is unlikely to question instructional materials. If students are not complaining, and teachers and administrators have selected materials and are using them, parents and other public representatives assume the materials are sound. Even when parents are educators themselves, or content experts, they are reluctant to interfere in their children's school experience apart from helping them with their homework. Parents quickly abdicate responsibility for helping their children with their studies once the material such as the math or science becomes too complicated.

When students do complain or parents do not understand what is in the textbooks, there is a flurry of consternation and the district administration defends the materials or abandons them. Frequently these controversies result in a reversion to older materials that do not inspire any controversy, thereby maintaining the educational status quo of the parents' generation. The loudest outcries, such as the one in Kanawha County, West Virginia, in 1974, have come from people who perceive that textbooks are undermining values and patriotism. In Kanawha County, conservative parents found some textbooks to conflict with Christian values, morality, and patriotism;

schools were boycotted. Finally the school board restored the previously approved books to quell the controversy.

Other controversies have arisen over how textbooks treat evolution and creationism or intelligent design, sex education, and appropriate literature. Many of these controversies erupt during the process of writing state standards. In 2005, the Kansas Board of Education developed science education standards that increased emphasis on uncertainties about the theory of evolution. In 2007, after four of the six conservative Republicans who had approved the 2005 standards lost their seats, the board voted to reject the amended science standards. In the spring of 2010, the Texas State Board of Education passed new high school textbook standards that amended the previous standards, which, among other things, deemphasized the teaching of the civil rights movement and slavery and increased emphasis on the conservative resurgence of the 1980s and 1990s. In 2010 an elementary school Virginia history textbook included the claim that thousands of blacks fought for the Confederacy during the Civil War, which is factually inaccurate. This error made national news and led to an indictment of using a website on the Internet as a sole source of information and the absence of historians reviewing and fact-checking textbooks.

While these controversies ignite public discussion and capture media attention, they do not address the effectiveness of the textbooks and the improvement of student understanding and academic performance. Adding a paragraph in a high school history book about the conservative movement will not fundamentally improve student understanding of or interest in history. Including intelligent design in one lesson of a science program that may or may not be taught does not develop student ability to consistently identify, explain, and apply scientific knowledge in a variety of complex life situations. Attention is paid to these political issues rather than to the increasing evidence that students in other countries dramatically outperform American students (OECD 2006).

In the 1960s Mel and Norma Gabler established a nonprofit organization, Educational Research Analysts, to review textbooks. In addition to values and patriotism, they also included a limited analysis of the effectiveness of different educational approaches and questioned the substitution of sight word reading methods for phonics and the introduction of new math. Educational Research Analysts remains one of the few significant reviewers of textbooks outside of state and district committees. Other organizations such as the Textbook League, which issues the *Textbook Letter*, focus on "false" science and history. The Mathematically Correct organization was influential in the 2000–2001 California math textbook selection, but has not remained active as an organization in textbook evaluation.

Apart from these organizations and as a result of the assumptions about textbooks made by students and teachers, once adoption committees review instructional materials and select them, there is rarely any discussion about them and certainly not about their effectiveness.

Furthermore, a new curriculum is expensive and once it is selected, districts celebrate the acquisition of new materials, expecting that they are better than the old because they are new and assume they will have a positive effect on education. Because it takes a couple of years to implement a new curriculum and because evaluating the impact of the curriculum is so complicated, there is rarely a school or district review of the effectiveness of curriculum materials.

Reluctance to Interfere with the Free Market and the Private Sector

In the United States, there is no national curriculum published by the government. Instead, from the early days of the country, textbooks were developed by privately owned publishers and sold to schools. Government entities are reluctant to interfere with the textbook development and selection processes. National, state, and local governments and schools set standards that outline what should be included in instructional materials, but they do not dictate how those standards should be organized, developed, presented, or assessed.

> One reason sometimes cited for the federal policy makers to shy away from curriculum is the Department of Education Organization Act of 1979, which prohibits the Department from endorsing or sanctioning any curriculum designed to be used in an elementary school or secondary school. Similar prohibitions have been included as boilerplate language in the Elementary and Secondary Education Act, the Individuals with Disabilities Education Act, and the Education Sciences Reform Act. (Whitehurst 2009)

The free market should help to identify the best instructional materials through competition. The most effective materials should be the best sellers and should be implemented in classrooms throughout the nation. That would happen if instructional materials were selected based on their effectiveness, but surprisingly, effectiveness may not be a top priority for the people who decide what materials are purchased. Meeting the standards is the number one criteria for approving a state textbook. Ease of use is the number one criteria for teachers who make the purchasing decisions. People who do attempt to evaluate effectiveness are often ignored. For example, Educational Research Analysts (Educational Research Analysts 1999) and Mathematically Correct ("Mathematically Correct Second Grade Mathematics Review" 2000) identified Saxon Math and SRA Real Math as most effective, but these evaluations did not translate into sales. Because for-profit companies provide curriculum, government and universities (unless they are part of state textbook selection committees) will not teach or critique specific curriculum for fear of promoting or condemning commercial products. Publishers suspect foul play and favoritism if a government agency advocates a particular philosophy or approach or promotes a particular product that includes the recommended approaches.

The free market is working, but not to the benefit of schools and students. Publishers are incentivized to cover standards and make the materials appealing and easy to use, but these elements rarely translate into effectiveness.

RESEARCH

It seems obvious that simple research studies could be conducted to demonstrate program effectiveness and inform district decisions about the selection of the instructional materials. Yet research studies seldom help to select the most effective curriculum for a variety of reasons.

Educational Research

The most well-attended conference for educational publishers might well be AERA, the American Educational Research Association. AERA publishes journals in which researchers publish their studies about the effectiveness of educational practices. Whereas many publishers attend IRA (International Reading Association) and NCTM (National Council of Teachers of Mathematics) conferences primarily to display and promote their products in the exhibit hall, few editors attend to learn about advances in curriculum.

Educational research tends to focus on specific methods. Scientific studies are done with random samples of classrooms to test whether, for example, focusing on the height of the ascenders and descenders of letters aids or detracts from decoding. Incorporating these research results in a comprehensive preK–6 reading program is adding a grain of sand to the ocean beach. It needs to be done, but these studies do not constitute a curriculum.

Program Effectiveness Research

Some studies have been conducted to evaluate the effectiveness of a particular program. With the emphasis on research inspired by the No Child Left Behind legislation, many publishers conducted or funded research studies. The publishers' marketing and sales departments have funded many of these. But because there are many variables in the implementation of a curriculum, virtually any strategy, curriculum, or method can show results under the right circumstances. Some of the most effective curricula fail if they are poorly implemented. The Success for All program, for example, will not accept an adoption unless a school agrees to a school-wide implementation and intensive training and professional development. If some teachers but not others implement a curriculum with fidelity, it may reflect poorly on the curriculum when, in fact, the curriculum may not be at fault. Publishers are very reluctant to submit their programs for a legitimate research study because they may find poor control of variables and fear that the consequences of poor results would be disastrous. Schools are reluctant to assign different classes to random trials if they believe that one group will receive inferior instruction.

In some cases publisher studies were forwarded for review to the What Works Clearinghouse that was established by the Department of Education after the No Child Left Behind legislation was passed in 2001. As a government agency, the What Works Clearinghouse was reluctant to endorse any particular program. Instead it evaluated the studies on particular programs to determine if the research practices in submitted studies were valid. Publishers did initially pay attention to the What Works Clearinghouse, but in its effort to be exhaustively scientifically accurate, it produced very little that was useful to publishers. The report on Elementary School Math, for example, published on July 16, 2007, looked at 237 studies of seventy-three curricula. Of the 237 studies only 9 met their evidence standards, 2 without reservations and 7 with reservations. Of the curricula only Everyday Math, a research-based program, was found to have "potentially positive effects on math achievement." The other curricula had no discernible effects on math achievement based on the studies reviewed (US Department of Education 2007). That there were no discernable effects on math achievement, coupled with the fact that the programs studied were all in new editions, plus the discovery that the report had no effect on sales, confirmed that publishers did not have to worry about the What Works Clearinghouse. If publishers are not punished for creating ineffective materials or incentivized for creating effective materials, building effective curricula will not be a priority.

WHY THE CURRICULUM ADOPTION PROCESS DOESN'T SUPPORT THE SELECTION OF EFFECTIVE MATERIALS

One would expect that the state adoption process and the process of selecting instructional materials would focus on identifying quality curriculum, but by and large they do not. In the United States there are two very different methods for selecting instructional materials. Twenty-two states hold textbook adoptions, and specific textbook sales are limited to the years of the adoption. The other states are open territory, with individual schools or school districts adopting materials on their own schedules. Textbooks are seemingly subjected to rigorous review by a host of experts to win state adoption. Yet, regardless of whether a state uses the adoption or the open-territory process, it is typically the teachers who will be using the books who make the final selections, and in the end teachers are not equipped to conduct a rigorous review.

State Adoptions

According to a study published by the Thomas B. Fordham Institute,

> the textbook adoption process was, in effect, born to twist American history and frustrate the development of a common civic purpose. Its origins trace to the aftermath of the Civil War, when most publishers had their headquarters in the North. Embittered ex-Confederates distrusted Yankee publishers and wanted Dixie schoolchildren to have their own textbooks—so southern states established textbook adoption processes to make sure anti-Confederate books stayed out of their schools. Northern publishers obligingly complied, publishing separate textbooks for schools in the South and North. For decades, Southern textbooks referred to the Civil War as "the War for Southern Independence" or "the War between the States." Today, nearly 150 years later, most adoption states are still located in the South and West. (Whitman 2004)

Adoption states include the following:

Alabama	New Mexico
Arkansas	North Carolina
California	Oklahoma
Florida	Oregon
Georgia	South Carolina
Idaho	Tennessee
Indiana	Texas
Kentucky	Utah
Louisiana	Virginia
Mississippi	West Virginia
Nevada	

The American Association of Publishers School Division (AAP) creates a document every fall listing the upcoming state adoptions. It outlines when each state will hold adoptions for different subjects and grades in the upcoming five years. Although this schedule is subject to change, it drives educational publishing plans. For example, if Texas has legislated a K–12 science adoption in 2011, publishers who decide to bid in the adoption begin preparing at least two years before. Texas funds its adoptions, which means that once a program is approved, schools and districts can use allocated state funding to purchase that subject. Many other state adoptions are unfunded. They may hold adoptions to review textbooks but schools are on their own to purchase them. That's what makes Texas such a highly coveted target for publishers. If a program is adopted and does well in Texas, the publisher is guaranteed to generate significant revenue.

Publishers strategize based on the AAP schedule. State adoptions create a huge market, especially if the state funds the adoption. Following the AAP schedule, Texas might adopt science in one year, along with West Virginia, Virginia, Oklahoma, New Mexico, and Alabama. Then California and South Carolina might call for science the following year, and Tennessee, Kentucky, and Georgia the year after that (AAP School Division 2009). In response, a publisher will plan on publishing a brand-new Texas edition of a science program targeted for the deadline for the Texas adoption. The publisher will incorporate the other states' guidelines and then produce a national edition for the open territory states and New Mexico. It would be cost prohibitive to create a completely different program for each state.

The following year, the publisher will revise its Texas/national edition and "Californiaorize" it to submit in the California adoption. Depending on how different the California standards are, the publisher may decide to make minor adjustments to the 2011 national edition it submitted in New Mexico to submit in the other adoption states, as well as open territory states. Of course each state may have a state specific cover and other elements, but the program is basically the same as that created for Texas or California. Publishers cannot afford to create individual programs for each state.

For a state adoption, the state department of education provides publishers with the state standards, any criteria for meeting the standards, and the deadlines for submission. In preparation for the adoption, states recruit teachers, curriculum specialists, and sometimes professors to review the submitted programs. These reviewers are trained by the state education agency to look for particular things in each program. In Texas the adoption committee's sole job is to make sure that every part of every one of the TEKS, Texas Essential Knowledge and Skills, is met at least the designated number of times in the student and teacher editions. In Florida, adoption committees are trained to look for standards coverage, but they also ask other constituents to review the programs and consider their recommendations.

The same is true in California, which invites teachers and content specialists to be IMRs (Instructional Materials Reviewers) and professors to be

CREs (Content Review Experts). In some cases the IMR committees heartily approve of a program but the CREs do not. In other cases the opposite occurs. Both parties vote on each criterion and try to reach consensus. California comes the closest to holding a comprehensive review of curricular materials, but too often the process degenerates into a confusion of individual preferences and loyalties.

The actual state adoption process can be a circus. In Texas the committees converge at a hotel for a week. Each committee has a checklist of the TEKS breakouts, the individual components of each standard. They are instructed to go line by line and look for coverage of each part of each of the TEKS. If they can't find something in the student or teacher edition, they may consult the publisher's correlation and check to see if they agree with a publisher's reference. The committees are all in a room, and they are instructed not to talk to any publisher. Representatives from the publishers wait outside for committees to finish their reviews. If the committee identifies omissions, the publisher has an opportunity to submit a rebuttal with an explanation of where the TEKS is covered or to submit replacement camera-ready copy to include the TEKS. The committee can accept or reject the publisher response. If rejected, the publisher has another opportunity to appeal to the textbook commission in the department of education or to the state board of education. This is not an evaluation of the quality of the curriculum. It is an evaluation of whether the specific people reviewing the materials believe a standard has been met. "The process of reviewing the guidelines in Texas is very open, but what happens behind the scenes after that is quite different. . . . The publishers just want to make sure they get their books listed" (Shorto 2010).

Publishers make a huge investment in state adoptions and are willing to do whatever they can to get adopted. If a program is not adopted, state funds are limited for it and the program is tainted with a bad reputation. Selling materials to recoup a publisher's investment is nearly impossible if a program is not listed in the states for which it was developed. Behind the scenes, if the state adoption committee has an objection or cites an omission of a standard, even if the publisher disagrees, the publisher will add content to the text to ensure it is adopted.

In California, textbooks are sent to each IMR and CRE before the deliberations. The adoption consists of each committee coming together to discuss and then vote on whether a program meets the standards and the adoption criteria.

In some states teachers converge in a location and review all of the textbooks in one day. They may or may not have had an opportunity to see the programs in advance. There is no way a thoughtful review of a curriculum's quality can be determined in such a short review. These types of processes encourage reviewers to make critical decisions based on design or other appeal.

Following the guidelines for review and selection, the public typically has an opportunity to comment on the submissions before the state board of education approves the final list. In these public reviews, ethnic groups, religious organizations, antidefamation groups, parent groups—anyone with an interest in education may comment.

Once the adoption list is set, salespeople begin a process of sampling and marketing to individual school districts. Some states require that publishers provide extensive samples of their programs. The cost of sampling is prohibitive for smaller publishers or those who do not have programs that can compete with the design, features, and number of components that a major publisher provides. If a salesperson has not already built a relationship with a district, he or she will have a difficult time meeting his or her sales quota. Much of the sales effort depends on the long-term relationships and deals and favors that have occurred in the past.

Unfortunately state adoption committees are not always qualified to critique a program's quality or effectiveness. They mainly evaluate whether the state standards are included in the program. And outside of a very few organizations, there are no consumer product reviews. Even when adoption committees include content specialists, these people typically evaluate the accuracy of the content, rather than whether the instructional strategies are effective, whether the program incorporates the latest research on best practices, or if the scope and sequence makes sense and follows developmental progressions.

This is vitally important because once a program is approved for use in the state or district regardless of its ultimate effectiveness, everyone assumes that it will be as effective as any other program in meeting the standards. Unfortunately quality and instructional effectiveness are rarely considered in state adoption situations.

Because publishers must make large investments in programs to increase their chances of getting on an adoption list, they are adverse to any risk that may jeopardize their chances of being successful. As a result, innovations are curtailed and any element that is not specifically required or requested by the state or by potential customers is suspect. Some states, California and Florida, for example, are now rejecting programs that have extraneous content, that is, content that is not required in their state standards. A publisher has no incentive to produce anything different or innovative. The results are that all publishers can be counted on to deliver very similar types of materials.

Open Territory Adoptions

If the adoption states' textbook selection process is flawed, the open territory process is worse. In open territory states, individual school districts or schools may develop their own adoption schedules, invite selections, and may or may not appoint adoption committees to review them.

Publishers' open territory sales representatives have a completely different job from that of adoption state sales representatives. In adoption states, the reps know what the focus will be in each year and plan elaborate campaigns creating hierarchies of districts depending on the potential sales.

Open territory sales representatives must be prepared to sell any program in the publisher's book bag to any teacher or district at any time. It is a huge effort to identify when key districts are planning to begin the review process for new books. Open territory reps can easily miss out on big opportunities if they don't have an "inside scoop."

Many open territory states get short shrift from publishers. Publishers may submit programs that have state specific covers or state specific elements, but it is rarely profitable for them to create programs specifically for an open territory state because the needed investment is large compared with most open territory states' market size.

As a result open territory customers frequently get a version of the latest state adoption program, which has been tailored to another state's requirements. Even if an open territory state has different or higher standards expectations, it is cost prohibitive for a publisher to produce state specific materials for every state.

SCHOOL SELECTION OF INSTRUCTIONAL MATERIALS

Regardless of whether a school is in an adoption state or open territory state, the final selection of which instructional materials will be used in a classroom is left up to the school or district. A school may appoint a local adoption committee of teachers and parents, or they may have the curriculum specialist review the submissions, or it may be left to the teachers to decide which materials to adopt. There is a wide range of criteria for the selection process.

Some schools make a very conscientious effort to select materials and several pieces of information are evaluated. These may include the following:

- **Parent Input**—The PTA or PTO (Parent Teacher Association or Organization) may be asked to review or send a member of the organization to review the textbooks available. The purpose is for the parent organization to determine if there is any material in the textbooks that the community may find objectionable.
- **Teacher Review**—Subject area teachers are appointed, invited, or volunteer to serve on adoption committees. Their purpose is to review submis-

sions and recommend the instructional materials they believe to be best for the school or district's students.

- **Public Participation**—Some schools and districts invite the public to review instructional materials and provide feedback to the adoption committees.
- **Field Test**—Some schools or districts conduct field tests of different materials so teachers and students have an opportunity to try them out for a specific period of time. This has the potential of identifying differences in effectiveness.
- **Rubrics**—Rubrics or checklists to aid in the evaluation may be used to review textbooks. Teachers, administrators, or districts create some rubrics. Educators outside the district create others (Kame'enui and Simmons 2000).
- **District Textbook Adoption Committee**—Often approved by the local school board, these committees may include teachers and administrators. These people are selected to represent the subject area. The purpose is to review all the recommendations and recommend a textbook to the school board for adoption.
- **State Standards Correlation**—A correlation of the curriculum and the state standards is often part of the review, to demonstrate where the standards are addressed in the curriculum.

It would seem that in the best of all worlds, knowledgeable teachers and administrators would take their work very seriously and spend hours reviewing submitted materials and trying them out with students. These teachers have knowledge of best practices and can discern materials that have busywork from those that have effective strategies and practice. Regardless of design, price, or publisher incentives, these teachers would select the materials that would be most effective and promote student understanding, skill, and achievement. They would select the best materials regardless of whether the new program required them and their colleagues to substantially change their teaching methods.

Having all teachers vote on new instructional materials sounds like an even better idea than having a few teachers select new materials. After all, teachers are the ones who will be using the materials and know what is best for their students, and if they all agree, then they can collaborate on a successful implementation.

The reality of a final selection, however, is often far from ideal and most frequently leads to the selection of materials that are not at all superior to the ones the teachers are already using. All too often the following circumstances occur.

- A small group of teachers is assigned to the adoption committee. Even if they are positive about the assignment, none of them has adequate time to devote to a careful evaluation. The teacher with the strongest personal preference prevails. No one really worries because they determine that all the submissions are pretty much the same anyway, and they can make anything work for them.
- A group of very experienced teachers selects the textbook that is most like what they are already doing so they don't have to change their lesson plans or procedures.
- An administrator awards the adoption to the publisher with the lowest price or most free materials with the school's order to save money for the school or district. The rationale is that all the programs will be equally effective, especially if they have been approved in a state adoption.
- A teacher who has attended a recent conference advocates for the textbook that best reflects the latest fads and trends in education.
- The primary grade teachers select the textbooks that they feel their students will enjoy most, often textbooks with the least amount of text and the most appealing design.
- All-teacher votes rule out any extremes. Research-based programs may appear too difficult to teach. Computer-based programs may not seem to encourage enough classroom participation.
- Teachers select the textbooks they feel will be easiest to teach, ones that require the least amount of preparation.
- The teachers on the adoption committee each receive pallets of materials from the publisher and never open the materials to review because doing so is too overwhelming. They select the latest version of the curriculum from the publisher they had been using or sometimes choose another, even if their curriculum is effective, simply because they want something new and different.
- The publisher that provided the best presentation and treated the faculty to a good snack is awarded the adoption.
- The publisher representative that has the best relationship with the school is awarded the adoption.
- The curriculum coordinators, or the content specialists, select a program that they determine is the highest quality. When the faculty reviews the program and realizes it is dramatically different from current practices, they revolt and refuse to use the new curriculum. Curriculum specialists face the task of motivating teachers to embrace the new curriculum and learn how to use it to its potential advantage. This often results in curriculum supervisors teaching classes themselves.
- An administrator selects and pushes for the implementation of an effective curriculum and expends courage, coercion, political capital, and energy when teachers are not supportive.

The end result of this process most frequently is that teachers select the materials for superficial reasons. They may be the most visually appealing or require the least amount of change. The more experienced and successful teachers are, the less inclined they are to change what they are doing. Therefore, an innovative curriculum, even one with clear-cut demonstrated results, will be rejected and a curriculum much like the current one with updated labels will be adopted.

The conventional wisdom among publishers has been that the publisher with the most pages and most program ancillary components usually won the adoption. The cost of ancillary components—like extra workbooks, manipulatives, game packages—was built into the cost of the core student and teacher editions, so they could be marketed as "free with order." If teachers believe that all programs are equally effective, then the one with more pages or more components appears to be the better deal.

Experienced Teachers Do Not Select the Most Effective Materials

It seems counterintuitive to recommend that experienced teachers not select textbooks. Good teachers are revered. Most adults can easily name teachers who had a significant impact on them. Sometimes it's because the teacher believed in you, helped you, or was a great role model. Many teachers who are idolized are described as tough and challenging, but fair. People recall with respect those teachers who maintained discipline and kept the class in order and with disdain or pity those teachers who let them get away with too much. When summaries of what makes a great teacher appear, the following characteristics tend to emerge: (1) has a sense of humor; (2) is intuitive; (3) knows the subject matter; (4) listens well; (5) is articulate; (6) has an obsessive/compulsive side; (7) can be subversive; (8) is arrogant enough to be fearless; (9) has a performer's instincts; (10) is a real taskmaster (Starkey 2010).

Few would disagree with this list, yet all but one of these characteristics tends to be personality traits. Teachers are judged on how they connected to students or made learning fun. Rarely are they judged on how effective they are or how much students achieved or absorbed.

As Elizabeth Green explains, "Among the factors that do not predict whether a teacher will succeed: a graduate-school degree, a high score on the SAT, an extroverted personality, politeness, confidence, warmth, enthusiasm and having passed the teacher-certification exam on the first try" (Green 2010).

To this list of factors that do not predict teacher effectiveness can be added good curriculum writer or reviewer. Teacher education and training involve how to manage classrooms and deliver curriculum to students. The

qualities that make a good teacher seldom include that they are knowledgeable about the most effective practices identified by research, that they
thoroughly understand student learning trajectories in each subject area,
or that they have great analytical and critical judgment with respect to
evaluating curriculum effectiveness. Yet these are the qualities and skills
that would stand out on the resume of a good curriculum author or writer.
Many curriculum writers would make very poor teachers and many teachers would make poor curriculum writers. The occupations do not share the
same skill set.

Teacher presentations at conferences most often describe a particular lesson that is effective, not a curriculum. The idea that any teacher can translate
his or her success into a curriculum that other teachers will use to duplicate
the success ignores the expertise of content specialists, instructional designers, child development specialists, and curriculum writers. Teacher expertise
is in working with students and delivering curriculum, not in developing
curriculum.

Neither is teacher expertise in identifying and analyzing effective curriculum that will improve teacher and student performance. Time and again instructional materials with the most effective practices, informed by research,
lose out in local and state textbook adoptions to programs that appear to be
easy to teach. Easy to teach programs have minimal teaching strategies, little
or no innovation, pay lip service to education reform, often have extensive
graphic appeal, and a lot of components. As a result, publishers have been incentivized to make their programs look good and appealing to teachers rather
than produce effective results.

In those cases where a strong leader in the schools purchases an innovative
curriculum, there is often powerful resistance from teachers who do not want
to change. Many schools buckle under this pressure and resort to all-teacher
votes, but all-teacher votes empower the status quo.

If a leader is determined to change the curriculum, and a proven curriculum
is implemented, many teachers will become advocates after an initial period
of resistance. More than once, even experienced teachers will say, "I never
knew how to teach ___ until I used this program." Colleges of education
rarely teach their students how to recognize effective curriculum characteristics.

Unless a school is already top notch, effective materials should require
teachers to change what they do. But as a teacher, once you have figured out
how to survive and have a bank of lesson plans, you are very reluctant to
change and will select new materials that require the least amount of change.
Because experienced teachers hold the most sway in adoption committees,
the status quo prevails.

There is no intentional malice in this process. Why would a successful teacher want to change and potentially throw out his or her bank of lesson plans? So when new and different curricula are adopted, many experienced teachers simply ignore the new materials or adapt their lesson plans to accommodate the new materials. Either way the status quo is maintained.

CONCLUSION

With all the attention focused on improving education, it is remarkable how little analysis is given to curriculum effectiveness. Students, teachers, and parents assume that textbooks are accurate, cover required standards, and are effective. The government avoids imposing on the free market enterprise of selecting textbooks. State adoption committees review textbooks to discern if the state standards are covered. School adoption committees assume textbooks cover the standards and make selections based on appeal, ease of use, and costs. Because all textbooks appear so similar, experienced teachers, the strongest voices in selection committees, choose materials that require the least amount of change.

The free market does not work to select the most effective materials if the people selecting are not educated in curriculum design and best practices and are not trained to evaluate curriculum effectiveness. Although teachers are experts in working with students, they are not experts in curriculum. When they select materials, they typically select materials that have appealing design, are easy to teach, and have a large number of components and features. They do not select the most effective materials. Harriet Tyson-Bernstein explained how the textbook selection process was flawed in 1988, and her observations are still relevant today (Tyson-Bernstein 1988).

Yet, if student achievement is stagnant, improvements must be made in all the ingredients of education and curriculum is a key ingredient. Einstein's definition of insanity applies: "Insanity: doing the same thing over and over again and expecting different results." Selecting again and again curricular materials that don't require change will not help to improve education. Throughout American history curricular materials have played a significant role in improving education. The current environment requires a new generation of effective materials that will advance education. But unless the system for selecting curricular materials is reformed, educational publishers will continue to produce materials using the same criteria they have been using and growth will be stunted.

Chapter Two

The Educational Publishing Business and Profit Motive

Of the $8 billion spent annually on K–12 instructional materials in the United States, about $4 billion is spent on textbooks and digital products, according to figures from the Association of American Publishers.

—Dakarai Aarons (2010)

Educational publishing in the United States is a for-profit business. Because education has been and continues to be a national priority, educational publishing has flourished over the years. It is comforting to think that publishers create educational materials to improve education and the lives of children, but in fact they produce educational materials to make money and reinvest in the business. If they could make money by improving education and the lives of children, they would. Other countries may have state-sponsored or government-approved curriculum, but in the United States, as in many countries, free market forces determine the materials schools use. Like any business, publically owned educational publishers are responsible to their shareholders and motivated by profit. They will do what they need to do to maintain a profitable business model.

ABOUT THE EDUCATIONAL PUBLISHING BUSINESS

Published educational materials for grades prekindergarten to grade 12 come in basically two forms: *basal* materials and *supplemental* materials. Basal materials are primarily programs that provide comprehensive instruction for an entire subject area. Basal programs may span the elementary grades, providing a complete reading, math, science, or social studies curriculum. In high school, basal materials are defined by individual subject areas, such as algebra, US history, or chemistry. Basal programs are intended to meet all the required standards for that area at specific grade levels. A basal program may include student textbooks, workbooks, manipulatives such as geometric shapes for math, software, and teacher guides. Supplemental materials are designed to support a specific subject area that may have nonexistent or weak coverage within the basal program. For example, teachers may feel that the basal reading program does not provide enough practice with grammar skills and may supplement the reading instruction with a grammar workbook or software program. Some teachers who don't use basal materials, use an assortment of supplemental materials to create their own lessons.

Reading in grades K–6 is the largest market for educational materials. The most comprehensive basal programs are reading programs since they make up almost 25 percent of the textbook market. Reading has also been the highest priority for elementary teachers. Reading proficiency is widely tested and reading test scores typically determine a school's adequate yearly progress, which is related to school funding. Basal materials are also available in a wide variety of subjects, including auto mechanics, fine arts, and instructional technology. A publisher may spend $100 million or more on producing a basal reading program, $75 million on a mathematics program, but as little as $3 million on a fine arts program. Investments are made based on market spending. Core subject area spending may vary year by year depending on the economy or a particular adoption year, but they typically follow this pattern.

1. Reading, 24 percent
2. Mathematics, 20 percent
3. Language Arts, 13 percent
4. Science, 13 percent
5. Social Studies, 11 percent

Even with variations in the level of state and federal funding for education, educational publishing is a very stable market. Because educational publishing depends on government funding, its profitability depends on adequate government revenues. In an economic downturn, if states or schools delay purchases, publishers downsize and limit investments in new products. Eventually, however, schools will require new materials and purchases will be completed.

The goal of business is to maintain profitability by satisfying consumer demand. In the case of educational publishing the consumers, by and large, are teachers. Of course students use the materials, and taxpayers ultimately pay for them through school budgets, but it is primarily teacher committees who select educational materials and it is teachers whom publishers strive to please.

In the nineteenth and twentieth centuries the free marketplace served education well, providing materials that helped to standardize curriculum, offering a wide variety of educational choices, and helping teachers meet state and national standards. One could argue convincingly that the relationship of commerical publishers and public education has been extremely productive. Curriculum developed by the government could easily become dogmatic. Curriculum developed by universities or nonprofit organizations may not have the resources that a commercial endeavor could employ to create appealing, comprehensive materials.

Over the past thirty years, however, in an effort to maximize profit the educational publishing industry has undergone a massive consolidation. This has resulted in a monolithic industry that stifles innovation, squashes competition, drastically limits choice, and creates a risk-averse development process that at best perpetuates the status quo. Because customers do not demand diversity, choice, and proof of effectiveness, educational publishers have pursued paths to increased profitability.

THE HISTORY OF THE EDUCATIONAL PUBLISHING BUSINESS IN THE UNITED STATES

Educational publishers have a long-established history of marketing and selling goods and services in the form of textbooks, educational materials, and professional development to educational institutions. Education and the educational publishing industry have enjoyed a symbiotic relationship throughout the history of the United States.

Textbooks in the Nineteenth Century

Thomas Jefferson believed that the survival of democracy depended on an educated and informed population. Education was the essential ingredient of democracy. Jefferson's plan for education included these principles (Jewett 1996):

1. Democracy cannot long exist without enlightenment.
2. Talent and virtue, needed in a free society, should be educated regardless of wealth, birth, or other accidental condition.
3. Children of the poor must be educated at common expense.

During the early part of the nineteenth century, Jefferson's ideas were expanded and interpreted differently by those who wanted local control of schools and those who wanted more centralized control and state funding. As public education became a foundation of American democracy, educational materials were developed to support it.

Horace Mann carried the mantle of public education into the nineteenth century. He saw public education as the means for achieving the greatest good for the largest population and convinced business interests that public education promised benefits for them. He also promoted the idea that education led to upward social mobility and advocated for standardization and the creation of state boards as opposed to local boards of education. Among other responsibilities, these state boards selected instructional materials.

Although there is a tradition of instructional materials dating back to the Greeks, American textbooks developed out of the growing need to educate the American population. In the early years of the country, this involved the teaching of reading, writing, and mathematics. Early textbooks like *The New England Primer* were widely used. The *Schoolmaster's Assistant* by Thomas Dilworth was an arithmetic book that went through fifty-eight American printings. Noah Webster's *Blue Back Speller*, which eventually sold over 100 million copies, presented an American spelling system. The pedagogical goal of most of these books was a student's memorization of definitions, rules, facts, and spellings. Textbooks provided the lessons to memorize and teachers provided the discipline. These materials could be used with or without a trained teacher and many students, including Abraham Lincoln, were self-taught from these types of books.

The public school movement expanded as states began to fund local schools to promote equality and democracy. Public schools in turn promoted the idea of standardized textbooks. At the same time, educational theories were expounded and more and more teachers were educated in "normal schools," which were created to train high school graduates to be teachers. With this emphasis on education, textbooks became commodities and textbook marketing and competition ensued. To stay ahead of the competition, for example, the *Blue Back Speller* added more woodcut images. To support the Americanization of the population, textbooks like the McGuffey Readers, which eventually sold over 122 million copies, began to include moral tales that taught children how to read at the same time they introduced them to American ideas and morality. As public school enrollments grew from 7.6 million in 1870 to 12.7 million in 1890, educational publishers innovated to respond to customer needs and competition.

Many of today's major publishing companies got their start in the eighteenth and nineteenth centuries. For example, Thomas Longman founded Longman in London in 1724, and a Longman family member controlled the company until 1972. Longman is now an imprint of Pearson Education

(Pearson Education 2010). Houghton Mifflin had its start in 1832 as Ticknor and Fields, publisher of Emerson, Hawthorne, and Thoreau. In 1880 Ticknor and Fields merged with Houghton and Mifflin. In 2007 Houghton Mifflin merged with Harcourt Publishing that had its start in 1905 as World Book Company. McGraw-Hill was founded in 1888 and is headed today by Harold W. McGraw, a descendant. The textbook industry was profitable in the nineteenth and twentieth centuries because it provided educators with organized, structured, and comprehensive curriculum in different subject areas.

Educational Publishing in the Twentieth Century

With the influx of immigrants in the early part of the twentieth century, schools took on the job of vocational education to produce a competent workforce for America's industries. For this purpose high school was extended to all children and truancy laws were instituted. Schools expanded their offerings to provide both academic and vocational tracts. Textbooks were developed to support the different curricula.

Textbooks continued to support the Americanization of the immigrant population by introducing newcomers to American culture and society. For example, Scott Foresman's Dick and Jane reading series provided models of suburban life. In the last half of the twentieth century, attention to including people of different races, ages, and ethnic backgrounds as a modern reflection of American life was expressed in educational materials.

The textbook industry grew as enrollments increased as well. In 1905 only one-third of children who enrolled in first grade enrolled in high school and only a third of those graduated from high school, with even fewer attending college. By 1920, 17 percent graduated and by 1930 over 45 percent graduated from high school. In 2006, 68.6 percent of American children graduated from high school (National Center for Higher Education Management Systems 2006). Educational publishers responded to the needs by producing a wide variety of academic and vocational materials, and textbook companies flourished, even during the Great Depression. Textbooks provided curriculum as diverse as home economics, engineering, auto mechanics, electricity, and Latin. With its contribution to standardizing curriculum and setting standards in each subject area, educational publishing leant credibility to a high school diploma, which many employers use as a prerequisite to employment.

The Elementary and Secondary Education Act (ESEA), enacted in 1965, had a profound effect on American education and affected the expansion of instructional materials. The ESEA, which has been reauthorized every five years since 1965, with the No Child Left Behind Act serving as the reauthorization in 2001, provides substantial funding for professional development, instructional materials, and other resources to promote American education. The legislation included the following initiatives that focused the funding and development of educational materials. If educational materials satisfied requirements, schools could use federal funds to purchase them.

- Title I funding to assist in the education of low-income families
- Title II funding for school library resources, textbooks, and other instructional materials
- Title III funding for supplementary educational centers and services
- Title IV funding for educational research and training
- Title V grants to strengthen state departments of education
- Title VI in 1966 aid to handicapped children
- Title VII in 1967 funding for bilingual education programs

The 1994 reauthorization of Title III included specific funding for Technology in Education, and Title II included funding for professional development. Federal funds could then be used for electronic materials and teacher training. In 2001, No Child Left Behind required states to develop assessments in basic skills to increase school accountability to meet adequate yearly progress, which resulted in federal funding spent on state assessment programs.

With increased focus on all these different areas, publishers developed instructional materials to respond to the needs of projects that would receive federal funding. As educational theories about how to teach different subjects and research were promoted throughout the twentieth century, textbooks began to reflect new instructional practices. In reading, theories included whole word, sight word, phonics, and whole language approaches, and reading programs were developed for a whole language approach, a phonics approach, a linguistic approach, a whole word approach, a sight word approach, and other potentially effective methods. For each approach, educational publishers responded with completely different series to fit the desires of a school district. In math education, when new math was popularized in the 1960s, math textbooks reflected new math lessons. As differentiation and individualization emerged as concerns, educational materials provided strategies to address them.

Educational materials were profitable in the twentieth century because they addressed the wide diversity of curriculum needs. They met the need of providing curriculum for the enormous variety of subject areas that schools offered in both academic and vocational arenas. Within a subject area, curriculum materials were created to address different philosophies and teaching methods. Educational publishers were able to find niche markets for a wide variety of materials.

The Twenty-First Century:
From Specialization to Commoditization

The textbook business is difficult to enter. It requires a major upfront invest-ment of human and monetary resources, typically two to three years before the products are sold into the market. As a consequence, educational publish-ing comprises companies that started in the eighteenth and nineteenth centu-ries and have fought their way into the twenty-first century. A key to survival is to have a substantial backlist of previously published materials that are still in print with enough residual sales, such as workbooks that are repurchased every year, to pay the bills and provide for investments in new products and revisions of older successful programs.

As public education grew in the nineteenth and twentieth centuries, the de-mand for instructional materials grew and spawned hundreds of educational publishers. As the need for materials expanded to vocational education, pub-lishers rose to fill that need.

Throughout the nineteenth and twentieth centuries educational publishers were, for the most part, specialized and many small publishers flourished. Laidlaw Brothers was a language arts publisher with strong ties in the Catho-lic schools. Charles E. Merrill had strengths in science. Addison Wesley had strengths in mathematics. Steck-Vaughn and Modern Curriculum Press were supplemental publishers, providing extra practice workbooks in phonics and math (Whiting 2010).

In the last two decades of the twentieth century, educational publishers were increasingly incentivized to create comprehensive programs in each of the core subject areas (reading, math, science, social studies) rather than smaller pro-grams that addressed specific philosophies or niches. Larger programs began to incorporate subjects that had previously been taught separately. For example, reading programs incorporated handwriting, spelling, and writing instruction. Some reading programs also claimed to cover science and social studies stan-dards. Publishers began to spend enormous amounts of money to produce these programs and looked for ways to consolidate and economize.

Today, as a result of this consolidation only three educational publishing companies account for over 75 percent of all instructional materials in the United States: McGraw-Hill, Pearson, and Houghton/Harcourt. Each of these publishers has its roots in the nineteenth century. Over the past thirty years, however, there has been a steady consolidation as larger companies sought to grow and increase their market share through an acquisition strategy. The three companies have swallowed up much of their competition. Although ever changing, table 2.1 identifies some of the key acquisitions of the three major publishers by the end of 2009.

Table 2.1. Consolidation of Educational Publishers as of 2010

McGraw-Hill (founded in 1888)	Pearson (founded in 1724; Thomas Longman published the first book typeset by Benjamin Franklin)	Houghton Mifflin Harcourt (founded in 1832 with Ticknor and Fields)	Still Independent
Barnell Loft	Addison Wesley	American Heritage	America's Choice
Bennett	Addision-Wesley Longman	Broderbund	Cambium
Benziger	AG	Brooks/Cole	Davis Publications
Contemporary	Alemany Press	Cengage	Hampton Brown/
Creative Publications	Allyn & Bacon	Clarion	National Geographic
The Grow Network	altonaED	Classroom Connect	John Wiley & Sons
CTB (California Test Bureau)	Celebration Press	Course Technology	Kendall Hunt
Dolch	Chancery Software	DataDirector	Key Curriculum Press
Economy	Cisco Press	D.C. Heath	Learning.com
EDL Educational Development Labs	Cobblestone Publishing	Delmar	The Math Learning Center
Everyday Learning	Computer Curriculum Corporation	Earobics	Mondo Publishing
Glencoe	Cuisenaire Company	Edmark	Sadlier Oxford
Gregg	Dale Seymour	Education Media and Publishing Group International	Scholastic
Ideal/Instructional Fair	DDC Publishing	Edusoft	Zaner-Bloser
Jamestown	Dominie Press, Inc.	Gale	
Laidlaw	eCollege	Great Source	
Landoll	Educational Management Group	Harcourt School	
Lippincott	Ellis Horwood	Heinemann	
Living & Learning	ELLIS	Heinle	
Macmillan	Family Education Network	Holt, Rinehart, Winston	
McCormick Mather	Fearon	Houghton Mifflin Learning Company	
Meeks Heit	Ginn & Company	Mariner Books	
Merrill	Globe Fearon	McDougal Littell	
Mimosa	Harper & Row		
National Textbook Company	Interstate Publishers		

Open Court
Optical Data
Palmer
Random House
RGA/Lowell House
SRA
Thompson Learning
Tribune Learning
Webster
Wright Group

Janus Book Publishers
Lange Medical Publications
Little, Brown & Company
Longman
Macmillan Computer Publishing
Macmillan Publishing
Markt & Technik
Modern Curriculum Press
National Publishers
NCS
Peachpit Press
Philip Allan
Prentice Hall
Promissor
Psychological Corporation
Que
Quercus Corp.
Regents Publishing
Scholar Inc.
Scott Foresman
Shepards
Silver & Company
Silver Burdett
Silver Burdett, & Ginn
Simon and Schuster
W.C. Brown
William Collins
Ziff-Davis Press

Psychological Corp
Rigby
Riverdeep
Riverside Publishing
Saxon
Schirmer
SkillsTutor
South-Western College
Steck-Vaughn
Sunburst Communications
Thomson Learning College
Ticknor and Fields
Wadsworth

Sources: McGraw-Hill Companies 2010; Pearson Education 2010; Hougton Mifflin Harcourt 2010.

As a result of the consolidation, each of the three big publishing houses has at least four key divisions that provide print and digital educational materials: preK–8 elementary basal, 6–12 high school, supplemental, and testing. Further consolidation continues to occur.

CAUSES OF CONSOLIDATION

Educational publishing is a business. There are a few nonprofit companies that got their start in universities with grant funding, but the lion's share of publishers have a responsibility to their shareholders to provide profit. Over the past thirty years most educational publishers moved from specialization to commoditization strategy. Companies that had strengths in one area were purchased by other companies that had specializations in other areas to create a complete product line under one umbrella. Economies of scale in all areas of the business were established to consolidate product development, financial resources, and sales functions.

Given that publishers are for-profit businesses and only a few publishers have maintained their independence, several factors contributed to the massive consolidation of the industry over the past thirty years.

State Adoptions

One significant reason for the consolidation of the educational publishing industry is the nature of state adoptions. State adoptions drive the educational publishing schedule. The big three adoption states (Texas, California, and Florida) adopt new materials on a five- to eight-year cycle. The sales for these big adoptions occur in the first and/or second year of the adoption. A reading publisher that makes a substantial investment in a program for Texas must find other avenues of revenue for the nonadoption years. This need inspired publishers to acquire other publishing companies that had other specialties so that they would have offerings for each and every adoption in the big three states. If a publisher wanted to expand its business into another subject area, it could purchase another publisher with a reputation in that area. This occurred when Macmillan, later Macmillan/McGraw-Hill purchased Merrill Publishing for its science programs and when Silver Burdett, later Pearson, purchased Addison Wesley to expand into math in the 1990s.

Homogenized Standards

Over the past thirty years, the emphasis on and development of educational standards and the requirement that publishers meet these standards have also had a dramatic effect on the educational publishing industry. As standards began to define curriculum, the elements that made individual publishers distinctive, including unique philosophies and specific authors were de-emphasized. If a curriculum must meet all the standards before it will be considered by a state for adoption or a school for purchase, educational publishers have no incentive to create innovative materials or to create materials for which there are no standards. Materials that do not address specific state standards will not sell.

Because most state standards are based on some version of national standards, for example the National Council of Teachers of Mathematics standards, all publishers must include much of the same content in their programs. It is difficult for a publisher to create or support two different profitable programs that teach the same subject matter.

Investment Costs

If a textbook program is successful in the marketplace, publishers stand to make a lot of money. Because reading is so fundamental and potentially lucrative, representing 25 percent of all instructional materials purchased, a publisher may invest upward of $100 million dollars to create a basal reading program. Mathematics comes second. Yet even for a subject like fine arts, which is taught on average once a week in the 50 percent of American schools that teach art, publishers may invest up to $5 million dollars in development costs alone.

As programs became increasingly bigger to address more state standards, investments increased. Publishers that did not have the resources to create multimillion-dollar programs could not compete and were either dissolved or acquired by bigger companies.

To be adopted and be able to sell materials in key states, a program must meet all of the state standards. That requirement eliminates small, targeted publishers that do not have the resources to meet all the standards. A large company would seldom consider investing in a small, targeted program if they were already developing a larger program for the subject area.

Competition

Competition has encouraged the expansion of individual programs and as a result has pushed many publishers out of business and reduced choice. Customers assume that all programs that have been adopted by the state cover the standards and will all be equally effective. Because of this, customers look for other reasons to differentiate and select materials. The most obvious and easily explained is to provide components or features that other programs do not have. Bigger publishers have a major advantage over smaller publishers in this arena because they can employ already published resources from some of their other programs. For example, science biography cards created to support a science program can be repurposed for the publisher's reading program. These cross-curricular connections are very appealing to teachers. This has caused the size of programs to mushroom exponentially since publishers feel they must have every component and feature that other publishers have to be competitive.

Many publishers could not compete with increasingly larger investments and as larger publishers acquired smaller publishers, competition shrank. For example, Holt and McDougal were competitors in the high school educational market, but once they were under one umbrella, they no longer threatened each other's market share and eventually the parent company published only one program instead of two.

Because the best-selling programs offer convenience and ease of use rather than effectiveness, publishers focus their efforts on those qualities. The most successful programs in recent times are those that have these elements:

- Largest page count. The perception that an increased page count offers more in-depth material and greater choice and coverage inspired a competitive race among publishers to see which program could have the largest book. This has translated over the past two decades into multivolume student and teacher books.
- Emphasis on cross-curricular connections. Cross-curricular features and content such as social studies and science connections in a reading or math program appear to help teachers make connections among the subjects and address standards in other subject areas that may not otherwise be addressed. Whether the cross-curricular connections are used or actually address the intention of a content-area standard is of less importance.
- Greatest number of components. If one publisher offers a trade book library or a software practice game with its program, the other publishers will quickly offer other components to level the playing field.
- Minimal teaching requirements or innovation. The programs that offer teachers greater convenience and the most resources while at the same time not requiring that teachers change their practices have been the most successful in the marketplace.

Profit Pressure

Because of the increased investment costs due to standards and competition, publishers have faced increased pressure to be profitable. Founders of companies, like Robert Laidlaw and John Saxon who had a vested interest in education, were replaced with managers having backgrounds in sales, marketing, or finance. Their experience has to do with increasing profitability rather than promoting a particular philosophy or strategy. If profit can be made by developing effective materials, that is all well and good. More important, however, are the features that appeal to the teachers who select the materials, including design and a variety of features and components that give the impression that there are a multitude of resources for teachers to use.

Companies also maintained profitability by acquiring other companies. Not only does an acquired company provide the purchaser with a complete product line for adoptions, once an acquisition is made, costs are minimized by consolidating human resources, warehousing, manufacturing, accounting, marketing, and sales. For a time a company may keep a separate salesforce for different divisions, particularly if the divisions have different instructional philosophies, but eventually the pressure to merge to save costs usually prevails.

EFFECTS OF PUBLISHING INDUSTRY CONSOLIDATION

Limited Choice

One effect of consolidation of educational publishers has been a dramatic decrease in the number and diversity of publisher offerings and customer choice. In contrast to the more than twenty-five basal reading programs available in the 1960s, basal reading now has only three major contenders: McGraw-Hill School, Houghton Mifflin Harcourt, and Pearson.

Further consolidation is continually occurring within each publishing company. For example, for the 2007 math adoptions in Texas and California, McGraw-Hill submitted three programs from the different divisions: SRA Real Math, Wright Group Everyday Math, and the School Division Math Connects. In the 2009 Florida math adoption, McGraw-Hill submitted only one program, a revision of Math Connects. It was not deemed cost-effective to revise three programs since the investment must be in line with the size of the potential market. The research-based programs, like Everyday Math, Real Math (McGraw-Hill), Investigations (Pearson), Math Expressions (Houghton Mifflin Harcourt), Math Trailblazers (Kendall Hunt), or Math Learning Center's Bridges, would have been eliminated if they were not revised to meet Florida's standards. Plus they may have had limited appeal to the teachers who select the books. It is not cost-effective for a publisher to submit them for adoption. With submission, the publisher must incur marketing, sampling,

and inventory costs. A large company would naturally put its energy and resources behind one program with the largest target market appeal instead of
trying to support two different programs.

Limited Subject-Area Coverage

As smaller companies have been incorporated into larger ones, specialties
and niche publishers have been eliminated. With the emphasis on creating
large programs for each core subject area, it is no longer worthwhile for a
major publisher to use financial and employee resources on products that will
bring in limited revenue.

Spelling is an excellent example. In 1985 there were almost thirty well-
known spelling programs on the market. At the time many adoption states
limited and ranked their final approved programs to the top ten, top five,
or top three to help teachers make selections. Some spelling programs were
basal programs. Others were supplemental. Many had very different philosophies and organization. Some were more effective than others.

As the industry consolidated, McGraw-Hill acquired at least seven different spelling programs (Barnell Loft, Laidlaw, Macmillan, Merrill, Random
House, SRA, and Webster). Houghton Mifflin Harcourt acquired D.C. Heath,
McDougal, Riverside, Harcourt, Steck-Vaughn, and Houghton Mifflin spelling programs. By 2000, each company produced only one spelling program.
With this consolidation came the absence of alternative approaches, any
diversity, or broader choice.

In 2010 only two spelling programs were submitted for the potentially
lucrative Texas adoption for grades 1–6: Zaner-Bloser, a family owned publisher, and School Specialty Intervention. Many states have stopped including
spelling as a separate subject on their adoption lists. Having built spelling into
their basal reading programs, the big three publishers decided not to invest in
separate spelling programs. The programs they each acquired over the years
already are or may soon be phased out of print. If teachers wanted to teach
spelling using a research-based word list, organization, and strategies, they
would have very few options. School Specialty eventually dropped its bid
for adoption when several of its levels did not meet the Texas criteria. As a
result, one spelling program was approved in Texas in 2010, and the major
publishers may succeed in having Texas reconsider funding the adoption,
since spelling is now incorporated in their reading programs.

Bland Materials

With huge investments to create huge programs at stake, educational publishers are very concerned about giving any potential customer cause to

reject a program. As a result, publishers are careful to balance references to age, ethnic, and racial groups so the population is adequately represented. They also carefully review materials to avoid any controversial topics or controversial literature. In the same vein, publishers ensure that a program addresses all concerns, all trends, and all approaches so every customer will find something they like—a one-size-fits-all approach. The inclusion of all instructional approaches and philosophies, however, is almost the same as having no philosophy or approach.

At one time, authors such as John Saxon in mathematics or William Kottmeyer in spelling wrote programs based on their successful experiences and expertise. These programs were very distinctive and advocated a specific approach to the subject. Not everyone liked the programs, but those who did found them to be highly effective. Because marketing departments argue that teachers will not purchase programs that are too different from what they are currently using, today's major publishers find well-respected authors to contribute to a program, but often minimize their contributions in order to promote marketing concerns over research and effectiveness. The result is that the major programs have no vision or consistent philosophy that will motivate teachers and students.

Lack of Concept Development and Innovation

With all the profit pressure in today's major educational publishing companies, it is very difficult to get new or innovative projects approved. Salespeople who have significant influence over the publishing plans look back to the last most successful campaign and want to match it rather than create new strategies. They promote the idea of copying a successful competitor. Financial staff is risk averse. They will be skeptical of establishing and entering any new market because the publisher has no track record. They may be skeptical of entering an existing market because the competition is too fierce. They will not want to reinvest in a product that didn't sell well with the why-pour-good-money-after-bad point of view. And many resist investing in revising a profitable program because if it's not broke, why fix it? This is often the opposite of the philosophy behind why many companies were originally established: a visionary had a great idea and developed it into a profitable product.

Now that more and more curricular materials are digitized, the major publishers are looking to repurpose the materials they have already created. Huge databases of lessons, images, and practice and assessment items have been created so that instead of producing new materials, publishers can select from materials that have already been created. If publishers are not incentivized to rethink their approaches and create new, innovative, and effective programs, they will likely make use of their digital assets and contribute to maintaining the status quo.

A striking example is the comparison of a current algebra program with one from 1965 (Dolciani, Berman, and Freilich 1965; Burger et al. 2011). Newer should be better, and teachers and administrators assume new instructional materials and new editions are superior to the old, but this is often not the case. Granted, a newer program may reflect the newest trends, have an updated design, and match the competition point for point, but there have been no incentives for ensuring that the best practices and the most effective instruction and the most engaging and challenging exercises and activities are included.

A comparison of math books from 1965 to 2011 demonstrates the following points.

- Books almost doubled in size (564–920 pages).
- Today's books are much more colorful, from 2-color to 4-color.
- The percentage of each page devoted to design elements and graphics has dramatically increased in the newer editions.
- Teacher editions include many more features (organizers, warm-ups, differentiating instruction, math humor).
- There is much more emphasis on assessment and standardized testing. There is no mention of standardized tests in the 1965 edition. Huge sections of the student and teacher editions in the current books are devoted to test preparation.
- Current editions promote a wide variety of options for managing a diverse student population with Lesson Tutorial Videos addressing every example in the student edition differentiated instruction, assessment, and intervention. The program includes online editions, Spanish editions, and DVD editions of the student book, along with twenty-eight additional components, including a $667 classroom manipulative kit. The 1965 edition has a student edition, a teacher's edition, and a set of transparencies.
- A comparison of the tables of contents will demonstrate that the topics covered in the books are very similar (see table 2.2).

The point is not that we should return to the days of old because life was so much simpler. Surely the emphasis on differentiated instruction and the extra resources for teachers to explain concepts and the technology access for students are welcome, but is the instruction superior? After forty-five years of research in how people learn coupled with teacher experience, one would expect the concept development in newer editions to reflect that. Certainly with the emphasis on early algebra, a lot of research has focused on this topic. Yet publishers have been rewarded for design and additional components in the quest to make teachers' lives easier. They have not been incentivized to improve the content or teaching methods.

Table 2.2. Comparison of Algebra Tables of Contents, 1965 and 2011

	1965		2011
Chapter 1	Symbols and Sets	Chapter 1	Foundations for Algebra
Chapter 2	Variables and Open Sentences		
Chapter 3	Axioms, Equations, and Problem Solving	Chapter 2	Equations
Chapter 4	The Negative Numbers		
Chapter 5	Equations, Inequalities, and Problem Solving	Chapter 3	Inequalities
		Chapter 6	Systems of Equations and Inequalities
Chapter 6	Working with Polynomials	Chapter 7	Exponents and Polynomials
		Chapter 8	Factoring Polynomials
Chapter 7	Special Products and Factoring	Chapter 10	Data Analysis and Probability
Chapter 8	Working with Fractions		
Chapter 9	Graphs		
Chapter 10	Sentences in Two Variables		
Chapter 11	The Real Numbers		
Chapter 12	Functions and Variation	Chapter 4	Functions
		Chapter 5	Linear Functions
		Chapter 11	Exponential and Radical Functions
		Chapter 12	Rational Functions and Equations
Chapter 13	Quadratic Equations and Inequalities	Chapter 9	Quadratic Functions and Equations
Chapter 14	Geometry and Trigonometry		
Chapter 15	Comprehensive Review and Tests		

Commonality and Competition

Educational publishing is a highly competitive industry. If a publisher invests $100 million to develop a reading program, the publisher must mitigate as many risks as possible to recoup its investment and make a profit. Intensive energy is expended at every publishing company to study subject-area requirements and the competition, and identify and counter strengths and weaknesses. Because there are only three major publishers, if one publisher produces a popular new element into a program, the other two usually add a similar element quickly.

To command market share, the big three companies believe they must duplicate features and components that other successful programs have. So today's programs have grown astronomically large with an overwhelming number of pages and components. Yet the programs cover the same standards and disguise unique elements that might cause teacher customers to object. Instead of variety in approach or sequence, the companies attempt to differentiate in design and extra components that come free with an order. New ideas and new approaches, even those proven effective, have little chance of reaching the market if they are not required and supported by the states. California even penalizes publishers for having extraneous content, that is, content that is not required in their standards. The investments, up to $100 million and more, to produce a basal reading program are so large that educational publishers are unwilling to take any unnecessary risks of doing something that has not been successful in the past or does not prove popular in focus groups of teachers. The competition is monopolistic, in that the three companies publish products that are very similar in spite of their attempt to use advertising, branding, and packaging to convince customers that their products are different. In the end the main basal programs are virtually interchangeable.

"Just seven math curricula constitute 91 percent of the curricula used by K–2 educators. Should these curricula differ substantially in effectiveness, the implications for policy and practice would be significant" (Whitehurst 2009).

CONCLUSION

In 1991, the consolidation of the textbook industry was discussed with concern about the consequences (Altbach et al. 1991). Today the issues are even more pronounced.

Educational publishing has had a long symbiotic relationship with public education. Over the years educational publishers helped to standardize curriculum and bring equity and equal opportunity to schools. Educational publishers have contributed to the depth and breadth of educational experiences by providing comprehensive curriculum in a wide variety of subject areas.

Over the past thirty years, educational publishers have focused on increasing profits and market share by consolidating their products and processes. This has resulted in a dearth of customer choice, a reluctance to innovate, and huge programs that are barely distinguishable from one another. Today the major publishers that account for 75 percent of the materials used in schools are each producing similar programs with similar instructional strategies, strategies that do not require teachers to change their practices significantly. This would be all well and good if the status quo was acceptable, but it is not.

Lack of choice is not good for education. Competition should inspire constant innovation and improvement. Cell phones of just five years ago are vastly inferior to the cell phone of today. One cell phone company increases sales because it offers better features and faster service. In contrast, instructional materials are bigger but not better than they were five years ago. Publishers are not incentivized to create increasingly effective materials because their customers do not use effectiveness as a criterion for evaluation and purchase.

Education is the foundation for a better future. There is little chance for innovative and more effective materials to reach the classroom without a change in the way curricular materials are reviewed and selected, which would incentivize publishers to create more effective materials, and schools to adopt and learn to use them with integrity. Without free market incentives, publishers will likely continue to maximize profits by minimizing competition, consolidating resources, and concentrating on superficial marketing factors, such as design elements, larger page counts, and features that don't contribute to improving education and student achievement.

Chapter Three

Educational Materials Publishing

Players, Process, and Priorities

The textbook adoption and selection process has a direct effect on publishing priorities in producing educational materials. Although there are many points in the publishing process where concern about effectiveness could take priority, this is overshadowed by the criteria the customers use to select the materials: meeting state standards, marketing concerns about design, ease of use for teachers, and competitive advantages.

To analyze why the publishing process does not make effectiveness a priority requires an understanding of the process itself, the many players involved in it, and their competing priorities and interests. This analysis reveals the key decision points that potentially could, but most often do not, emphasize the importance of producing educational materials that will actually be effective in the classroom.

It is easy to assume that K–12 educational publishing is like other types of publishing in that an author writes a manuscript and then confers with an editor to finalize the content. After the author and editor are satisfied, a copyeditor corrects any errors in the manuscript; then the manuscript is sent to be designed, produced, printed, and released for sale.

Although some aspects are the same, educational publishing is very different from other types of publishing. For one thing, no one author or team of authors would be able to write all the thousands of pages that even one grade level of a basal series would require. One volume of a typical teacher's guide, for example, includes over a thousand pages. Many grade levels of a basal reading or math program include up to six teacher edition volumes. This would take years for one author to write. It is not possible or advisable for the authors to write all the materials. The author should direct the writing of a first grade reading program, but it would not be a good use of the author's time, for example, to painstakingly select decodable words and ensure adequate repetition of phonetic patterns.

Another reason the curriculum development process is so involved is because of the number of constituents that must be satisfied.

INSTRUCTIONAL MATERIALS CONSTITUENTS

Before a writer begins to write, he or she must consider the intended audience. All instructional materials have many constituents whose ideas, concerns, and needs must be addressed if the materials stand a chance of being widely used in classrooms. Sometimes the constituent concerns are the same. Sometimes they are in opposition. Most of the time they are just different.

- **Teachers** are concerned with ease of teaching and appeal to students.
- **School administrators** are concerned with cost, teacher satisfaction, and improving test scores.
- **Government officials** are concerned with academic progress.
- **Parents** are concerned with student satisfaction and achievement.
- **Public interests** are interested in how the textbook addresses concerns such as accuracy, controversial topics, or ethnic and gender representation.
- **State adoption committees** are concerned with how effectively the materials address their particular state's guidelines.
- **Students** are concerned that the materials are comprehensible and manageable.

It is easy to see that the key concerns of the major constituents do not include how effective the materials will be in promoting student achievement. Effectiveness may be assumed, but it is not a priority among many of the constituents.

INSTRUCTIONAL MATERIALS PLAYERS

Because of the complicated nature of the curriculum development process, many different players are involved. These players often have competing and conflicting interests. Some are obsessed with creating effective materials. Others focus on creating profitable materials. Some are mainly concerned with meeting the schedule. Some are only worried about the design. Others are focused on making sure the required standards are addressed. The competition among the players results in what the final product reflects.

Understanding the role, priorities, and influence of each of the players helps to reveal how the priorities for an educational program are translated into the final product.

The publishing players fall into four categories: development team, production team, sales team, and upper management. The specifics of each role may vary from publisher to publisher, but the responsibilities and tasks exist regardless. Each of these players takes his or her responsibility seriously. The tensions among the teams could lead to a well-designed, competitive, and highly effective program, but too often, because customers do not demand it, program effectiveness is not a priority.

Development Team

The development team is responsible for generating the program scope and sequence, design, and content. The educational publishing development team translates an idea into a manuscript. The team consists of authors, editors, writers, and designers. A publisher's development *team* is different from a development *company*, which is an external company that provides editorial and production outsourced services to a development team.

Authors

An author of an educational curriculum is usually *not* the writer of the curriculum. In educational publishing, writers carry out the authors' and editors' directives. Authors of textbooks are usually university professors who have made their reputations as experts in specific areas of the curricula. The author represents an educational product and his or her educational philosophy and reputation are on the line.

Years ago in commercial publishing, the author might have been the visionary—the educator who has the idea for an effective curriculum. This is still true in some nonprofit publishing houses. In those cases, particularly if a project is funded through a grant, the author may not be concerned with appealing to teachers or adoption committees. The author may not be concerned with design, inconsistencies, or even readability.

In today's for-profit, commercial publishing companies, the publisher typically identifies and selects textbook authors. Rarely are authors selected from a submission of an unsolicited manuscript. Publishers desire people, usually academics, who are well-known researchers and spokespersons in their subject areas. The most desired author is one who is published in academic circles and presents at educational conferences. He or she may not have had any experience writing or developing curriculum, but the publisher is interested in the credibility of the author. Publishers look to authors for their expertise in both content and effective instructional strategies. Well-known authors can add a great deal of prestige to a curriculum and are called upon to represent the program.

Once an author is under contract, he or she engages in meetings with the publisher and establishes the program vision, guidelines, and objectives. Authors may even help to plot out the scope and sequence. As the program is developed, authors critique the manuscript. Authors rarely have input on the design or marketing of a program.

Author Priorities.   More than any of the other players, authors are concerned with the integrity of the instruction and its effectiveness. Their highest priority is translating their research into material that teachers can and want to use.

Author Influence.   For the most part, publishers depend on authors to provide knowledge of what research has been done to identify the most effective strategies and concept development. In nonprofit and grant-funded publications, authors do have a significant role to play and often direct the development team. In commercial publishing, however, the author's role can be almost insignificant. One math author working at a major publisher relayed the story of working with the editorial team on restructuring an entire curriculum to conform to research on the developmental progressions in mathematics. During an author meeting, a marketing manager entered the conference with news from the latest focus groups. He told the team that teachers cared only about making sure manipulatives were pictured and could care less about the progressions. Plus, the marketing manager claimed, customers would be annoyed if the scope and sequence changed too much from what they were used to because it wouldn't make sense to them. The editorial team decided to abandon the effort. If authors are not commanding and demanding, their input is easily mitigated by other concerns. Author input typically occurs at the very beginning of development. After that, other concerns can take precedence over the quality of the curriculum.

Writers

Textbook writers are typically commissioned to follow specific guidelines for creating lessons, based on guidance from authors and editors. This is "work for hire," so their names are generally not attached to the materials. In the past, publishers may have employed many writers. Today freelance writers are usually commissioned directly by the publisher or by a private editorial development house that provides publisher services. Some writers are former teachers who know a subject area or grade level. Some are people who have writing experience but no specific expertise in education or a subject area.

Writers are hired to write a particular grade level, component, or feature of a program. The editors, in an effort to reflect what the authorship has outlined, create the guidelines for the writers. Some writers produce very engaging materials that meet the guidelines for readability, skill development, and length. When writers fail, the in-house editors are responsible for completing the manuscripts.

Writer Priorities. The priorities of the writers on a series are to meet the editorial guidelines and complete the project on time.

Writer Influence. Writers have very little influence on the effectiveness of a curriculum if the editorial guidelines do not require it.

Editors

Textbook editors have difficulty explaining what they do. Their responsibilities vary widely. In short they are responsible for the content development of instructional materials. Their task may include developing a project business plan, writing guidelines, and reviewing, copyediting, and writing the manuscript. They are responsible for knowing the market, conducting market research, instruction, reviewing educational research, analyzing the competition, and ensuring state guidelines are addressed and that the manuscript is complete. They are also responsible for fact-checking and reviewing the manuscript to make sure there is a fair representation of women and minorities and that there are no unnecessary sensitive issues included that would distract from the learning objectives. To do this, they must communicate with people in marketing, design, sales, and finance, as well as upper management.

When commercial publishers were specialized before the industry consolidation of the last thirty years, many publishers employed dedicated full-time editorial staff members who knew the products inside and out. At a publisher such as Websters or Saxon, the editors worked closely with the authors to realize the authors' vision (Whiting 2010). Today, most publishers prefer a small full-time editorial staff that manages a project using contract employees to edit the written manuscript. The contract editors follow specific guidelines. Today much editorial work is outsourced to editorial development companies that may also have contracted for writing the manuscript. These players seldom interact with the program authors.

Contract editors and outside development companies cannot guarantee content expertise. Even in-house full-time editors, particularly at the elementary level, may be moved from one department to another so that they lose their specialties. If editors do not have a content specialty and do not understand a program philosophy or market, they have no way of gauging if the product will be effective or not.

After a manuscript has been outlined by authors and written, editors are responsible for ensuring that it meets program guidelines, state standards, and fits into the design template.

Editor Priorities.   Editors are responsible for working with authors, designers, marketing managers, production managers, and salespeople to produce materials that meet the project requirements. Editorial priorities shift as a project progresses. At the beginning of a project, they may make author concerns and effectiveness a priority, but as a project progresses, intense schedule and budget concerns often cause them to change their priorities.

Editor Influence.   Editors, particularly executive editors, have substantial influence on the effectiveness of a curriculum. They work with authors and translate author vision into writer and editorial guidelines that writers follow. Editors must, however, manage the different constituents and negotiate with the authors, marketing, management, production, and designers to produce a program. Editors are ultimately most influenced by what potential customers want. They learn this from market research and their communications with marketing and sales personnel, rather than contact with authors.

Designers: Art, Design, and Photo

Designers are responsible for the look of the materials, including the color palette, the typography, the amount of text on a page, the style of headings, width of text, feature design, photos, covers, logos, and artwork. They are responsible for translating the manuscript into appealing, appropriate material that highlights key features. After reviewing competitive materials, designers develop prototype cover and student and teacher lesson designs that are reviewed by editorial, marketing, and management. These designs are often market tested in focus groups. Once a design has been chosen, designers develop design templates for each component and grade level and identify illustrators to produce the artwork. When the manuscript is ready, photos and artwork are secured, and the elements are "poured" into the design template. This work is often outsourced to production companies. In-house designers review completed page samples to ensure that the design maintains integrity.

Designer Priorities.   Because designers are responsible for the look of the product, and key customers may judge books by their covers, a designer's main priority is the look of the material but not the content. An excellent program can be a marketing failure because of a poor design, and a poor program can be a market leader because of a good design. Designers often try to stretch the limits on design, by using nontraditional colors, fonts, or design elements, but they are frequently dissuaded by sales, marketing, and management input that does not want to produce material that a customer might dislike. Designers rarely read the content and because they may work on a variety of projects and usually do not have content expertise, they tend to be concerned only with the look of a program and are not in a position to be concerned about its effectiveness.

Designer Influence. In many publishing companies, there is a hostile relationship between editorial and design. Designers expect the text to fit the design template. Editors and designers battle over the amount of text on a page and editorial changes, especially changes late in the process that impact the design. Because design is so important to the sales of a product, designers have a significant influence on the final product. For example, content may be sacrificed to accommodate design concerns or writers are forced into putting features into a manuscript that may not make sense, but are needed for the design.

Production Team

The production team is responsible for producing the program, developing the manuscript into the final format, be it print or multimedia. The production team consists of production editors, people who produce pages, and manufacturing buyers.

Production Editors

Production editors take responsibility for the schedule and for making sure the material is complete and meets production and printer deadlines. They are responsible for a program style guide, which involves decisions about what terms will be used, how punctuation will be employed, and word and character counts. They may also be responsible for proofreading final manuscript and designed pages. Production editors are also often responsible for project communication and are often frequently the liaison between editorial and design and between the development and the production teams.

Production Editor Priorities. Production editors are concerned primarily with schedule, accuracy, and completeness. They may read materials, looking for errors and inconsistencies, but because they do not have content expertise, they rarely pass judgment on the content, which is the responsibility of the editorial team.

Production Editor Influence. Production editors work closely with editors at the beginning of a project in developing the schedule and the style guide. As the project proceeds, production editors necessarily assert their responsibility for meeting the schedule. When deadlines are looming, many procedural steps, such as levels of proofreading, checking for consistency, or making additional changes may be abandoned. If a deadline is firm and no manuscript is available, features, pages, or whole sections of a program may be cut.

Manufacturing Buyers

The buyers work with outside vendors such as production companies that develop and print pages. They are responsible for selecting paper for printed books, meeting binding and manufacturing specifications for hardbound or softbound books, and packaging for all program components. Buyers are basically responsible for all manufacturing and getting the completed product to its destination on time. In times past, to produce printed books, buyers worked with typesetters, film developers, and printers. Today vendors may be page makeup software specialists, software developers, and electronic printers. Much of the work is being done in India or China to control of the cost of labor. The buyer is responsible for taking the final files and producing the final product. This part of the product development process requires no content expertise.

Buyer Priorities. Buyers are concerned with receiving complete materials from the development team on time. Their jobs are complicated if the materials require additional changes, are missing elements, or are late. Buyers schedule printer time well in advance based on certain product specifications. If those specifications change or deadlines are missed, the product end date may be in jeopardy.

Buyer Influence. Buyers can have a significant influence over decisions made in the last phase of development if a schedule is in jeopardy. Missing or wrong artwork and blank or missing pages are indications that the schedule had to take priority over quality.

Marketing and Sales Team

The marketing and sales team is responsible for ensuring that the proposed product meets a significant need in the marketplace so the product will be profitable.

Marketing

In educational publishing, the marketing manager is responsible for communications between the sales and editorial teams and for market research. The marketing department represents sales and marketing interests and promotes those interests in the development of the program. In turn, the marketing manager is responsible for communicating the program particulars to the sales team so that sales can represent the product accurately. The marketing manager works with editorial to develop the description of the product and the market overview, including the customer profile. They establish sales forecasts and review program business plans to ensure they reflect the sales expectations. They review program components and develop pricing models and marketing plans. They are responsible for launching the product to the salesforce and supporting sales efforts with national advertising and marketing campaigns.

Marketing Priorities. The top priority for marketing is to ensure that the product will be competitive and profitable. They are very concerned with what customers want and what sales representatives need to be successful. Their bonuses are often dependent upon product sales. If the customers are teachers who want products that are easy to use and do not require much change, marketing will lobby for those interests regardless of whether a product promotes student achievement.

Marketing Influence. Marketing often has a profound influence on the product design, the makeup of the author team, and the success of a product. Marketing critiques product proposals and design and recommends changes if they do not meet perceived customer expectations. Marketing may also recommend people to the author team who are popular with customers or who might have influence in a particular state or region. For example, educators from Texas or California often appear as authors on programs that are submitted for adoption in those states. How the program is marketed and the information delivered to the salesforce about a program can also have positive or negative effects on the success of the program.

Sales

The salesforce is responsible for building relationships with customers, selling, and supporting the sales in their territories. Sales is also responsible for meeting with potential customers and communicating their needs back to the home office. Salespeople are assigned a territory, which may be in an adoption state or states, or open territory states. They may represent elementary or secondary product, all grades, one subject area, or a variety of subject areas depending on the publisher and size of the territory. In some cases sales representatives are freelance and may represent the products of more than one publisher.

Sales representatives are the ones who hear firsthand about product problems. Field sales representatives travel from school to school to meet with customers. They are responsible for knowing the school district needs and for tailoring sales efforts to maximize the potential of their sales budgets. For example, a small district in a territory may not garner the same attention as a large district. Although some salespeople have former teaching experience, they are typically not content experts. For presentations, sales representatives may schedule consultants to deliver product overviews or implementation workshops to train the teachers after a sale is made.

Sales Priorities.   The salaries and bonuses of sales representatives are based on meeting sales goals. Their priority is to have a product that customers want more than they want a competitive product. Sales representatives dread product problems that impact customers. Errors, mismatched printings, controversial subject matter or artwork, materials that fall apart after students use them, or late product are particular nightmares for sales representatives. Sales representatives advocate for competitive features, attractive design, and products that meet all of the local or state standards and requirements. Product effectiveness is not a priority for sales unless customers demand it.

Sales Influence.   Sales representatives can have significant influence over whether a product is produced. If the representatives don't think there is a market or there is too much competition, they will resist any publishing plans. Sales representatives often advocate for program components or elements that were competitive issues in previous sales campaigns. During development, sales may lobby for particular features to compete with other programs. If sales does not embrace a program and make efforts to promote it, the product will not be successful.

Consultants

In educational publishing, a team of consultants supports a company's products by working with the salesforce in the field to make sales presentations. They also work with teachers after a sale, conducting in-service and implementation workshops in support of a product. Sales consultants may be content specialists and represent only one subject area, such as math or reading, or they may represent all products in the company bookbag. There are both regional consultants who work in only one sales territory, and there are national consultants who represent products in any region. A consultant's schedule is dictated by the salesforce.

Consultant Priorities.   Because consultants are necessarily product specialists and work with teachers who are using a product, along with the same concerns as sales representatives, they have a vested interest in a product's effectiveness. Consultants encounter product usage issues and product shortcomings and work to find solutions for customers. If a product is easy to use and effective, the consultant's job is much easier.

Consultant Influence.   Consultants spend their time in the field supporting the sales team. They tend to have minimal contact with the home office. Most of their concerns are channeled through the sales representatives who represent customer interests.

Finance and Management Team

Finance

The financial people in a publishing house are responsible for analyzing the program costs submitted by the development and production teams, along with manufacturing costs, pricing models, and the sales forecast from marketing to establish a profitable plan. They monitor project spending and sales and produce financial reports, including profit and loss statements. Finance is responsible for controlling investments and balancing investment costs and sales.

Finance Priorities. Finance is mainly concerned with managing risk in estimating and forecasting product costs and sales to fit a company's business and profit model. Once a product is approved, finance is then concerned that the product budget is maintained and the product achieves or exceeds its sales goals.

Finance Influence. Finance has a profound influence on whether publishing projects are approved. If the financial models do not work because the manufacturing costs, the sales forecast, or the development budget is out of line and cannot be reconciled, the project will most likely not be approved for development. Finance has very little concern about whether a program is effective unless effectiveness leads to increased sales.

Upper Management

Upper management is responsible for the health, future, philosophy, and profitability of a publishing company. Upper management oversees finance, design, sales, and the development and production team managers, and relies on their recommendations and advice to make the publishing decisions for the company. Upper management teams consist of the company CEO (chief executive officer) or president, the CFO (chief financial officer), the vice president publisher in charge of product development, and the vice president(s) of sales and marketing. There may be other members in upper management as well, including vice presidents of manufacturing or design.

Upper Management Priorities. Educational publishing companies have a vested interest in long-term growth and profitability. Because many had their start in the eighteenth and nineteenth centuries, they want to remain healthy into the foreseeable future. The nature of the publishing business is that a company must make a substantial investment in a product long before it can actualize sales. The priorities of upper management reflect these characteristics. Upper management is concerned with making smart long-term investments in products that will be profitable.

Upper Management Influence.   At one time the upper management in many publishing houses comprised or represented the program authors, who helped to define the publishing house. In 1911, for example, Prentice Hall was formed by a New York University professor and his student, who named the company in honor of their mothers' maiden names. If successful, upper management supported the interests of the authors who dictated what was published. As publishers grew and published more products, upper management began to reflect the interests of the development, production, or sales and marketing teams. Prentice Hall is now an imprint of Pearson Education. Today, managers who come from the sales ranks, as many upper managers in publishing companies do, are often more sympathetic to the concerns of the salesforce.

The analysis of each of the publishing player's priorities demonstrates how easy it is for a product's effectiveness to be a low priority. Although authors may be concerned about that, if customers are not demanding that the program be effective, the players are poised to assert their own priorities. As a result, quality instruction may be sacrificed for design, financial, or competitive reasons.

THE PUBLISHING PROCESS AND ITS PRIORITIES

The players engage in the publishing process to produce an educational product. A small, simple project takes a minimum of six months for a publisher to produce, if everything goes smoothly. A large project can take two or more years to produce. The educational publishing product development process consists of a series of steps that attempt to ensure that a product will meet market needs and fulfill sales expectations. The entire process is devoted to creating products that customers want. If customers do not demand effective materials, materials that promote student achievement, the publisher has no incentive to create them. Outlining the publishing process reveals the many points where decisions are made that could impact the effectiveness of a product.

Publishing Plans and Product Proposals

All publishers develop publishing plans. The publishing plan is often the responsibility of the vice president publisher or the development team but usually must be approved by upper management and frequently sales and marketing. Publishing plans may be one-year or multiyear plans. The immediately upcoming years may include products that have already been approved and will most likely be published. The outlying years may involve ideas for products that have not yet been approved and are subject to change. Once the plan is established, the sales and marketing team and the finance and upper management team review it. In these reviews, products may be added, replaced, or moved from one year to another.

A publisher places product ideas on the plan or schedule for many different reasons. Frequently the products on a plan reflect state adoption cycles. Other products may be on the plan because they need a copyright update to remain competitive. Publishing plans may comprise both revisions and new products.

New Products on a Publishing Plan

The new product ideas that are placed on a publishing plan can come from a variety of sources but typically emerge from a publisher's editorial department. On rare occasions, new product ideas come from established authors. Rarely are new products developed from unsolicited manuscripts that individual teachers submit to a publisher. The following sources are typical inspirations for new products.

State Adoption Cycles. Most publishing plans at major publishers reflect the Texas, California, and Florida adoption cycles. If one of these states is calling for instructional materials in a specific subject area, the major publishers will plan a publication to compete in the adoption. Accommodations for other state adoptions will be included, as will accommodations for the national market. For example, if Florida calls for science one year and Indiana calls for it the following year, a publisher will produce a major program for Florida and then adapt it the following year to meet the Indiana specifications. A national version will be produced based on the initial publication created for the state adoption.

Because programs produced for major state adoptions require such a large investment, publishing plans at major publishers may include *only* state adoption programs. It is not worthwhile for a major publisher to produce a program without the potential of a state adoption. Even though only half the states in the United States are state adoption states, they still drive the publishing plans. Unless a major state calls for a program, it is nearly impossible to get a publisher to consider placing a new product on a publishing plan.

The state adoption cycle has two profound consequences for major publishers. First, it precludes any new or innovative curriculum from being considered unless it can be part of a larger program. Small programs that might address a new curricular area, such as twenty-first-century skills, law, technology, anthropology, or medicine, do not stand a chance of being published, regardless of how effective they may be. Second, the state adoption cycle restricts major publishers from creating materials that do not specifically address the major state standards. Major publishers argue that they cannot take a risk on investing major resources into an innovative product. Smaller publishers do not have the investment dollars to build a competitive program and market it successfully. As the publishing industry has become more consolidated, fewer and fewer innovative programs are being published.

Competition. Some new products may be placed on the plan to respond to a competitor that has produced something that grabs market attention. Although most often this results in competitive features in a larger program, a publisher might consider developing an entire program to match the competition.

Funding Sources. Funding sources for purchasing new products are required before a product would be placed on a publishing plan. When federal funds were tied to the Reading First initiative, which advocated and funded the teaching of vocabulary, phonics, phonemic awareness, comprehension, and fluency, many publishers created vocabulary programs or phonics programs to meet those needs. If a funding source cannot be identified and there is no state adoption call, a publisher may assume there is no demand. Unlike many other industries, the publishing industry tends to follow the market and does not try to create demand.

Revisions on a Publishing Plan

Publishing plans also include revisions of existing products. The typical life cycle of an educational program is five years, but it may be shorter if there are significant changes in the market or one of the major adoption states is calling for a new subject. If a product is successful, it may get a facelift at the end of its life cycle. The Houghton Mifflin Write Source program is an example of a program that has been through several revisions. McGraw-Hill's Everyday Math is another example. Pearson's Reading Street and Envision Math are new editions of previous programs, as well. On the other hand, publishers are often inclined to produce entirely new programs (although they may have some assets from previous programs) for state adoption submissions. Since Envision Math was submitted for the Texas math adoption in 2006, most likely Pearson will have a completely new math program the next time Texas holds a math adoption.

Interestingly, both Write Source and Everyday Math were created in the mid-1980s before the major consolidation of publishing companies. Write Source was initially developed by teachers as a supplemental handbook. The latest version, however, is designed to compete in the Texas language arts adoption and has grown exponentially. Everyday Math was a curriculum developed by the University of Chicago School Mathematics project. It too has been submitted in state adoptions.

Successful textbooks are revised for several different reasons.

Outdated Content. Outdated content can be an extremely urgent reason for revision. For example, when a publisher designed math covers that featured the *Challenger* space shuttle, the publisher immediately recalled the covers before the books were printed when the disaster occurred. New science books all now reflect the consideration that Pluto is no longer considered a planet. History and science books must be particularly sensitive about this. Reading programs are also evaluated based on the currency of their reading selections. All instructional materials need to reflect the current standards and trends or they will seem outdated.

Pedagogy Changes. Pedagogy includes the strategies and style of instruction that a teacher employs. Trends in pedagogy influence what teachers want in textbooks. In the 1990s, for example, during the whole language movement in reading education, there was a trend for the teacher not to teach explicitly, but to be the "guide on the side." Textbooks attempted to support this type of pedagogy, providing questions instead of instruction for teachers. As another example, for a time, there was a movement for teachers to be sure to activate prior knowledge at the beginning of a lesson. Textbooks included strategies to help teachers with that.

New Research. The phonics debate in reading instruction is a great example of how textbooks adapt to new research when there is funding supporting the purchase of materials that reflect the research. In the 1980s the whole language movement held that surrounding children with print and seizing on teachable moments instead of explicit methodical instruction was a far superior and much more interesting way to teach reading, instilling a love of reading in children. Basal reading programs spent inordinate amounts of money buying rights to authentic literature, literature written for the general public rather than written for a reading program, and organizing it to help children discover reading. Except for some phonics workbooks and a small number of alternative basals, phonics instruction could not be found in basal reading textbooks. Some teachers continued to teach phonics despite this because they knew students needed it. When research that unequivocally demonstrated the advantage of explicitly teaching phonemic awareness and phonics emerged in the early 1990s, and the Reading First initiative began funding the purchase of scientifically based materials, basal reading textbooks were completely revised to reflect this. Without the funding behind the research, however, the phonics movement would be dead because teachers would not demand it. Many teachers bemoaned the reemergence of phonics instruction because the whole language methods were so much more fun to teach, even if student reading skills suffered.

Trends Emerge. Education is rife with trends and fads. Fads occur typically when an educator writes a book that becomes popular. Then educational conference sessions are devoted to explaining the new trend. New teachers become excited and engaged and begin to look for support in instructional materials, which quickly follow suit. Sometimes trends and fads have a positive effect on education. Other times they have a negative effect. Very often they have a negligible effect. Seasoned teachers joke about these things that seem to come and go. Many teachers know that if they wait long enough the fad will change. Examples of some of the trends of the last fifty years include the following.

- **1950s–Present Reading Instruction**—Reading trends have emerged from whole word, sight word, high-frequency words, whole language, and phonics methods. Reading instruction has been the subject of a series of trends over the years and reading textbooks have changed with every one of them.
- **1960s New Math**—New math introduced by the mathematics community following *Sputnik* to advance mathematics skills advocated conceptual development and mathematical structures. Parents and many teachers did not understand it, could not help their children, and complained that it had no real-world application. The trend was over by the end of the decade.
- **1960s–Present Science Instruction**—As in reading, the science community has swung back and forth between promoting hands-on science curriculum, to reading about science through literature, to constructivism, to guided discovery, and to textbook science.
- **1970s Mastery Learning**—This short-lived movement advocated that children master each new concept before moving on to the next concept.
- **1980s Learning Modalities/Styles**—Visual, auditory, and kinesthetic modes of learning were seen to be the answer to learning for all students. As a result, teacher editions included three different strategies for introducing or reinforcing concepts. Recently research has proven that devoting a lot of effort to addressing learning styles has little or no effect, but those teachers who believe in this approach are not swayed by the research (Wolpert-Gawron 2010; Stansbury 2010).
- **1980s Math Manipulatives**—Hands-on math was believed to help students make math concrete and understandable. Manipulatives such as pattern blocks of different geometric shapes, scales, counting rods, and base-ten blocks were purchased for use in classrooms across the nation. Countless math manipulatives can be located in school storage rooms because teachers did not know how to use them to teach mathematics.
- **1990s Multiple Intelligences**—Howard Gardner's work on multiple intelligences, often confused with learning styles, inspired some schools to completely change their structure and curriculum to accommodate the different intelligences. Many teachers embraced this romantic view of children regardless of whether it demonstrated results.
- **Differentiated Instruction**—Carol Tomlinson struck a nerve outlining how teachers could *differentiate* instruction for English language learners and students at, above, or below grade level (Tomlinson 1999). All programs produced after her work was published included differentiated instruction.

Publishers had routinely included teaching strategies to meet the needs of students above and below grade level, so in many cases, these strategies were simply relabeled as differentiated instruction. Intervention and Response to Intervention are recent trends that have been treated similarly.

- **Teaching Models**—From time to time an educator gains attention for the development of an organized teaching model. Madeline Hunter presented an outline for instruction in the 1980s (what is the objective, what standards are addressed, an anticipatory set, teaching, guided practice, closure, independent practice) (Hunter 2007). There have been others including the 5E Model (Engage, Explore, Explain, Elaborate, Evaluate; Pashler et al. 2010). When these models take hold, even as obvious and commonsensical as they may be, publishers rush to include them in their teacher editions.
- **Digital Solutions**—The most recent fad is the promotion of digital solutions to replace classroom instruction. A example of this temporary fad is the Kahn Academy, which advocates using a "flipped" teaching method in which students watch the Kahn lecture before the teacher introduces a concept in class so they can work on the content in class. But the lecture videos are no better than what an inexperienced first-year teacher would explain with minimal preparation using a chalkboard. They do not address the needs of students at different grade levels; are filled with errors; promote misconceptions and procedural thinking; do not address state or national standards; and have no evidence that they have been effective with any groups of students, particularly students who need instruction. Teachers will embrace this, schools will waste billions of dollars trying to implement it, and educational publishers will try to copy it—only to find out after all these efforts that it is completely ineffective and may even be detrimental in promoting student achievement.

Unless a product has been criticized for a particular problem, the pressure not to change much in a revision is intense. Publishers stand to save a lot of money if they make few changes. If they can reuse artwork, exercises, and whole components, editors are encouraged to do so. Costs of revisions are usually based on percentage of change, so even if the materials could be substantially better, they are not revised if at all possible.

Publishing Plan and Product Proposal Priorities

Placing a product on a publishing plan is a key decision point. It would seem that increasing student achievement in a subject area would galvanize publishers to recruit experts as authors, align their efforts to conduct research on best practices, and produce a program that specifically promotes student achievement. Student achievement, however, is not a major consideration in the product proposal phase.

Publishers who are profitable cover state standards to ensure they are on state adoption lists. Then they have design, feature, and trend appeal to satisfy the teachers who make purchase decisions. A program that looks boring, regardless of how effective its teaching strategies and content, will not sell. If customers cannot distinguish an effective program from an ineffective one, and do not demand that use of materials translate into increased student achievement, publishers have no incentive to concentrate on producing effective materials. As a consequence, the programs that are placed on the publishing plan are those that the development, sales, marketing, financial, and upper management teams agree have the greatest potential to be profitable.

PREPRODUCTION PROCESS

Regardless of whether a product is a revision or a new product idea, once a product is on the publishing plan, the publishing process begins to follow a trajectory. A successful product will go through all phases of the process, but often products hit roadblocks that may cause delays or cause them to be eliminated from the publishing plan.

The publishing process starts with the preproduction phase of a project, which involves gathering data with market research, developing and testing prototypes, and creating a convincing business plan. The whole thrust of preproduction is to get approval to move forward with the project.

Preliminary Market Research

The initial steps in the preproduction process involve market research. Usually the marketing and editorial managers conduct market research to determine if there is a market for the proposed product. An author search may also be conducted to find willing and appropriate authors.

This preliminary market research concentrates on key issues:

1. **Market Description**. The market description identifies the subject area, upcoming adoptions and required standards, the number of teachers who teach the subject, market trends, and a customer profile that describes what a potential customer will expect to see in the product.
2. **Market Size**. Many sources report on market sizes in different states with demographic numbers of how many schools, teachers, and students are in a particular area. The marketing departments use this information to develop sales forecasts.
3. **Competition**. The business plan requires an analysis of the competitors already in the market, their product description, and their strengths and weaknesses.
4. **Product Description**. The nature of the program, the number of components, and required elements that are needed to be competitive in the described market are identified.

5. **Market Share**. The market share that can be expected based on the product description, competition, and market size is determined.
6. **Preliminary Costs and Forecast**. Estimating costs establishes ballpark figures for how much a competitive product will cost in the marketplace along with a preliminary sales forecast.

These efforts focus on *market* research, not *educational* research. How the program will promote student achievement is not addressed unless a competitor has made it an issue or a state has required a particular method or strategy, such as teaching explicit phonics. If the market research does not support the product proposal to the satisfaction of the marketing and editorial managers, the proposal may be changed or abandoned.

Preliminary Authorization

Once the preliminary market research has been gathered, the marketing and editorial managers use it to request preliminary funding and authorization to develop prototypes and continue market research. At this point the finance and upper management teams review the funding request and judge whether they agree in its profit potential.

Finance compares the request to other proposals and analyzes the company commitment in light of the entire publishing plan and company expenditures. The upper management team considers if the product is compatible with the company profile and will help build the company foundation.

The product's potential to promote student achievement rarely, if ever, is part of this discussion.

BUSINESS PLAN AND PROTOTYPE DEVELOPMENT

If preliminary authorization is acquired, the editorial and design team begin work on a prototype. The editors may work with authors or freelance writers to write a sample of the program. Once they are satisfied with it, the designers create a design prototype that reflects the key elements of the program. The prototype may be a page, a lesson, a chapter, or some other section of the program that potential customers and other constituents can review to understand what the program is all about. Marketing managers are often involved in prototype development.

At the same time, the editorial and marketing managers begin development of the business plan. The business plan includes a detailed description of the program, including program philosophy, authorship, target market, component descriptions, market research plan, and costs. Marketing and manufacturing contribute sales, pricing, and printing costs based on the specifications in the plan.

To develop major sections of the business plan, initial author meetings flesh out the program philosophy, pedagogy, and scope and sequence of skills and content to determine how they will be reflected in the program design. Authors contribute findings from academic research. Editors and marketing managers contribute information about the demographics of schools and competition.

This is the stage of the development process in which the authors and editors are most likely to address a product's potential effectiveness, if they review educational research and find ways to include best practices and other research findings in the program. If these features are baked into the prototype and are either ignored by or are received positively in subsequent reviews, they stand a chance to be reflected in the product. If they stand out and are not understood by those who review the product or do not meet teacher expectations, they have a good chance of being eliminated, regardless of how effective they are. It is critical that the editors communicate the significance of the key product elements in the prototype to the designers so that the design can represent them favorably.

Market Research

Once the prototype is complete, editorial and marketing conduct market research. Market research can take the form of competition analysis, surveys, interviews, and focus groups comprising teachers or curriculum specialists, people who will make purchasing decisions.

Competition Analysis. A major effort at any educational publisher is competition analysis. Publishers are very crafty in acquiring other publishers' materials. Competition analyses involve counting pages and components, as well as features. The goal is to identify any advantages a competitor may have and neutralize them. For new products and new submissions, competition analyses are conducted on competitors' previous editions.

Focus Groups. Publishers budget thousands of dollars to hire market researchers to conduct focus groups to test design concepts. The researcher recruits educators in key cities to attend a one- to two-hour session in which they are shown different cover and interior lesson designs. Sometimes multiple designs of the same content are tested against each other or against a previous edition of the program. Other times prototypes are tested against materials from competing programs.

Through this process, publishers have become experts on labeling and cover and lesson design so that customers will be able to see what they want to see. A publisher's sales, marketing, and editorial staff typically observe the focus groups behind a one-way glass.

It is in these sessions that publishers confirm that teachers rarely care about program effectiveness when weighed against a perceived useful design. The most effective, research-based programs almost always fare poorly in focus groups if they have poured their efforts and resources into effectiveness rather than design. A program can fail if teachers determine that the program requires too much reading, too much work, or is too different from what they are currently doing. Furthermore, if the teachers simply decide that the design may not be appealing, they conclude that their students won't like it. Interestingly, when curriculum specialists are in the room, they almost always prefer the research-based materials, but realize it would be an uphill battle for their teachers to accept them.

What Publishers Learn from Market Research

The market research phase almost always confirms that research and effectiveness are not important to potential customers. Based on observations from focus groups, the following are the key lessons that publishers learn again and again (Saperstein 2000).

Design

- Simple features like covers influence adoption decisions.
- First impressions are the screen through which everything else is perceived. If teachers like the cover, they will look inside to confirm their positive impression. If they don't like the cover, they look inside to confirm their negative impression.
- Visual overload hides important features and concept development.
- Labels are vital. Labels must communicate quickly and directly.
- If features are not highlighted or labeled, they do not exist to the customer.
- Teachers often dismiss programs for trivial reasons, for example, colors or font size, or a picture on one page.
- To teachers most books look pretty much alike. Often no textbook secures a majority of votes and ratings are close.
- Most programs adopt their competitors' unique features almost immediately. There is a six-month window for unique features. As soon as competitors publish a new edition, a publisher races to copy any unique features to mitigate any sales advantage.
- The most commonly heard complaint about instructional materials is that they are cluttered or difficult to navigate. The second most common complaint is that the teacher's guides are too big.
- New books always seem superior to what is currently being used.

Teacher Desires

- **Easy to Use**. Teachers want programs that are easy to use with information at point of use. Teachers don't want to flip around or have to find or develop other resources. Easy to use means easy for the teacher to use. In many cases it means that the teacher can teach from the student materials and will not have to consult the teacher's guide. If steps are not labeled for the teacher or there is too much reading, the program is not easy to use.

- **Simplify Teaching**. Teachers want new programs to have features that make their lives easier. This means that instead of requiring teachers to change, new materials simplify the task of teaching by making it more efficient. Teachers get excited about something they haven't seen before that fills a need they have. That's what evokes their passion.
- **State Standards**. Teachers want explicit connections to the state standards they are required to cover, although they often don't want to do what state guidelines demand because they feel they know what is best for their students.
- **Test Preparation**. Teachers want new materials to include thorough preparation for state tests because student performance on state tests is how teachers and schools are evaluated.
- **Realistic Readability**. Teachers are concerned that their students won't or can't read the student book, so they want lots of graphics and features to communicate content so even nonreaders can get something out of it.

Focus Group Observations

- Teachers are human and make decisions on imperfect knowledge.
- Some teachers don't always know that they don't know what they don't know. They don't have time to read up on the latest educational research or what the best practices are for the subjects they are teaching.
- Teachers believe that they can make any program effective, so design and features become more important in decision making than pedagogy and content.
- Teachers are constantly faced with implementing new standards, integrating emerging technology, and content shuffling such as teaching algebra in eighth grade. Consequently there is a huge need for ongoing teacher education.
- Interest grows in technology every day. Technology is expected as part of a program, but it must be optional because of computer availability in school and at home. Simple usage models for technology must be provided because teachers won't know how to use it.

Market Research Leads to the Development of Ineffective Materials

Market research is critically important in developing a competitive product. Publishers will focus test, revise, and focus test again until their products "win" a focus group. If the development team cannot develop a prototype that appeals to teachers, there is little chance that the product will be approved for publication. Yet conspicuously absent from a publisher's market research efforts are key areas that could inform the development of *effective* rather than *appealing* materials. Although they spend tens of thousands of dollars on focus groups, publishers do not fund these types of studies.

1. **The History of the Subject Area**. Understanding the development of a subject and how it has been taught in the past can provide vital information to the publishing process. Understanding the different movements in reading instruction, for example, can guide publishers away from repeating past mistakes and will enlighten why strategies and materials have evolved in the ways they have. Understanding how geography was or wasn't taught in the past can inform what the needs are today.
2. **Analysis of Previously Used Materials**. Although publishers will analyze competitive materials, they do not look back over the strengths and weaknesses of curricular materials that have been used in the past. Older teachers will often fondly recall materials that were effective or books they used when they were students, but publishers rarely take those into account when developing new products unless, of course, they are able to reuse assets and reduce their development costs. Many times publishers think they have created a new, unique feature only to find out it was part of the curriculum years before.
3. **Educational Research**. Educational research is in a constant state of revelation. Every day new studies emerge that shed light on effective and ineffective practices. Yet, unless authors make it an issue, publishers, for the most part, do not consider educational research when they develop educational materials.

If publishers learn only the lessons from focus groups and competition analyses, they are incentivized to deliver products that teachers say they want after only a cursory review in an artificial situation in comparison to copies of competitive materials. As a result of focus group market research, publishers fill their books with well-labeled features, features like random curricular connections that a teacher in a focus group thought was interesting. These features are believed to help sell the program.

Often as a result of focus group market research, publishers remove good content to make room for appealing features that are not particularly useful. Instead of focusing on providing a student edition with a logical narrative that builds along a learning trajectory, publishers provide "magazine" type formats because teachers in focus groups say this format type will appeal to their students. Narrative passages in a student social studies or science book are broken up into captions for images because without reading it, teachers in a focus group have determined it will be easier for their students to read. In many cases, it may be easier to read the words, but harder to discern the meaning. Plus, no matter how well designed a textbook is, it is still a textbook, and most children will not voluntarily look at it unless it is assigned or it provides useful information.

Market research conducted to develop publishing business plans too often ensures the status quo is maintained and curricular materials will not reflect current research or promote any advancement in education. With the absence of any other data, publishers convince themselves again and again that they are delivering what the customer wants and the market needs. Yet without change, there will be no increased achievement.

"We have to change, because what we are doing now is not working," said Kristy Kuches, a seventh-grade math teacher at Heritage Middle School in Deltona who earlier this month was named Volusia County's Teacher of the Year. Although student achievement in math has been climbing slowly over the past 10 years, far too many kids still don't understand math, officials say. (Weber 2010)

Business Plan

The creation of the business plan for an education product is a key decision point but it rarely includes a discussion of educational effectiveness. Using the information they have gathered and created about the program, the market, market research, and costs, editorial and marketing present the business plan to finance. Finance reviews the plan based on the company financial model. If the numbers don't work, the plan is returned for a revised forecast, cost cutting, or other revision. If the numbers work, the business plan is routed for approval to managers in editorial, marketing, sales, finance, and upper management.

Writing, Editing, and Design

Once the project is approved, the company is authorized to spend money to begin the writing and editing phase. In some companies this stage is financed under the preliminary authorization.

Before writing begins, authors and editors meet to confirm the program philosophy and breadth of the content. Editors develop a program scope and sequence that plots the skills and concepts that will be developed at each grade level.

In the best of all possible worlds, design refines and develops the prototype design and then gains design approval from sales and upper management. Next the designer creates a design template that indicates type size at each grade level and amount of text on each page or screen. Design also creates, tests, and gains approval for the program logos and covers.

Using the design, editors develop specific writer guidelines and convey them to the writers. Writers deliver initial manuscripts and editors review them to ensure they conform to the guidelines. As the manuscript is developed by the writers, a schedule of review, including author, expert reviewer, and editorial review is established.

As this phase of the project continues, writers produce manuscripts based on guidelines; authors, reviewers, and editors review the manuscript; and editors revise it based on comments, rewriting as necessary or adding any missing copy. Before the production phase begins, production editors send the manuscript out for copyediting and revisions are made.

During this phase the program philosophy, design, and features are set. It is very difficult to change any of this at this point and increasingly difficult hereafter. If student achievement and effectiveness were not priorities earlier, they will not be now. A change in priorities would require that materials be completely rewritten and reviewed. That is too costly and unnecessary if customers do not demand it.

Book Production Phase

Once a manuscript is basically written, it moves into the production phase in which it is "poured" into the design template. During this phase, editors review the pages to make sure the program specifications are met. They work with art and photo editors to select appropriate images.

Production editors review pages to make sure they fit and that spelling, punctuation, and grammar are accurate. Designers review pages to work out problems with art and design issues. All revisions are reviewed. Once the pages are complete with design, text, art, and photos, the files are prepared for printing and shipped to the printer. The printer then produces bound books and ships them to the warehouse.

Over the years, technology has changed these processes dramatically, shortening the writing, editing, and production phases. Often much of the work is outsourced. A publishing company may hire freelance writers, proofreaders, designers, and typesetters. They may also hire development, design, production, or full-service companies to produce the materials. A substantial amount of production work is now being done in India.

During the production phase, there is no concern about how effective the final product will be in the classroom. The entire focus is on getting the program into the warehouse. At this point everyone assumes that the product reflects the approved business plan that describes a program that will be effective. Anyone who disrupts the schedule with editorial changes is roundly criticized for not doing his or her job up front. As the development progresses, the pressure on authors and editors not to make changes or revisions becomes more and more intense.

If the effectiveness of the program is not a priority at the beginning of the project, it certainly is not during production.

Technology Development

Software products, or software that supports a print program, follow a similar progression, although software production may follow the print development and consequently may be the last pieces to be developed. Because technology involves additional layers of development and quality assurance, there is even less patience for changes.

MAJOR CONSIDERATIONS DURING PRODUCT DEVELOPMENT

Throughout product development, the development team has to balance three concerns: quality, schedule, and cost, and these concerns switch priority as the project progresses. The goal is for a project to be high quality, delivered on time, and on budget.

Quality

Through the writing and editorial phase, the quality of the product is the highest priority. But quality is not effectiveness. Instead quality is defined by the following:

1. Does the project meet the state standards so it will be adopted?
2. Does the project meet the program guidelines?
3. Is the manuscript complete?
4. Will the manuscript fit in the design?
5. Is the material age-appropriate with appropriate reading level, amount of text, and artwork?

Editors will address author or reviewer comments related to instructional integrity and effectiveness, but their primary considerations are on whether the state standards are met. The rationale is that instructional integrity is a usage issue and will be difficult to ascertain, if it ever is, and they must ensure that the book is adopted and salable. Most writers and editors are good writers and editors but they may not be in tune with current research in the subject area, nor are they experts in pedagogy or educational philosophy, so whatever is not reflected in the writers' and editors' guidelines is not given significant consideration.

Once the project moves into the production phase, the definition of quality changes to whether there are grammatical or spelling errors, whether the requested illustration and photo program is complete and matches the text, or whether the design has been compromised. As the production process moves into its final stages, the definition of quality begins to be related to physical manufacturing issues, such as paper weight or whether softbound covers curl up or not.

Schedule

Schedule is a concern throughout the development process but becomes an increasing concern as the project moves through production. Schedules may be delayed if a state has not published its requirements or if a project has not been approved internally by the company publishing board. Schedule frustrations pass down the line as the project moves from editorial to design, to production. In adoption situations with legislated deadlines, there is no wiggle room and publishers abandon rounds of pages or proofing if they need to in order to meet the deadlines. If an adoption state project with a steadfast deadline is running behind schedule, the time factor takes priority over quality and budget. If the program is not submitted on time the program will not be considered and millions of dollars of investment is for naught.

Cost

Cost is a major concern for product development. Costs are carefully balanced with sales forecasts in detailed financial analyses, which is part of an approved project business plan, which is part of the overall company business plan. If the costs are higher than projected, the project will go over budget and sales may not make up for it. If costs are too low, the company financial projections are off. Cost overruns most often occur if schedules are tight and extra help is needed, or if decisions are made to adjust the business plan to address competition or sales concerns. Cost overruns become a huge issue in company postmortem discussions when analyzing the profit and loss. At that time, all the decisions that were made in the heat of battle to get the project done are forgotten and cost becomes the highest priority, especially if the program was not successful in the market.

CONCLUSION

Analyzing the players and the processes of textbook publishing reveals how very little opportunity there is for an educationally effective program to be created. Almost all the players in the publishing process are focused on profitability or meeting the schedule. Potential profitability is tied to what the customers want and the market research that publishers conduct leads them to the conclusion that customers are interested in appealing design and ease of use, not student achievement. Even if curriculum specialists recognize more effective materials, they are overruled by others on the adoption committees.

On a publisher's development team, the people most likely to prioritize developing the most effective program are the authors, yet their role is often marginalized in the publishing process. Editors must concern themselves with meeting the standards and program specifications. Other members of the development and production teams must concern themselves with completing the project on time and on budget. Upper management, sales, and marketing are concerned with appeal and profitability.

Interestingly, when interests of the different players conflict, customer priorities do prevail. If an editor wants to rewrite a section to include more information, the question will be, "Will it matter to the customer?" If the customer does not demand that publishers produce effective materials for use in the classroom, publishers will not make it a priority because their other priorities take precedence.

The history of educational publishing demonstrates the lengths publishers will go to meet market needs and compete with other publishers to earn business. With all the money spent on instructional materials and all the benefits they can provide, examining how these materials can be more effective is critical to advancing education.

Effectiveness is difficult to determine. There are many factors and it really takes several years to determine if a curriculum has raised student achievement. Yet, if customers demand effective materials that incorporate the latest educational research, educational publishers would focus on creating those types of materials.

Chapter Four

Standards and Testing Don't Increase Student Achievement

Education is the cornerstone of democracy and the avenue to equal opportunity for all. For the most part, the American education system has succeeded in preparing generations of students from diverse backgrounds for a place in American society. Where it did not, the economy had a place for people who were willing to work hard even without the skills of formal schooling. In this process, expectations varied from school to school and student to student, but the job got done.

Now the job has changed. The demands of today's society are different. We need graduates who can compete in the global economy. We need adults who can use the knowledge and skills they acquire in school to deal with the complex issues of their own communities and of the world.

To fulfill the old promise of American education—that all graduates will be prepared to take their place in society—requires a new promise— that all students will be held to high academic standards.

—National Education Standards Improvement Council, 1993

With each new wave of concern about academic achievement, proponents argue for higher standards. Some even argue as if no standards have previously existed. Others claim that "for the past half-century, the standards represented in texts and tests have reflected the commercial market for 'dumbed-down' resources to a greater degree than they have reflected any public consensus on what teachers should teach and students should learn" (Lewis 1995).

Even others claim that setting high standards is the answer to improved academic achievement.

Solid standards matter because they are the foundation of standards-based reform, the dominant education policy strategy in America today. They have become even more important in the NCLB era, when weighty consequences

71

befall schools that do not rise to meet the standards (at least in reading and math). While the pros and cons of testing and accountability get most of the ink in newspaper debates, the standards themselves exert enormous influence over what actually happens inside classrooms. (Finn, Julian, and Petrilli 2006)

Governments and organizations are motivated to set academic standards when they find there is too much inconsistency from one program to another or from one district, school, or state to another. They are incentivized to create high standards when there is economic motivation to improve education, or when academic performance is weak in comparison to other schools, other states, or other countries.

Following the development of standards, standardized tests are then created to try and gauge whether standards are being met. Since the passage of the No Child Left Behind legislation in 2002, there is more emphasis than ever on testing. This testing is, at least in theory, aligned with the standards so students are being tested on what they were taught.

In 2010, after fifteen years of energy expended in creating *world class* high academic standards, involving the efforts of thousands of educators, including researchers, academics, teachers, administrators, politicians, and lay people; after a rigorous study of international comparisons; after an analysis of how children learn, we have an impressive canon of academic standards. After two hundred years of controversy between proponents of centralized and local control of education, we even have a set of Common Core Standards that almost all states already have or will adopt.

With the incredible attention to higher standards, measures of performance, and pressure on schools to meet adequate yearly progress, one would assume that American students' academic performance would have significantly improved.

Unfortunately, publishing a standard that fourth graders should be able to "explain major differences between poems, drama, and prose, and refer to the structural elements of poems (e.g., verse, rhythm, meter) and drama (e.g., casts of characters, settings, descriptions, dialogue, stage directions) when writing or speaking about a text," a fourth grade Common Core Reading Standard, does not make it happen (Common Core State Standards Initiative 2010a). Testing to see if a student can do this does not teach students to do it. Mandating that all students will take algebra in eighth grade does not automatically make teachers able to teach algebra at the eighth grade level and students to understand it. "Universal eighth-grade algebra is creating more problems than it solves, with 120,000 students not learning the mathematics that they need to know and hundreds of thousands of their classmates paying an educational price along with them" (Loveless 2008).

High standards and the resources to test whether or not students are achieving the standards are important, but they do not make the difference in student achievement. The National Assessment of Educational Progress has reported scores on long-term reading assessments for ages nine, thirteen, and seventeen from 1971 to 2008 and mathematics from 1973 to 2008. More than twenty-six thousand public and private school students were assessed in each subject area. From 1973 to 2008 there was intensive activity in developing higher standards. Yet, although scores have increased marginally for nine- and thirteen-year-olds, and there are signs that the racial score gaps are narrowing, the average reading and math scores for seventeen-year-olds is not significantly different from that in the 1970s (National Assessment of Educational Progress 2009). The United States' performance on international assessments has been flat to slightly up over the past twenty years.

A look at the history of the standards movement and how curriculum developers address them reveals why standards have not had a significant impact on student achievement.

WHAT ARE ACADEMIC STANDARDS?

Americans are familiar with safety standards that ensure the safety of products, including toys and cars. We're familiar with air quality standards, fuel emission standards, and technical standards. A standard is something established by an authority as a custom, a model, or an example. If a product is substandard, it is not as good as the model. If a product meets the standard, it is as good as or better than the model.

Academic standards were established when the first schools were organized, laying out what would be taught and what would constitute substandard, adequate, and superior achievement. Standards have been debated and have changed considerably over time. The debate over what should be taught, how it should be taught, and how it should be evaluated is very important. Many different parties have an interest in these concerns, including those of parents wanting to maximize their children's future opportunities, the academic community to prepare young people for further study, the business community to prepare young people for gainful employment, and the government to prepare young people to be productive citizens. From Thomas Jefferson to the current president, Americans have considered an educated population the foundation of democracy.

Over time different types of academic standards have been developed.

Content standards identify what students should know and be able to do in each subject area. A content standard is a statement of the knowledge students are expected to have.

Performance standards, like rubrics, identify what students can *do* to show that their work meets the content standards. A performance might indicate the form of the evidence, such as an essay, a science experiment, or a mathematical proof and the quality of that demonstration. Some think that performance standards are required to determine whether a content standard has been achieved. Performance standards are not the skills themselves, they are the standards of quality that assess whether a performance is substandard, achieves the standard, or exceeds the standard.

Curriculum standards describe what should happen in the classroom to achieve the content standards. Because content and performance standards do not dictate curriculum or teaching methods, curriculum standards have been developed to address effective *instructional strategies* for helping students meet the content and performance standards.

Professional standards focus on what teachers should know and be able to do in regard to their attitude toward student achievement, their knowledge of their subject matter, classroom management, and their continuing education. Professional standards are different from curriculum standards. Instead of identifying instructional strategies that would be effective in teaching specific content, professional standards set standards for professional behavior.

Benchmarks provide a learning target for a grade or span of grades. A benchmark sets a marker beyond which students cannot go (usually grades 4, 8, and 12) without demonstrating proficiency in the content or performance standards.

Assessment standards provide the criteria to judge assessments that evaluate progress toward standards. They describe the quality of the assessment practices.

Standards-based assessment is critical to the implementation of standards. If tests are aligned to the standards and schools care about how their students perform on tests, they will ensure that their curriculum is aligned to the standards so students have a better chance of doing well on the tests.

There are even standards for the standards. For example, standards should be

World Class, or as challenging as those of other leading industrial countries;
Important, representing what a consensus has determined are the most important knowledge and skills within a discipline;
Useful, for employment, citizenship, and lifelong learning;
Understandable, so teachers, parents, and students can understand the expectations;

Accurate, reflecting sound scholarship;
Balanced between the necessary skills and the conceptual foundations in a discipline;
Developmentally appropriate, challenging but attainable at each age; and
Assessable, so people can determine if they have been met.

These are lofty expectations for establishing high standards. "The National Council of Teachers of Mathematics (NCTM) has remained committed to the view that standards can play a leading role in guiding the improvement of mathematics education" (National Council of Teachers of Mathematics 2000).

Well-written standards hold the promise of focusing instructional and learning efforts. If everyone knows what needs to be addressed, and curriculum materials are designed and selected based on the standards, it would seem that implementing a new set of high standards would lead to improved student achievement. Yet, throughout history, setting higher standards has never really had that promised effect.

HISTORY OF EDUCATIONAL STANDARDS

Reading information about academic standards, it is easy to believe that academic standards are the result of the concerns raised by *A Nation at Risk,* published in 1983, which called for schools to "adopt more rigorous and measurable standards, and higher expectations, for academic performance and student conduct" (National Commission on Excellence in Education 1983). This inspired the creation of standards written by professional organizations like the NCTM standards, a new look at state standards, and most recently the Common Core Standards. Academic standards, however, had been developed, implemented, and revised long before these recent efforts. It is valuable to review the history of standards and standardized assessment to understand the present situation.

Early Content Standards

Educational standards have been a mainstay of American education. Early colleges like Harvard, founded in 1636, the College of William and Mary in 1693, Yale in 1701, and Princeton in 1746 set high educational standards for their attendees. As early as 1647, the Massachusetts General Court required towns to establish schools with teachers to ensure children could read (Hoffer 2006).

Thomas Jefferson lobbied to "diffuse knowledge more generally through the mass of the people" with the promise that "the ultimate result of the whole scheme of education would be teaching all the children of the State reading, writing, and common arithmetic; The general objects of this law are to provide an education adapted to the years, to the capacity, and the condition of every one, and directed to their freedom and happiness" (Jefferson 1904–1905). Although his legislation was not enacted until later, Jefferson set the standard for the concept of public schools.

Horace Mann, the father of the Common School Movement, carried the torch from Jefferson, and through his advocacy of public education, laid the foundation for the standards of public education today. Before Mann, schools offered only the bare minimum of education and mostly to those families who could afford it. Mann advocated teaching to all boys and girls, regardless of their background, a common body of knowledge and a set of values that were essential to American citizenship. Mandatory education laws were a means of social advancement and eliminating poverty. Central to his philosophy was teacher training and established standards for teaching reading, spelling, and arithmetic. He also promoted the importance of teaching music and physical education (Eakin 2000). By 1900, thirty-one states required children to attend school from the ages of eight to fourteen.

The standards for grading practices emerged in the nineteenth century as well. Yale started using a four-point scale in the 1780s and by 1897 the letter grade system that is widely used today was established at Mount Holyoke College.

Early educators and curriculum writers set standards, too. In 1783, for example, Noah Webster, a Connecticut teacher, published the *Blue Back Speller*, which set standards of American spelling and pronunciation that were different from British English.

The United States Office of Education was established in 1867. The goals of this department were to collect statistics and facts that might show the condition and progress of education, to publicize information about schools and methods of education, to promote efficient school systems, and to promote the cause of education in the country. With the Office of Education, the government established itself as a source of academic standards for American education.

Throughout American history academics have been engaged in setting standards for education. In 1892, the Committee of Ten led by Charles Eliot, the president of Harvard, recommended the standardization of American high school curriculum. Out of this committee came the structure of eight years of elementary education and four years of high school and established the practice of teaching English, mathematics, history, and biology, chemistry, and physics in successive years in high school.

In 1899, the Department of Normal Schools of the National Education Association set broad professional standards for teacher education. These standards included requirements for teachers to have demonstrated proficiency in completing a grammar school course that represented a complete course of study (Edelfelt and Raths 1998).

To standardize and ensure the quality of high school education, in 1906 the Carnegie unit was established in American schools. A committee of the Carnegie Foundation set standards as a measure of the amount of time a student had studied a subject. Fourteen units constituted the minimum required for four years of high school. This established the five 55-minute periods of instruction that structured the high school curriculum.

The *purpose* of schooling has been an issue from the very beginning of American education. The tension between academic preparation for university studies and technical/vocational training became more pronounced in the twentieth century as more and more students attended school. Standards were established for both types of education, which included academic track course requirements and vocational track requirements.

Immigration also had a profound effect on curriculum standards that were established to promote American citizenship. By 1918 all states had compulsory attendance laws requiring all children to attend school at least through elementary school. Standards were continually being updated and higher standards were demanded. In 1949, for example, Dr. Earl J. McGrath, the new commissioner of education, outlined two problems: the need to raise educational standards among teachers and the need to revise the high school curriculum to train for citizenship (Fine 1949).

Content standards were constantly being established and revised throughout the twentieth century by local districts and states; and textbook companies developed more and more products to address the states' standards. A 1956 McGraw-Hill educational catalog lists hundreds of educational titles. Because investments, particularly for the numerous high school courses developed to address both academic and vocational education, were not prohibitive, textbook companies offered many different types of curricula (McGraw-Hill Books Catalog 1956).

Professional Standards

Both content and professional standards were revised throughout the twentieth century. In 1946, for example, the Commission on Teacher Education concluded that "the improvement of teacher education is of the greatest national importance in our times." The commission set standards for all aspects of teacher preparation including subject-matter preparation, student teaching, curriculum, and in-service training. Significant efforts to develop professional standards occurred in 1961 with the National Commission on Teacher Education and Professional Standards, in 1976 with the Commission on Education for the Profession of Teaching, in 1986 with the Carnegie Forum's report of its Task Force on Teaching as a Profession, and the National Council for Accreditation of Teacher Education (NCATE), which has been operating since the 1950s (Edelfelt and Raths 1998). Today approximately forty states require the PRAXIS™ professional skills tests for licensure. This test series administered by the Educational Testing Service (ETS) is required by state departments of education for colleges and universities to measure the academic achievement and proficiency of those entering the teaching profession. PRAXIS measures the content and pedagogical knowledge necessary for beginning teachers. The work of the NCATE and the National Board for Professional Teaching Standards (NBPTS) along with state requirements is turning teaching into a standards-based profession (Lewis 1995).

State Standards

Under education law, all states are required to provide a school system, and each state develops and operates its own educational program. The federal government distributes federal aid for education and ensures equal access. In the United States, states and local districts have control of their schools. Each state constitution establishes the guidelines for education with general supervision of the state's elementary and secondary schools. By this power each state establishes its own academic standards. States also have county boards of education and some states, such as Ohio, have local school boards for designated districts within a county. The Virginia Constitution, revised and approved in 1971, for example, mandates that "standards of quality for the several school divisions shall be determined and prescribed from time to time by the Board of Education, subject to revision only by the General Assembly." Furthermore, Section 5 outlines the powers and duties of the Board of Education: "the Board shall divide the Commonwealth into school divisions . . . as will promote the realization of the prescribed standards of quality" (Virginia 1971).

States and local boards of education make most key education decisions. These state-level decisions are related to standards for curriculum content, general accountability, testing requirements, graduation requirements, teacher preparation, school financing, and the length of the school year. The local level determines specific curriculum content, choice of textbooks, student discipline, teacher hiring, job requirements, professional development, and school schedules, class sizes, and budgeting.

There have been significant differences among states with regard to their academic standards. For example, only eleven states require full-day kindergarten and only half require students to pass an exit exam before receiving a high school diploma. Some states require only two courses in math to graduate from high school; others require four (Center on Education Policy 2006).

States establish and revise their standards on different timetables. Some states write standards for each grade for some subjects. Others have written them for grade spans. Some states write standards for specific subjects such as keyboarding. Others write standards for core subjects only. Ohio has Academic Content Standards for thirteen different areas including international education and library guidelines. California has standards and academic frameworks for ten areas including English-language development. Texas has Texas Essential Knowledge and Skills (TEKS) in thirteen areas, including economics with emphasis on the free enterprise system and its benefits. Virginia has Standards of Learning (SOLs) in twelve areas, including driver education. Montana has content standards in thirteen areas, including workplace competencies. Each state now has its own website where its state standards can be accessed.

In addition to specific subjects that one state may cover but other states do not, states also include standards specific to each state. Most states, for example, have standards for state history in grade 4. A Tennessee standard states, "Summarize the contributions of people of various racial, ethnic, and religious groups in the development of early Tennessee" as part of its fourth grade social studies standards (TN.GOV 2011). Other states include state specific standards among their science curriculum. For example, one of Arizona's fourth grade science standards is "Compare weather conditions in various locations (e.g., regions of Arizona, various U.S. cities, coastal vs. interior geographical regions)" (Arizona Department of Education 2009).

Although there is no such thing as Arizona math or Nebraska English, until the recent Common Core Standards in English and mathematics there was no consistency in what was taught in each grade across the country. If a family moved from one state to another the school experience of their children could be very different. In some states standards are minimum requirements and teachers are expected to exceed the standards. In other states standards are maximum standards and teachers are expected to teach to the standards.

National Standards Initiatives

Our Nation is at risk. Our once unchallenged preeminence in commerce, industry, science, and technological innovation is being overtaken by competitors throughout the world. This report is concerned with only one of the many causes and dimensions of the problem, but it is the one that undergirds American prosperity, security, and civility. We report to the American people that while we can take justifiable pride in what our schools and colleges have historically accomplished and contributed to the United States and the well-being of its people, the educational foundations of our society are presently being eroded by a rising tide of mediocrity that threatens our very future as a Nation and a people. What was unimaginable a generation ago has begun to occur—others are matching and surpassing our educational attainments. (National Commission on Excellence in Education 1983)

The modern era of standards began with the publication of *A Nation at Risk* in 1983. This inspired a wave of standards writing efforts and standardized test creation to align with the standards. The chronology that follows chapter 7 documents the major initiatives in standards development since 1983.

STATE STANDARDS COMPARED
WITH NATIONAL STANDARDS

The passage of Goals 2000 in 1994 and the No Child Left Behind legislation in 2002 shepherded in a new round of state standards, as if none had previously existed. All states were responsible for writing their own standards. States legislated the writing of state standards and commissioned the creation of state proficiency tests to measure whether the standards had been met. As a result of No Child Left Behind, schools are required to annually test and meet performance goals for all students in grades 3–8.

Most states consulted the national standards that were developed by professional organizations in each discipline, as well as other state standards, and then, depending on the makeup of the state board of education, developed their own. In most cases there wasn't much variation. Some states, however, rejected national standards. Virginia, California, and Arizona rejected the NCTM standards and wrote standards that emphasized skills and mathematical procedures over problem solving and the ability to understand mathematical theory. Texas attracted attention in 2010 when it modified its history standards to de-emphasize Thomas Jefferson and add more information about religious leaders.

A great deal of energy has gone into developing state standards in every state. Every state has created standards writing teams that are charged with updating, revising, or rewriting the state standards.

An example of one of the six standards from Florida's New Generation Sunshine State Standards Math 2007 identifies a grade 1 Big Idea, a standard, and four benchmarks for that standard (see textbox 4.1).

TEXTBOX 4.1.   GRADE 1 BIG IDEA: FLORIDA GRADE 1 ADDITION AND SUBTRACTION STANDARDS

Standard 1: Develop understandings of addition and subtraction strategies for basic addition facts and related subtraction facts. (MA.1.A.1)

1. Model addition and subtraction situations using the concepts of "part-whole," "adding to," "taking away from," "comparing," and "missing addend." (MA.1.A.1.1)
2. Identify, describe, and apply addition and subtraction as inverse operations. (MA.1.A.1.2)
3. Create and use increasingly sophisticated strategies, and use properties such as Commutative, Associative, and Additive Identity, to add whole numbers. (MA.1.A.1.3)
4. Use counting strategies, number patterns, and models as a means for solving basic addition and subtraction fact problems. (MA.1.A.1.4)

Source: Florida Department of Education 2007.

The Texas TEKS for grade 1 related to addition and subtraction is different. In Texas there are thirteen TEKS and specifics like items A and B in textbox 4.2.

All of these standards are articulated across the grade levels. For example, in Florida the Big Ideas are developed across the grade levels and the Benchmark Standards articulate how the Big Ideas should be developed in each

---

TEXTBOX 4.2.   TEXAS GRADE 1 ADDITION AND SUBTRACTION STANDARDS

Texas (3) Number, operation, and quantitative reasoning. The student recognizes and solves problems in addition and subtraction situations. The student is expected to

(A) model and create addition and subtraction problem situations with concrete objects and write corresponding number sentences; and
(B) use concrete and pictorial models to apply basic addition and subtraction facts (up to $9 + 9 = 18$ and $18 - 9 = 9$).

Source: Texas Knowledge and Skills (TEKS), Texas State Board of Education 2006.

---

grade. There are fourteen math standards in grade 1, twenty-one in grade 2, and seventeen in grade 3, for example. Florida has eighty-three standards in reading/language arts in grade 1 and seventy-five in grade 3.

The two examples demonstrate the morass of standards across the fifty states. In Florida, the first grader must, for example, describe addition and subtraction as inverse operations, although this is not required in Texas. In Texas the first grader must use concrete and pictorial models to apply addition and subtraction facts, although this is not required in Florida. Considering that every state has different requirements, creating a curriculum for first grade mathematics to be sold across the country encourages breadth of content coverage, rather than depth of content knowledge.

Effectiveness of State Standards

When each state creates its own standards for each subject, some are bound to be more effective than others. In 2006, the Fordham Foundation looked at state academic standards following the enactment of NCLB. At that point thirty-seven states had updated or revised their standards in at least one subject, but Fordham determined they were just as mediocre as ever with the exception of California, Indiana, and Massachusetts, which received high scores. In 2011 the Fordham Institute compared US History standards across the states and determined that the majority of state standards were "mediocre-to-awful." Only one state, South Carolina, had standards strong enough to earn an A. Only nine states were rated B (Stern and Stern 2011).

> Standards-based education reform involves many elements—testing, accountability systems, cut scores, to name but a few—but the success of each ultimately rests upon getting state academic standards right. So far, however, the states that have produced exemplary standards are greatly outnumbered by those whose standards are weak, nebulous, watered-down, content-free or otherwise unable to bear a real burden. (Jacobs 2006)

National Common Core Standards and State Standards

The new Common Core Standards are the national standards for English reading/language arts and mathematics. In 2010 Fordham compared the new Common Core English and math standards to existing state standards. They found that the Common Core standards are clearly superior to those currently in use in thirty-nine states in math and thirty-seven states in English. Common Core Standards were superior in both math and reading in thirty-three states. Only Indiana and California had standards that were clearly superior to the Common Core (Carmichael et al. 2010).

As an example, the Common Core standards for addition and subtraction in first grade are much more specific than most state standards (see textbox 4.3).

TEXTBOX 4.3. COMMON CORE MATHEMATICS STANDARDS FOR GRADE 1 ADDITION AND SUBTRACTION

Represent and solve problems involving addition and subtraction.

1. Use addition and subtraction within 20 to solve word problems involving situations of adding to, taking from, putting together, taking apart, and comparing, with unknowns in all positions, e.g., by using objects, drawings, and equations with a symbol for the unknown number to represent the problem.
2. Solve word problems that call for addition of three whole numbers whose sum is less than or equal to 20, e.g., by using objects, drawings, and equations with a symbol for the unknown number to represent the problem.

Understand and apply properties of operations and the relationship between addition and subtraction.

3. Apply properties of operations as strategies to add and subtract. *Examples: If 8 + 3 = 11 is known, then 3 + 8 = 11 is also known. (Commutative property of addition.) To add 2 + 6 + 4, the second two numbers can be added to make a ten, so 2 + 6 + 4 = 2 + 10 = 12. (Associative property of addition.)*
4. Understand subtraction as an unknown-addend problem. *For example, subtract 10 – 8 by finding the number that makes 10 when added to 8. Add and subtract within 20.*

Add and subtract within 20.

5. Relate counting to addition and subtraction (e.g., by counting on 2 to add 2).
6. Add and subtract within 20, demonstrating fluency for addition and subtraction within 10. Use strategies such as counting on; making ten (e.g., 8 + 6 = 8 + 2 + 4 = 10 + 4 = 14); decomposing a number leading to a ten (e.g., 13 – 4 = 13 –3 – 1 = 10 – 1 = 9); using the relationship between addition and subtraction (e.g., knowing that 8 + 4 = 12, one knows 12 – 8 = 4); and creating equivalent but easier or known sums (e.g., adding 6 + 7 by creating the known equivalent 6 + 6 + 1 = 12 + 1 = 13).

Work with addition and subtraction equations.

7. Understand the meaning of the equal sign, and determine if equations involving addition and subtraction are true or false. For example, which of the following equations are true and which are false? 6 = 6, 7 = 8 – 1, 5 + 2 = 2 + 5, 4 + 1 = 5 + 2.
8. Determine the unknown whole number in an addition or subtraction equation relating three whole numbers. *For example, determine the unknown number that makes the equation true in each of the equations 8 + ? = 11, 5 = _ 3, 6 + 6 = _.*

Source: Common Core State Standards Initiative 2010a.

Most states have voluntarily adopted the Common Core Standards that have been written to date, although states are allowed to make some modifications to them. In order to qualify for federal funds, states were required to rewrite their standards. The Common Core Standards initiative saved states time, energy, and money by providing solid standards in the two core academic areas, English/reading/language arts and mathematics. As Common Core Standards are developed in other subject areas, including social studies and science, states will have the opportunity to adopt them, as well, and forgo re-creating their own versions.

STANDARDIZED TESTING

Contrary to popular belief, standardized tests, like standards, have a long history as well. Legitimate test results give an accurate picture of student performance and provide valuable information that helps to shape policies and strategies for academic improvement. Tests can inform parents, educators, and policymakers about curriculum strengths and weaknesses. Poor test results can encourage schools to identify weaknesses and address them with improved methods and curriculum. In 1994, California was a national leader in progressive education when the National Assessment of Educational Progress showed that the state had the lowest scores in fourth grade reading. This galvanized the state to rewrite its standards that were used to create a new state test, and dramatically change curriculum (Jacobs 2006).

A standardized test is a test that is administered in a standard way. Every student takes the same test and is given the same time to complete each section of the test. To standardize the testing environments and control variables, the temperature and lighting are controlled as much as possible, and the people who proctor the tests are given specific instructions about what they can and cannot do.

Standardized tests enable the analysis of comparisons across the public education system. The Elementary and Secondary Education Act of 1965 required standardized testing in public schools, and the 2001 reauthorization of that act, No Child Left Behind, tied public school funding to standardized state tests.

Historically, standardized tests comprised multiple choice and true-false questions that could be scored by computers. Open-ended and essay assessments are difficult to score. Yet today state proficiency tests developed to align with state standards that have strengthened their writing standards beyond grammar, usage, and mechanics routinely include writing assessments. These are scored by teams of evaluators trained to look for specific criteria in each response.

Categories of Standardized Tests

There are three basic categories of standardized tests. Until NCLB, most standardized tests were *norm-referenced* multiple choice tests that measure what each test taker knew in comparison to what other test takers knew about the same topic. Results are typically reported in percentiles showing the percentages of students who scored higher or lower on each topic. Most college entrance exams are norm-referenced.

Typically *criterion-referenced* tests were the types of the tests and quizzes written by teachers to show whether students had learned specific material. With NCLB, states set standards and developed standardized tests that were standards based or criterion referenced. These tests are also mainly multiple choice, but test takers are measured on how well they achieve the standards, regardless of how other test takers perform. Most state achievement tests are criterion referenced. These tests measure whether students have achieved the state standards.

A third type of standardized test is the *ipsative* assessment in which a test taker's score is compared to his or her previous performance, such as attaining a higher score in a computer game or in physical education. These types of standardized tests are often used in special education.

National and International Standardized Tests

Many standardized tests have been administered over the years. Baby boomers may remember taking the Stanford-Binet intelligence test, which used a single number, the intelligence quotient or IQ for the score. This score was a combination of the mental and chronological age (Fletcher 2009). Giving students their IQ scores, which were said to be static, in elementary grades was highly controversial. The Iowa Tests of Basic Skills (ITBS) for grades K–8 were developed in 1935 at the University of Iowa for the purpose of improving instruction. New versions of the tests are widely used in public, parochial, and private schools throughout Iowa and in other states as well. The California Achievement Test (CAT), the Terra Nova developed by CTB/McGraw-Hill, and the Metropolitan Achievement Test (MAT) developed by Harcourt were the main tests at the K–8 levels. These are norm-referenced tests as opposed to criterion-referenced tests in that the scores are compared to other students. Private, for-profit companies publish and score the tests. The Scholastic Aptitude Test (SAT) and American College Test (ACT) are the two major college exams. Advanced Placement (AP) tests are given to high school students who want to place out of introductory courses in college.

National Assessment of Educational Progress (NAEP)

First administered in 1969, the National Assessment of Educational Progress (NAEP) is the largest nationally representative assessment of student achievement. NAEP assessments are conducted in mathematics, reading, science, writing, the arts, civics, economics, geography, and US history. Test questions are based on rigorous, challenging content standards and performance standards. The results are expressed in achievement levels (advanced, proficient, basic, and below basic). NAEP is a criterion-referenced test, designed to show how well students know the content and skills according to a specific criteria. The test is given to representative samples of students across the country at grades 4, 8, and 12.

International Comparison Tests

There are two international assessments that are widely administered in the United States: the Trends in International Mathematics and Science Study (TIMSS) conducted by the International Study Center (IEA) and the Programme for International Student Assessment (PISA) conducted by the Organisation for Economic Co-operation and Development (OECD). These are the two measures that provide international comparisons of student achievement with the goal of improving teaching and learning. TIMSS is based on the curricula from participating countries, but is not aligned to the standards or curricula of any one country.

TIMSS, a criterion-referenced test, provides data on the mathematics and science achievement of an international comparison of students in grades 4 and 8. Since 1995, every four years TIMSS evaluates student achievement in school mathematics and science and provides trend data for countries that have participated in all of the assessments. More than a half million students from fifteen thousand schools in over forty-five countries participated in TIMMS in 1997, and sixty countries participated in 2011. This includes approximately thirty-three thousand students from more than five hundred schools in the United States. The tests include both multiple choice and free-response exercises and collect data from the achievement tests, questionnaire responses, curriculum analyses, classroom instruction videotapes, and case studies of policy issues. The data allow for the ability to rank countries according to their student achievement, and the curriculum analyses and video-taped lessons allow for international comparisons of standards, curriculum, and teaching methods that contribute to the strengths and weaknesses in each country. TIMSS makes serious efforts to ensure that the comparisons are legitimate, scrutinizing participation rates, and ensuring the random selection of participants.

PISA, a norm-referenced test first administered in 2000, measures reading literacy, mathematics literacy, and science literacy every three years. In 2000, forty-three countries participated in PISA and by 2010, over seventy countries participated. In the United States approximately 5,300 randomly selected students from 165 schools and weighted to be representative of the nation participated in the test. PISA measures the ability to apply what has been learned to real-world situations.

Standards-Based State Tests

Until the 1990s standardized tests were not aligned to state standards. The ITBS, CAT, and MAT were norm-referenced tests and used nationwide. Because there were no national standards and every state had a different set of standards, it would have been impossible to administer standards-based, criterion-referenced tests nationwide. With the Goals 2000 legislation, in 1994 state legislatures enacted laws that mandated the creation of new standards and proficiency tests aligned to the standards. State boards of education made serious efforts to create an alignment among the state standards, the curriculum used in schools, and new state proficiency tests.

With Goals 2000, teachers were required to teach to the standards. The tests aligned with the standards. Schools, especially after NCLB was enacted, were evaluated on whether they made adequate yearly progress as measured by their state tests. As a result, teachers and schools got very serious about teaching to the standards.

When the No Child Left Behind Act mandated that states develop rigorous standards and administer standardized tests aligned to those standards to evaluate adequate yearly progress, states moved from administering tests like ITBS, CAT, and MAT to state proficiency tests. Many states developed their own tests, including the Florida Comprehensive Assessment Test (FCAT), the Texas Assessment of Knowledge and Skills (TAKS), California's Standardized Testing and Reporting (STAR), New York's Regents Exams, and Virginia's Standards of Learning Tests (SOL). Some states joined forces. Four states (Maine, New Hampshire, Rhode Island, and Vermont) participate in the New England Common Assessment Program (NECAP).

Each of the state tests measures student performance in different subject areas at specific grade levels. For example, Virginia tests reading in grades 3, 4, 5, 6, 7, and 8, and science in grades 3 and 5. Each state uses its state standards, such as Virginia's Standards of Learning (SOL), Texas's Essential Knowledge and Skills (TEKS), or the NECAP's Grade Level Expectations (GLEs) as the criteria by which students are measured.

CRITICISMS AND CONTROVERSIES
RELATED TO STANDARDS AND TESTING

From the early days of American education, standards have been controversial. Horace Mann confronted resistance from Boston schoolmasters who disapproved of his teaching standards, parents who did not want to give up education to the schools, and parents who resented mandatory school. Controversy still rages between people who want the schools to teach religion and those who do not. Catholics opposed to secular common schooling went so far as to create their own private schools. There have been publicly fought controversies over the teaching of evolution, sex education, and reading selections.

Since 1983, there have been major controversies over the development of academic standards.

Local versus Federal Control

Because education is the domain of the states, there has been significant resistance to the development of national standards. All of the standards developed by professional organizations after the Goals 2000 legislation were voluntary, and as a result, only had significant impact insofar as they affected the development of a state's standards. The NCLB legislation promoted local control of education, which meant that fifty states each wrote their own standards and own standards-based tests. Some states and local communities feel that the government is imposing on them and that standards should be made on a local level where local school boards and parents decide what their children should and should not learn.

Content versus Performance Standards

Another controversy has been whether standards should be content or performance based. Advocates of content standards want clear descriptions of standards in terms of knowledge and skills. Advocates of performance standards claim that standards should describe the behaviors that demonstrate competence.

Cost of Resources

Some voices have been critical of the amount of money that has been spent on the development of standards and standardized tests when classrooms lack instructional resources.

Teaching to the Test

Some of the loudest critics have argued that the emphasis on high-stakes tests linked to graduation or adequate yearly progress encourages teachers to "teach to the test" rather than teach important skills and concepts. Studying the previous tests, teaching test-taking strategies, and drilling on specific test items seem like good ideas until students take the test and find different test items than they had anticipated and studied. Any given test on any given year only covers a fraction of the standards in each discipline. There is no way a school or teacher, let alone a student, could anticipate which standards might be covered. This has not dissuaded countless schools and individual teachers, and, for that matter, parents, from investing in test preparation materials. Practicing multiple choice items, however, is no substitute for practicing authentic reading and writing, which is what the test is actually attempting to evaluate.

Standardized Tests Are Not Accurate Measurements

Many people, particularly parents and educators of students who are not successful on standardized tests, argue that standardized tests are not good measures of what students know and are able to do. These people maintain that tests measure test-taking ability rather than knowledge and skills and appear to promote memorization over creative thinking.

Accountability Anxiety

Some critics see the standards movement as the antithesis of quality education in that instead of promoting curiosity and a love of learning, it promotes test anxiety on the part of students, teachers, administrators, and politicians.

Standards Represent a Previous Trend

Some critics who have been in education for a period of time have criticized the standards movement because of the similarity to trends that they experienced in the past. They claim the standards are being promoted as new and improved, when they appear to be similar to yesterday's standards, which were not effective in promoting change and student achievement. The attention to writing performance standards in a specific way, for example, reminds critics of the behavioral standards that were promoted twenty years before. The standards from the Partnership for 21st Century Skills, with its emphasis on communication and collaboration skills, seem like those from the 2004 Department of Labor's Secretary's Commission on Achieving Necessary Skills (SCANS), and so on.

Content Controversy

Even with all the transparency and compromise in developing standards, there are critics of the content of the standards. For example, in 1996, the Senate voted to reject the National History Standards because conservatives had claimed that they focused too much on women and minorities to the exclusion of prominent historical figures. The history standards never quite recovered from the negative public perception. In 2010 historians objected to the 2010 Texas history standards, which they claimed distorted the historical record.

Number of Standards Overwhelming

Many educators look at the huge array of standards, even if only focused on one state and one grade, and feel overwhelmed. As an elementary teacher, who teaches all subjects, it is intimidating to make sure that you are addressing the intent of all the standards in every subject. Many teachers feel that they are on their own to figure out how to implement the standards. They think they must write a curriculum themselves or they are inundated with materials they must evaluate to determine if they meet the standards. The standards that were created with great effort by conscientious people seem too overwhelming to use in the classroom. Instead of relief, standards committees, like the New Jersey committee quoted below, make it seem that teachers must make sense of the new standards, throw out everything they know, and develop their own curriculum using the sample teaching strategies, adaptations, and background information given.

> The New Jersey Academic Standards were created to improve student achievement by clearly defining what all students should know and be able to do at the end of thirteen years of public education. To assist teachers and curriculum specialists in aligning curriculum with the standards, the department provides local school districts with a curriculum framework for each content area. The frameworks provided classroom teachers and curriculum specialists with sample teaching strategies, adaptations, and background information relevant to each of the content areas. In addition, the statewide assessments were aligned to the Core Curriculum Content Standards. This alignment of standards, instruction, and assessment was unprecedented. (New Jersey Department of Education 2004)

Mile-Wide, Inch-Deep Standards

A major criticism of standards is that standards writing committees won't leave anything out. The people who make up the committees each have skills and concepts he or she feels are important, and everyone on the committee has a different list of concerns. After standards have been through the review process, more concerns are addressed. By the time the standards are published, they reflect a wide range of topics at each grade level that are impossible to teach meaningfully in one year. If educators cover them all, they will provide superficial coverage. If they don't, they risk not preparing their students for the standardized tests.

Standards Stifle Creativity

Some critics believe that teaching to standards stifles teachers' creativity and limits their ability to promote and explore student interests. These people feel there is no time to do anything else except teach to the standards.

Vagueness of Standards

Many standards are criticized because they are too vague and open to different interpretations. For example, a grade 5 geography standard states, "Students will make and use different kinds of maps, globes, charts, and databases." As written, this standard could be addressed with an experience involving fifteen minutes with a road map, a map of the school, a globe, a growth chart, and building a spreadsheet of five rows and two columns. Or it could involve a week's worth of work reading and creating different types of maps, comparing maps and a globe, and another week collecting data and then learning how to use charts and databases to analyze the data. A ninth grade language arts standard has the same vagueness problem, "Students will analyze the relationships of pairs of words in analogical statements (e.g., synonyms and antonyms) and infer word meanings from these relationships." Teachers and students, and for that matter, curriculum developers, have a great deal of difficulty discerning what the expectations of the standards writers were.

Standards Rigor

Some standards are criticized for being too easy. Others are too challenging. Standards can cause high-achieving students to become bored and other students to become discouraged. The brightest children may be unchallenged and the neediest children may be condemned by low expectations.

Basic Skills versus Concepts

Some states have experienced controversy over whether the standards promote basic skills or concept development. Advocates of basic skills are concerned that students will not have the foundational skills they need. Advocates of conceptual development maintain that skills are only valuable in the context of understanding and the emphasis in education should be on understanding, not skill building.

Alignment

Another criticism has been that standards have not been aligned to curriculum or to the state tests, so it is up to the teachers to ensure they are aligned or face students' failure. If teachers are using one set of standards and the tests are not aligned to the standards, scores will not reflect what students know and can do.

Confusion between Academic Standards and Teacher Expectations

There is some confusion between academic standards and the standards or expectations a teacher has for his or her students. When parents discuss rigorous standards, they often are concerned about teachers imposing standards of quality for student work. If a teacher does not correct spelling errors or does not require students to produce much written work, that teacher is characterized as having low academic standards. A teacher who is particular about accuracy and assigns a lot of homework and makes students work and think is said to have high academic standards. Many people, outside of the educational community, may be unaware that academic standards even exist.

LIMITATIONS OF STANDARDS

All of the criticisms levied against standards and standardized testing complicate the development of educational materials developed to teach the standards and prepare students for standardized tests. Curriculum developers must provide adequate instruction, practice, and assessment for each standard, but when standards are vague, are not rigorous, or are not aligned properly with standardized tests, the instructional materials will be lacking. The standards are not the curriculum and as such have serious limitations that must be addressed by curriculum developers.

Writing and Implementation of Higher Standards Takes Time

For a society that wants to see the results of change, implementing a standards-based curriculum is a very frustrating experience and it is easy to lose interest. Even the framers of the National Education Goals Panel expressed a concern. They recognized that not all students would meet the standards rapidly and that no one knows exactly what needs to be done to reach the high standards. They also acknowledged that raising educational performance is a long-term, systematic effort that will take decades. However, the standards define realistic high goals and they are a critical first step toward raising educational performance (Goals 3 and 4 Technical Planning Group 1993).

Writing standards and tests, developing curriculum to reflect those standards, educating teachers in the new standards, implementing the curriculum, and then testing the results is a multiyear process at best. Because of this, it is really difficult to measure the effectiveness of any of the efforts. Only a historical analysis can provide that information—whether important standards were written and assessed, whether curriculum reflected the standards, whether teachers were adequately trained, whether they implemented the standards and curriculum with fidelity—all of these variables have to be considered in any analysis. It is very difficult to find these types of analyses on standards implementations, so new standards efforts always seem to be starting from scratch.

Standards Do Not Prescribe Curriculum or Teaching Strategies

Neither content nor performance standards, nor for that matter, professional or assessment standards, prescribes a curriculum or even a scope and sequence of skills. Teaching strategies and activities are the domain of the curriculum. Neither do standards prescribe a particular curriculum. Schools choose the curriculum they determine will help students meet the standards.

> Standards are not curriculum. This initiative is about developing a set of standards that are common across states. The curriculum that follows will continue to be a local responsibility (or state-led, where appropriate). The curriculum could become more consistent from state to state based on the commonality of the standards; however, there are multiple ways to teach these standards, and therefore, there will be multiple approaches that could help students accomplish the goals set out in the standards. (Common Core State Standards Initiative 2010b)

Some standards are accompanied by examples of teaching strategies to meet the standard, but these do not constitute a curriculum. Curriculum developers are on their own to interpret the standards, order concepts, and develop activities and strategies to teach them. In turn, teachers must choose and implement appropriate curriculum. There is a vast, wide-open plane of interpretation in these efforts.

Standards Are Difficult to Learn and Apply

Ohio State University is one of the top education institutions in America and has graduated thousands and thousands of education majors who have become teachers. OSU prepares its students to become licensed teachers in the state of Ohio. Here is a description of the Masters of Education program for potential grades 4–9 middle school teachers.

> The Middle Childhood M.Ed. is a full-time, sequential program of professional courses leading to initial Ohio teacher certification/licensure in grades

four through nine. The sequence may vary from campus to campus and can be completed in five quarters. Students engage in a coherent series of courses in adolescent development and learning, middle school philosophy and organization, teaching methods, technology, diversity, field experiences, an internship, a research and inquiry component, and a culminating project and/or examination focused on critical issues in education. Most of the professional courses and fieldwork are open only to those students who have been admitted to the program. The goal of the program is to prepare dedicated individuals to apply their knowledge and skills of learning theory, problem solving, critical thinking, creativity, and interpersonal communication in the middle childhood school setting.

The M.Ed. teacher preparation program is a full-time, graduate program. Students interested in middle childhood education must choose a minimum of two of the following subject areas in which they wish to teach and complete specific course work for each:

- Mathematics
- Reading & Language Arts
- Science
- Social Studies (Ohio State University 2011)

Although there is a research and inquiry component, there are no courses devoted to learning standards, interpreting standards, selecting curriculum materials that reflect standards, or teaching standards. It would be difficult for a college or university to teach one state's standards when there are fifty different sets of standards. Not only that, the students may come from a variety of different states and plan to start teaching in other states.

New teachers with fresh teaching certificates must figure standards out on their own in their first teaching experiences. Even if a new teacher had a strong background in standards, once he or she is faced with the school environment, classroom management, discipline problems, and social pressure from other teachers, there is little guarantee that the standards will remain a high priority.

For experienced teachers who have witnessed lots of trends come and go, new standards are put in the context of what they are already doing with the hope that they will not cause much change. New standards may be the topic of an afterschool professional development training or a school or district presentation on a professional day, but if the educational materials teachers are using do not change, experienced teachers are on their own to learn, interpret, and implement new standards.

Standards Do Not Translate

There have been several documented cases that showed that although students in a state have shown improvement on the state proficiency tests, they do not show the same improvement on national tests, such as NAEP. In 2005, to meet adequate yearly progress using their state-created standards and tests, states reported that large percentages of their students were meeting their high standards. It makes sense if, in fact, high standards were in place, teachers effectively taught the standards using standards-based curriculum, and tests were aligned with the curriculum. Interestingly, the scores on the NAEP test were far lower than states were reporting on their state assessments. Idaho, for example, reported that 90 percent of its fourth graders were proficient in mathematics. Yet the NAEP results showed that only 41 percent of Idaho students reached the basic level of proficiency. Georgia reported that 87 percent of its students were proficient in reading, but only 26 percent of Georgia students reached proficiency on NAEP.

It is easy to conclude that because of the political high-stakes nature of the test results, states may have intentionally or unintentionally embraced low standards and grade inflation to make themselves look better (Ravitch 2005). It is also plausible that states did a good job of creating, teaching, and testing to standards that were not comparable to other state, national, or international standards. As a result students may achieve proficiency in one state and be below proficiency in another. It would also account for America's poor performance in international comparisons. The "50 states, 50 standards, 50 tests" strategy outlined in the NCLB legislation has not improved student achievement on national and international measures.

STANDARDS AND ACHIEVEMENT

There is no question that many sincere efforts have been made to create rigorous curriculum standards by states, by national organizations, and by collaborations. And millions of dollars have been spent on creating and administering tests aligned to the standards. The results of these efforts are unclear, at best.

The Center on Education Policy analyzed trends over a four-year period for those schools and districts that did not make adequate yearly progress (AYP) on raising student achievement under NCLB. From 2005 to 2009, one-third of the nation's schools did not make AYP, an increase from 29 percent in 2006. More than one-third of the nation's school districts did not make AYP in 2009, up from 29 percent in 2006. The percentages of schools and districts that did not make AYP fluctuated from year to year within the same state and varied greatly across states (Center on Education Policy 2010).

To date, the mere creation of standards, any type of standards, has not had an effect on student achievement. "School achievement appears astonishingly persistent. Nearly two-thirds of low-performing schools in 1989 are still low performers two decades later" (Loveless 2010).

On the 2006 NAEP US History Assessment, not even half of twelfth graders achieved a basic level and only 13 percent were proficient. Although every state requires students to study American history and every state has at least minimal standards, only thirteen states include any history or social studies as part of their high school exit exam.

If standards were the key to student achievement, one would expect that the state standards rated highest by organizations such as the Fordham Institute would result in the highest achievement, but they do not. In both 2003 and 2011 the Alabama state history standards were rated A and A− by Fordham respectively, but Alabama students rank far from the top in history.

The Fordham study admits this in its evaluation of the latest state history standards.

> We readily acknowledge that standards, in and of themselves, do not yield student achievement. We've ample evidence that standards, even good standards, absent proper implementation and accountability, do little more than adorn classroom bookshelves. Academic standards are simply the recipe with which the education system cooks; educators supply and mix the essential ingredients. But without clear, consistent standards, you can expect learning goals, curriculum, and instruction to vary wildly from district to district and school to school, and few students to graduate high school knowing all they should about their country's past and thus its present. . . . Let us repeat, however, that great standards alone don't produce superior results. Several states with exemplary history standards still aren't serious about course requirements, assessments, and accountability. (Stern and Stern 2011)

If history is not taught well and it is not tested on high school exit exams, students will not be proficient, regardless of the existence of rigorous standards.

It is very tempting to spend time developing higher standards, which may seem to make a difference, but experience shows higher standards would have little effect on achievement. Many history standards are already in place, and some of them are bound to be rigorous. Setting rigorous standards is important. To make improvements in student performance, however, the educational practices related to teaching need to change in schools across the country. History shows us that making only improvements to standards will not lead to significant improvements in student achievement.

Regardless of the complete lack of evidence that higher standards result in improved student performance, people continue to advocate for more rigorous standards and aligning testing to them. These initiatives, however, cannot be expected to raise student achievement.

EDUCATIONAL PUBLISHERS AND STANDARDS

With so much attention and effort devoted to academic standards, especially in the past twenty-five years, anyone would expect that creating curriculum that teaches state standards in the most effective way would be the major preoccupation of educational publishers. Yet publishers are motivated by profit, and once a state adoption committee has approved a curriculum, everyone assumes the standards have been covered. The competition for sales is based on other factors, such as how easy the program is to teach, appealing design, or enticing features and components. The purchasing decisions rarely, if ever, are based on the superiority of standards coverage in one curriculum over another. Even when schools claim to review the state standards coverage in a program, the publisher's marketing materials, rather than a thorough review of the curriculum, is accepted as proof that the program meets the standards. Many programs win in purchasing competitions because they have better standards *correlations*, not better standards coverage.

A major part of the responsibility of editors in educational publishing is to ensure that the company's curricular materials meet state standards. This seems like a straightforward task, but it is not. For one thing, states have different definitions of what it means to "meet" their standards. Second, authors and editors may interpret the standards differently from the intentions of the standards writers. Third, the people who review curriculum for standards coverage may not understand the intention of the standards writers. Finally, partly because there have been fifty different sets of standards, educational products have not been developed from any set of standards. Instead, typically, curriculum is developed and then standards are correlated and any holes are filled.

Meeting State Standards

Every state has a different definition of what it means to meet the state standards. Some states require that a curriculum meet 100 percent of every part of its state standards. Teachers in other states expect to supplement each new curriculum with additional content in order to meet the state standards and prepare students for their state tests.

Partial Coverage

Most states do not require that all their standards be met in a publisher's curriculum. They expect the teachers in the state to understand the standards and fill in any gaps. Open territory states such as Iowa or Maine recognize that they do not have the clout to demand that a publisher meet every single one of their standards in a particular area.

Partial coverage may also mean that standards topics are mentioned, but they may not be fully developed. Consider, for example, the grade 5 geography standard: "Students will make and use different kinds of maps, globes, charts, and databases." Many states and school adoption committees would accept this standard as having been covered if a program included two kinds of maps and had a one-sentence teacher direction to have students compare them. The maps may appear in a student book or not. The directions need only appear somewhere in the program. The rationale is that the teacher is given the opportunity within the program to teach the standard.

One Hundred Percent Standards Coverage

At the other extreme are states like Texas that require 100 percent coverage of every part of every standard three to five times in the student book. Using the geography example, the Texas state adoption committee would look for three instances where students used different kinds of maps, three instances where students used different types of globes, three instances where they used different types of charts, and three instances where they used different types of databases. In Texas if a publisher misses one instance of one part of one standard, the program will not be approved as meeting all standards. The Texas adoption process allows publishers an opportunity to add missing content to meet a standard but not make major revisions. California has a similar requirement.

These states that have major sales potential have also moved to eliminate extraneous content from approved materials. This is an attempt to ensure that publishers create curricula for only one state. States want to reduce the size of their students' textbooks and provide a more focused curriculum. Yet it is cost prohibitive for a publisher to create fifty different curricula for each subject.

Some states require publishers to create state specific correlations of the state standards to the curriculum so that reviewers can see where the publisher has met the standards. Publishers may be required to identify the top three to five instances of each standard or they may highlight all instances of a standard within a curriculum.

Standards Interpretations

Many standards, even if they are more specific than others, are open to wide interpretation. Educational publishing editors spend a great deal of time discussing what a standard means and what qualifies as coverage. In the high-stakes states, publishers often contact the state for clarification. Once a curriculum has been developed, adoption committees may have a differing interpretation and not accept a publisher's coverage of a standard. In some cases the state department of education officials must intervene.

Once a curriculum is purchased, the educators must interpret the standards and determine whether students are meeting them. If not, students may not be successful on the state's standardized test, which represents another interpretation of the standards.

Of course by aligning the standards, curriculum, and tests, there is a much better chance that instruction will be in range of the intentions of the standards writers than if there was no alignment.

STANDARDS AND EDUCATIONAL
PRODUCT DEVELOPMENT

Standards do not constitute a curriculum. Standards are the list of concepts that must be included in a curriculum, but they do not dictate in what order the concepts should be taught, what activities are most appropriate to develop the concepts, or how to evaluate student progress toward meeting the standards. The way concepts are ordered is critically important for student understanding. Many teachers and students have experienced the bewilderment when, for example, there are gaps or leaps between math concepts that are not carefully articulated. Students seem to be doing well with one concept and then are completely lost when they start the next chapter.

The order in which concepts are presented is important and so are teaching strategies. Experienced teachers may be used to presenting a concept or skills in a particular way and feel that students can understand that concept using that method. In addition, educational research is ongoing and continually identifying strategies that are more or less effective. A set of strategies for specific concepts, however, does not constitute a curriculum. One or even a series of great lessons or activities does not make a year's worth of curriculum.

Standards and strategies are components of curriculum but they are not the curriculum. That is one reason that publishers do not build curriculum from a set of standards and strategies. Another is that publishers are incentivized by cost considerations to reuse or revise assets they already have created. If a publisher had created a spelling program, and there is a new call for spelling, it is most logical that the first step in creating a new program is to review the old one to see if the new standards are addressed and how much revision it would take to make the old program conform to the new standards.

Covering standards then becomes a process of tagging the instances of each standard and adding content where needed to address any standards that are not covered. Only in some cases are older assets abandoned because they do not address enough of the new standards. Even then, there may be components of a program, such as teacher resource materials, extra readers, games, and activities from previous programs, that are tacked on to the new core program.

In those few cases where a completely new program has been developed to address a new set of state standards in one state, the program is reviewed for standards coverage for every other state. So, for example, if a publisher creates a new reading program for Texas one year, the publisher will try to include as many standards as possible from other states so that they can market the program to a larger customer base.

State Specific Editions

Publishers have been ingenious in creating state specific materials. In the 1980s publishers began creating state specific versions with a state cover and some state specific materials. A publisher might provide a separate workbook that included state specific content that was not covered in the core materials.

Teachers were very positive about this since they believed the publisher had developed the curriculum for their specific needs. By purchasing state specific materials teachers incentivized publishers to focus their efforts on state specific features, rather than effectiveness. This started an escalation of state specific features and the focus on competition. In addition to state specific covers, the next phase involved including state specific features that could be swapped out in other state editions. In a California science book, there might be pictures and captions or other small features that addressed California interests. A picture and description of the Golden Gate Bridge might introduce a chapter on water. In a Texas version of the curriculum the feature might be replaced with the Rainbow Bridge, or in Florida, the Seven Mile Bridge. As technology improved and mitigated the cost, publishers began to include the standards and state icons on every page of a book for the major states. The key adoption states (Texas, California, Florida) now not only expect but also require their own state versions of a curriculum.

Publishers often created "modular" programs for those instances, as in science, where one state called for earth science in fourth grade and another called for it in fifth grade.

States that are not as potentially profitable get different degrees of state specific treatment. Pennsylvania, an open territory state, might get a state specific cover on the student and teacher books and some introductory pages that provide the correlation to the Pennsylvania state standards. Pennsylvania educators are impressed by this and are more likely to purchase the state specific materials, even if another curriculum is more effective.

State specific editions have all but eliminated small publishing companies that cannot afford to customize their curricula for each state. National editions cannot win adoptions against editions that appear to be tailored just for the customer.

How Publishers Address Standards

Once the standards from all applicable states have been analyzed, editors begin the process of making sure they are addressed within the curriculum. In some cases chapters or sections are rewritten or reworked to reflect a standard or group of standards. For the most part, however, a paragraph here, an activity there, a few practice exercises, and some assessment items are all that are required to be rewritten or reworked. Editors are pressured to change only what is absolutely necessary to meet the standards to get past an adoption committee. The curriculum will be evaluated on whether a standard is included, not how effective the instruction is to develop the standard. There is little incentive to do more than add specific instances and be sure to use the wording of the state standard in the heading, the index, the table of contents, and the correlation so reviewers can find it.

Even though states like Texas and California have gone to great efforts to make sure that adopted curriculum materials meet their standards, the review process becomes an exercise in checking off instances of coverage rather than the quality of the instruction. Once the materials are adopted by the state and schools assume the standards are met because the curriculum has been adopted, the publishers win or lose sales on the basis of design, ease of use, and state specific elements. In open territory states without a state adoption to demand or review standards coverage, standards are much less of an issue in curriculum development.

Standards Correlations

Correlations of state standards to a particular curriculum are critical to a publisher's sales efforts. It is to the publisher's advantage to cover all the standards, and because interpretations of standards coverage varies so widely, publishers typically cite every conceivable instance of coverage in a correlation. Because there are so few reviewers who actually know a state's standards, and can identify that the standard is covered and verify the quality of the coverage, correlations documents become the proof of coverage. A good correlation that shows that every standard has been covered multiple times can make the difference in sales.

Publishers and the Common Core Standards

On one hand, publishers are positive about the language arts and mathematics Common Core Standards in the sense that they will no longer have to work as hard to coordinate different standards from different states. Addressing fifty different sets of standards was a major problem in curriculum development and a major cost factor. On the other hand, having state specific versions of curriculum has been a major competitive advantage for those companies that could afford to produce them. Although publishers long complained that it was difficult to create a science program, for example, when one state required astronomy in fourth grade and another called for it in fifth grade, unless they continue to create state specific covers and include state specific content, they will lose a significant point of competitive advantage.

Educational publishers' perspectives on the Common Core Standards show the ambivalence toward the standards. "For everyone, I think it brings a greater focus to the materials we are putting together," says Rose Else-Mitchell, the publisher for New York City–based Scholastic Education and its vice president of product development. There are likely to be challenges, some concede.

> "The competition will intensify among the industry. In a sense, you've got fewer customers," says Kathy Mickey, a senior analyst and the managing editor of the education group at Simba Information, a media-industry market-intelligence firm in Stamford, Connecticut. "But I don't think the publishers necessarily look at this as a negative in terms of the opportunity," she says. "They will always work with whatever the policy is." (Aarons 2010)

The educational publishers clearly don't see the Common Core Standards as initiating a radical change in education that would cause them to change their product development processes.

CONCLUSION

For the past thirty years America has been engaged in a comprehensive standards development effort. It is satisfying to write standards. It requires great intellectual energy and integrity. People who have been thinking of improvements in their disciplines enjoy the opportunity to employ their wealth of knowledge and express it in an academic exercise. Setting standards is an altruistic endeavor and many people eagerly take part in it. At the end of a standards writing project, there is an impressive published set of standards and a sense of accomplishment. That is probably one reason there have been so many efforts to write new standards over the years. Yet, after studying 130 years of professional development standards, Edelfelt and Raths found four patterns that could be true of all standards movements.

1. **Same Recommendations**. The recommendations for improving teacher education were remarkably similar over 130 years. They included brighter students, more competent faculty, more realistic classes, rigorous general education, serious (performance) evaluation, collaborative planning, and so on.
2. **Same Reasons for New Standards**. New standards writing efforts were motivated by three concerns: (a) the perception of dire national needs, (b) concerns that there is too much variation among programs, (c) the availability of new science or knowledge to give direction where it was absent in the past.
3. **No Historical Perspective**. Almost none of the reports acknowledge previous reports. Reports do not refer to previous recommendations or why the profession had adopted them without changing dramatically either the practice of teachers or the status of teaching.
4. **No Research**. Finally, although all the reports shared uncommon zeal for the standards they were promulgating, there was very little evidence in the reports or in the literature of the time to support the recommendations. Instead, the recommendations seemed to represent "self-evident" beliefs. (Edelfelt and Raths 1998, 20)

The efforts to set rigorous standards over America's history have resulted in an impressive corpus of standards. As Edelfelt and Raths found, however, most standards appear to have been created as if no standards previously existed. Setting new standards seems like such a reasonable and easy answer to increasing student achievement. In 2010, after all the standards initiatives of the past thirty years, when forty thousand teachers were asked what should be done to improve student achievement, two of their core recommendations had to do with standards and assessment.

Establish Clear Standards, Common across States—Teachers see the role standards can play in preparing students for their future, but want clearer standards and core standards that are the same across all states. Nationwide, 74 percent of teachers say that clearer standards would make a strong or very strong impact on student achievement, with only 4 percent saying they would have no impact at all. Sixty percent of teachers say that common standards would have a strong or very strong impact on student achievement, with only 10 percent saying that they would have no impact at all.

Use Multiple Measures to Evaluate Student Performance—From ongoing assessments throughout the year to student participation in individual classes, teachers are clear that these day-to-day assessments are a more reliable way to measure student performance than one-shot standardized tests. Ninety-two percent of teachers say ongoing in-classroom assessment is either very important or absolutely essential in measuring student performance, while only 27 percent say the same of state required standardized tests. (Scholastic and the Bill & Melinda Gates Foundation 2010)

There is no evidence that establishing more standards and using multiple measures to evaluate student performance would fundamentally change classroom practices that would improve student achievement. An emphasis on establishing more clear standards and more evaluation vehicles, when we are already inundated with standards and test results, distracts from the real change that is needed to make a difference.

The real issue is not the standards, but the need to change educational practices and curriculum. If teachers are not schooled in the standards and publishers are incentivized to produce materials that correlate to new standards but that do not change any practices, student achievement will stagnate.

In 1983 *A Nation at Risk* provided clear directives for what needs to be done to improve student achievement: "Evaluate educational materials on their ability to present rigorous and challenging material clearly and require publishers to furnish evaluation data on the materials' effectiveness" (National Commission on Excellence in Education 1983). The directives, however, were not realized. What currently passes for evaluation data are *correlations* to standards, not an evaluation of the effectiveness of the materials. If educators do not select materials based on their effectiveness, educational materials that do have legitimate evaluation data on their effectiveness often cannot compete with programs with state specific features, appealing design, and ease of use. If schools are to use more effective educational materials they must significantly change how they select and present curricula.

With the Common Core Standards there is a new opportunity to make changes that have the potential to significantly improve student achievement. In the Thomas B. Fordham Institute's analysis "Now What?," Finn and Petrilli discuss the need for improved curriculum to take the Common Core seriously.

Teacher groups have long complained—rightly, we think—that most instructors are left to figure out how to "implement" standards themselves. They are simultaneously drowning in a sea of materials (from textbooks to online lesson plan banks to modules from advocacy groups) and living in a curricular desert. What they want is a voluntary but thoroughly crafted curriculum that brings life to the standards, along with suitable textbooks, digital materials, supplemental readings, and so forth that they can use in their daily practice. They also need—and deserve—help from disinterested expert evaluators regarding which of the many instructional materials that will be described (usually by their vendors) as "aligned" with the Common Core are truly matched to its cognitive expectations and sequencing. Equally essential in the classroom are interim assessments (that break the full-year standards down into manageable but explicit chunks) and plenty of training in how to use all of this. (Finn and Petrilli 2010)

Writing standards is very hard work, but it pales in comparison to actually producing change in the classroom. Unfortunately, efforts have been focused on writing and rewriting standards and tests while publisher incentives for creating curriculum remained unchanged. Publishers will not create truly standards-based materials with rigorous and challenging material if the people making purchasing decisions are selecting materials based on design and ease of use. Unless potential purchasers employ reviewers who can judge the quality and appropriateness of textbooks, publishers will continue to provide impressive correlations and apparent studies that convince customers that the materials they are considering purchasing are new and improved, when they may not be.

Clear, focused content standards guide local curriculum development and help supply meaningful information about best practice to teachers and parents. Yet standards alone will not bring about the major improvements in student performance and school quality that are needed. (Progress of Education Reform 1996, 10)

Of course, we need standards, but standards are just one part of the lengthy equation. Improved student achievement involves the standards, the quality of the curriculum developed to teach the standards, and the methods schools and teachers use to implement the curriculum.

Chapter Five

Why Technology Hasn't Improved Student Achievement

Throughout the history of American education, there have been countless articles about new technologies in schools. On the one hand, some bemoan the loss of skills required to use the old tools and predict dire consequences. Others extol the benefits of the new technology and predict that technology will so dramatically change schools that they will no longer be recognizable.

In 1815 the use of paper, which had previously been cost prohibitive, gave students and teachers the ability to record and save lessons, yet schoolmasters were concerned that if students used paper, they would lose their knowledge of how to clean their slates, and then what would happen when the paper ran out?

In 1950 ballpoint pens introduced a more efficient and effective way of writing, but there was concern that disposable ballpoint pens were an expensive luxury that schools could not afford and students needed to retain their abilities to refill their inkwells.

In the 1960s, television in the classroom introduced a wide range of learning opportunities as students watched space launches and engaged in foreign language lessons, but many were concerned that it took away from foundational skill development.

Controversy still rages over the use of calculators in the classroom. For students developing math skills, calculators allow for efficient computations that will enable higher-level mathematics, but many are concerned that students will lose their ability to calculate numbers and understand mathematics concepts.

By 2010 digital technologies including desktop, handheld, and laptop computers, smartphones, MP3 players, iPads, and electronic books made significant inroads into education. Between 1983 and 1995, the ratio of computers to students in schools changed from 1 computer to each 125 students to 1 computer for each 9 students. By 2008, the ratio was 1 computer with Internet access to every 3 students. Even in 1994, schools spent almost $3 billion on computer and network based technology (Glennan and Melmed 1996). In the fall of 2008, 97 percent of schools had one or more instructional classroom computers and 58 percent had laptops on carts. In addition, handheld devices, LCD and DLP projectors, digital cameras, and interactive whiteboards are widespead (Gray et al. 2010).

Adapting to new technologies is part of the evolution of education. With the information and knowledge age brought about by the advancements in digital technology and access to information and communications, there are few who do not recognize the impact that digital technology has had in daily life. Technology enthusiasts have been predicting the dramatic changes that they expect in education and dire consequences if technology is not embraced. "If educators cannot successfully integrate new technologies into what it means to be a school, then the long identification of schooling with education, developed over the past 150 years, will dissolve into a world where the students with the means and ability will pursue their learning outside the public school" (Collins and Halverson 2009).

When a new technology is introduced, it is often accompanied by claims of fantastic results. In a case evaluation of its new 3D stereoscopic simulation technology, Texas Instruments claims that a group of students who received a lesson in 3D saw a 35 percent increase in their scores. The control group had only a 9.7 percent increase. Not only that, the lesson that normally requires two to three class periods to complete took only one class period (Gordon 2010). These types of results, however, fade as soon as a marketing campaign for the new product ends.

There is no question that technology has dramatically changed the way schools function. Yet throughout history new technologies have not had the effect on student achievement promised by their promoters and it appears that digital technology is no different.

FROM SLATE TO INTERACTIVE WHITEBOARD

Following the development of one type of technology provides insight into why technology in and of itself may improve some processes, making school life more effective and efficient, but may not necessarily have an influence on student achievement.

In the eighteenth and nineteenth centuries, students used slate boards. Paper was expensive and hard to get, so students had pieces of slate that they could write on with small pieces of slate, later chalk, to complete their exercises. In the late 1700s a Scottish teacher hung a set of slates on the wall, and the blackboard was invented (Makofsky 2011). This new technology had incredible advantages. Teachers could present their concepts and ideas to the whole class in a visual way. Instead of having to write math problems on every slate, students could copy them from the blackboard. By the 1850s, almost all schools had a blackboard and chalk. Chalk, a soft limestone, introduced another technology that was easier to use and easier to clean than pieces of slate.

By the 1960s green steel chalkboards were introduced. The green was easier on the eyes. By the 1980s businesses began using whiteboards with markers that eliminated the harmful chalk dust, and schools began replacing their chalkboards with whiteboards.

With computer technology, *interactive* whiteboards now use chalkboard visibility with a projector to display what is on a computer desktop and become a giant touch screen that teachers can use to demonstrate concepts and students can interact with. This technology can also project a movie, a PDF of a book page, an electronic presentation, or live television. At one time movie projectors, filmstrips, overhead projectors, and televisions provided enhanced educational experiences. Digital technology, projectors, and interactive whiteboards have made them all obsolete. Today blackboards, VCRs, audiotape players, videodisc players, and film projectors are used less and less frequently in schools.

The technology revolution has been taking place in schools in the same way cell phones represent a revolution in communications. Cell phones and interactive whiteboards are technology tools that facilitate communications among people and instruction in schools, but they are tools. In the same way that cell phones do not affect the quality of a conversation, interactive whiteboards and other digital technologies do not affect the quality or the content of the instruction. In education, it is curriculum developers who develop instruction and teachers who deliver it, using the tools that are available in an attempt to meet academic standards. It is the quality of the instruction, not the quality of the technology, that has an effect on student achievement. If it were the technology, there would have been significant advances in student achievement every time new technologies were introduced, but that is not the case.

BENEFITS OF TECHNOLOGY USE IN EDUCATION

There are a number of benefits that have been attributed to using technology in the classroom although they have not affected student achievement.

Student Motivation—Many students are excited about using technology in school, especially those who don't have home computers.

Individualized/Personalized Learning—Technology allows for a much higher degree of individualized instruction than a teacher working with groups of students can offer. When student responses are tracked, the technology can pinpoint strengths and weaknesses and provide immediate feedback or prescribe appropriate resources tailored to a student's needs.

Multimedia—Technology enables teachers to access a wide range of multimedia for a rich instructional experience. The difference, for example, between looking at a picture of cell division and watching a video of cells dividing adds a valuable dimension to instruction.

Information and Resource Access—Technology makes vast information resources available to teachers and students, more than any print library would be able to offer.

Efficiencies—Technology affords greater efficiencies in planning, scheduling, assessing, and evaluating than using previous methods.

Communication and Collaboration—Technology enables communications within the school environment.

Distance Education—Using technology, online self-paced e-learning courses can be made widely available to students who cannot attend school or who do not have local courses available to them.

Digital Content—To control costs, particularly in high school and higher education, the potential of electronic books that can be accessed online or books that can be published to fit the specific needs of a district is frequently promoted. One significant advantage of digital content is the ability to correct and update it quickly without having to wait for a new edition to be printed.

TECHNOLOGY USE IN SCHOOLS

As in the case of the introduction of the chalkboard, technology has been successfully adopted when it provided a clear advantage over older methods and is affordable and reliable. Too many applications are more difficult to use with technology. To be successful, technology must make educators' jobs more efficient. "We can't ignore the realities of school and teacher life when talking about technology. If computers don't support teachers where they work and the way they work, teachers are not going to find ways the machines can assist them in the classroom" (Dockterman 1997).

School Data Systems

A huge technology success story has been the use of school data systems for student enrollments, attendance, scheduling, bus scheduling, grade reporting, and school media center management. Eighty percent of teachers report that they use software sometimes or often for managing student records with only 9 percent reporting rare usage. This is in contrast to the 50 percent who say they use drill and practice programs sometimes or often with 23 percent who claim they rarely use these types of instructional programs (Technology Counts 2011). Even remote rural schools have some form of computer data management system to manage these services. Many schools now have automated call services, so every reported phone number is called to inform students and parents about an unexpected school closing like a snow day, a school emergency, or when a student is absent. The data systems allow for a massive amount of information to be recorded, stored, analyzed, and retrieved. There was some initial resistance to new systems, as there probably was when libraries introduced computer catalogs to replace card catalogs. There is a cost investment and an enormous investment in employee training. No one could argue that collecting, recording, and sorting all of the information by hand or calling each home individually is a superior process. By the same token, no one could argue that data systems directly improve student achievement, although they do provide information educators can use to inform instruction.

Classroom Management

Technology has made major advances in many classroom management tasks, including planning and recording and reporting grades. In days past, teachers had weekly planning books and grade books. These have been replaced by electronic planners and electronic grade books, which often are tied into the school data system. An added advantage is that if and when an administrator reviews teacher lesson plans, he or she can review these plans online.

Many electronic planners now have links to electronic resources, including teacher editions, textbooks, and multimedia resources. This allows teachers to preview and review resources and then drag them into the electronic planner.

Assessment

Anyone who argues that teachers are resistant to technology is not considering their embrace of electronic grading systems, including those that automatically score multiple choice tests. From electronic scanners that use specific types of recording sheets to online writing assessments, teachers have embraced those technologies that substantially improve their assessment processes.

There are several forms of technology used for both formative and summative assessment. Handheld clickers collect responses from all students to

questions teachers pose and display them for evaluation. This is very helpful in directing the teacher to address weaknesses in student understanding.
There are handheld devices that, for example, enable teachers to record
student responses during reading assessments, which helps teachers chart
progress. Assessments, including tests and quizzes, that students take online
provide instant feedback, scoring, and reporting functions.

These technologies are the interactive whiteboard equivalent to the slate.
They provide significant improvements in processes, but they have not been
responsible for an increase in student achievement.

Teacher Presentation

The slate to interactive whiteboard example demonstrates the technological
advances of teacher presentation technologies. From chalkboard to filmstrip
to VCR to interactive whiteboard, some technologies are used more in some
classes than others. Overhead projectors, for example, were widely used in
math classes because teachers could demonstrate solutions. Filmstrips and
video were more widely used in social studies, science, and English classes to
show events, demonstrate concepts, or dramatizations. In the past they were
displayed on movie projectors or filmstrips, whereas today they are delivered
via DVD or the Internet.

Electronic presentation tools are popular for upper grades to present or
review concepts, although they are not as widely used in high schools as
they are in university settings, where they commonly support lectures. Some
58 percent of elementary teachers and 73 percent of secondary teachers
claim they use presentation software sometimes or often. Yet 25 percent of
elementary teachers and 16 percent of secondary teachers report rare usage
(Technology Counts 2011).

Digital presentation tools to demonstrate science phenomena, work
through mathematical problems, analyze data, or model the writing process
support teachers and the way they work in a significant way.

Communications

Technology for communications is another area embraced by teachers.
Some teachers create newsletters on the computer that they either print and
send home or e-mail to parents. Most schools have websites that enable
parents to access school calendars, see student grades, and contact teachers. Every state provides public interactive report card information that
includes a school's demographic profile, test results, trends, graduation

rates, adequate yearly progress, district finances, and other information. Anyone can access this information for any public school in the country. This is a dramatic acceptance of technology to collect, sort, analyze, and report data. Yet no one would claim that this by itself raises student achievement.

Student Skill Practice

Much of the software developed by educational publishing companies over the past thirty years, other than school data or teacher management software, has been game based to motivate students to practice math, spelling, phonics, geography, or other skills. Programs like *Math Blaster* or *Grammar Games*, developed by companies that were eventually acquired by larger educational publishing companies, were considered "edutainment."

Gaming software has promised significant student achievement but there is little research that supports this result. With the exception of keyboarding software that teaches students how to type efficiently, most gaming software does not *teach* skills but rather has students practice skills like basic math facts and spelling. Teachers tend to allow students to play the software as a treat when they have finished with their work, but they have not adopted gaming software programs as part of the core curriculum. Much of this type of software is also available to the home market.

Student Work

Students who have computers at home or have access to computers in a library use computers to complete schoolwork. Above the primary grades, students routinely use word processing programs to compose and edit their school writing assignments. Students also use the Internet with and without parent supervision to conduct research. They may also use electronic presentation tools to build and present school assignments. For mathematics courses, students use calculators, advancing to graphing calculators in the upper grades. Spreadsheets and database software are used infrequently.

There is some evidence that the use of word processors improves student writing: "Students who use computers when learning to write produce written work that is about .4 standard deviations better than students who develop writing skills on paper. . . . They engage in the revising of their work throughout the writing process, more frequently share and receive feedback from their peers, and benefit from teacher input earlier in the writing process" (Goldberg, Russell, and Cook 2002).

Distance Learning/Online Classes/Blended Learning/Virtual Schools

Distance learning and online classes are gaining traction in high schools and adult education. These classes offer a range of courses that may not be available at a local school and provide the flexibility to complete them away from school. Online courses are a boon to students who want to take advanced placement courses, to students who have disabilities that prohibit them from attending school, and to students who might otherwise drop out of school, including pregnant students. Most recently, a "blended learning model" is employed. It combines face-to-face and online instruction. It enables schools to cut costs because students do not need to be on-site every day.

> The US market for Self-paced eLearning products and services reached $18.2 billion in 2010. The primary catalyst driving the strong virtual school growth in the US is the economy. State-run virtual schools used to target courses that were not offered in local districts or not available to rural students. Now, as a way to cut costs, they are targeting core curriculum and supplemental as well.
> The explosive growth of online enrollments in both academic segments in the US has created a boom market for Self-paced eLearning products in the PreK–12 and higher education segments. (Adkins 2011)

Online classes, sometimes called netcourses, are not a practical solution for elementary school students who need a lot of supervision, but features of online learning, including the ability to access and submit assignments during school absences due to illness or vacation, for example, have great appeal. Recently schools have implemented electronic school snow days that are employed when schools are cancelled because of inclement weather. Of course, students who do not have computers or online access at home are at a serious disadvantage.

> Overall, the students who do best in netcourses are focused, self-directed, independent, motivated, and comfortable expressing themselves in writing. While many students thrive on the experience, others have dropped classes because they've fallen behind or because they needed face-to-face interaction with their teacher and peers. . . . For a netcourse to be successful, teachers need to encourage substantive interactions among students, monitor and shape the conversation, and promote an atmosphere where students respond to others' work. That may require a far greater commitment of time and energy than some students are used to giving, and those that underestimate the work it entails can spoil a course for their students. (Engler 2000, 55–56)

Student Learning and Inquiry

When technology enthusiasts talk about technology transforming schools, they often ignore the transformations that have already taken place and focus on changing learning models. They argue that technology with its access to information will provide enhanced capabilities for learning.

> Enthusiasts suggest that putting students in situations where computer tools will be necessary to solve complex problems will kick-start schools to change basic instructional practices. Since simply putting computers into schools, as in the 1980s and 1990s, did not produce the revolution, enthusiasts have now turned to more sophisticated implementation models, such as the design of interactive learning environments. Learning environments are computer programs where learners are put in new situations and given appropriate tools and supports to learn how to deal with those situations. Sometimes these are personalized tutoring systems and sometimes several people may be learning together. (Collins and Halverson 2009, 13–14)

Technology enthusiasts describe environments in which students control what they want to learn and employ just-in-time learning models in which students find what they need to know as they need to know it. These models, they claim, will maximize customization to address individual learning, address scaffolding issues, provide the necessary support that students need to learn, and maximize social media for interactions among learners.

> In the enthusiast's view, computer-based environments promise a revolution in schooling of the same magnitude as the revolution in our culture set in motion by the Industrial Revolution. Technology enthusiasts favor a constructivist approach to learning, where students, rather than teachers, do most of the work. . . . Technology enthusiasts envision schools where students are working on realistic tasks and adults play a supportive role to guide them to new activities and help them when they encounter problems. (Collins and Halverson 2009, 27–28)

People who are enthusiastic about educational technology argue that technology will force us to rethink education for the technological age of knowledge and information, including rethinking the idea that learning takes place in school, rethinking what motivates students to learn and what is important to learn, and rethinking careers and the transitions from learning to work. They promote each new technology as the one that will make the difference: computer labs, mobile computer labs, a one-to-one computer ratio, iPods, smartphones for educational use, interactive whiteboards, touch screens, 3D experiences, Smart Tables, and iPads.

Yet, over the past thirty years, there have been many efforts to create computer environments to engage students in learning and promote student achievement that have not demonstrated significant student achievement.

Computer Assisted Instruction and Integrated Learning Systems

In the early days of the school computer, some companies developed computer assisted instruction (CAI) and integrated learning systems (ILS), which were a means of delivering individualized instruction through a computer network. CAI is an ancillary computer program that had limited materials and resources used for individual enrichment, practice, or remediation. ILS was aligned with curriculum and used as is or with the instructional planning. The promise was individualized instruction across all curriculum areas for kindergarten through adult learners, building higher order critical thinking skills and providing self-paced learning that tracked individual student progress. The benefits were the systematic exposure to the curriculum, the ability to track errors and reexpose students to instruction and practice to reach mastery, and provide an accurate and comprehensive record of individual progress. In addition, computer-based instruction claimed to provide motivation and interactivity in a game-like format.

What researchers found was that machines were not as effective as live teachers and the ILS teaching was impersonal. After initial excitement about using computers, students found the instruction boring and repetitive.

The costs were very expensive with the investment in computers, software, and training. After numerous implementations, CAI and ILS effects on student achievement were mixed (King 2000).

Game-Based Educational Programs

A variety of games has also been developed that help to create a computer environment for learning. In contrast to drill and practice software, other games have been problem-solving based. Some are independent games like *Oregon Trail*, in which the player takes the role of a pioneer and travels the Oregon Trail. Some provide enhanced reading experiences with electronic books that have an audio track, built-in highlighter and glossary, and embedded animations or movies. Some games have been simulation type software that allows students to virtually experience an experiment or explore an environment. Others require students to solve problems. System modeling games like *Civilization* and *The Sims* and massively multiplayer (MMO) games like *World of Warcraft* inspire enthusiasts to believe that students will develop rich problem-solving, interpersonal, and leadership skills if educators integrate these types of experiences in education.

> The difference in many of today's educational games is that they are online and social, allowing children to interact and collaborate to achieve common goals. Unlike the stand-alone boxed games of the 1980s and 1990s, the newest educational games are set up like services where children can enter a virtual world, try on a character and solve problems that may relate to the real world.
>
> Newer games work concepts of math, science or language into the actual game mechanics, rather than stopping for something that feels to the player like schoolwork, experts say.
>
> In Gamestar Mechanic, for example, KC had to use physics concepts to figure out how to get two players to arrive at the same point at the same time. He then had to defend his game's workings to other Gamestar Mechanic players. . . . Executives in this business are concerned with holding children's attention and avoiding the boring "chocolate-covered broccoli" model that prevailed in the 1980s and 1990s. Despite popular titles like Math Blaster, the educational games industry eventually collapsed because of price wars, misguided consolidation and an inability to keep pace with changes introduced by the Web. (Olsen 2009)

Although there are a few anecdotal reports of increased student achievement, to date there has been a lot of expectation and excitement, but not real academic achievement, related to using digital technology for student learning and inquiry.

LEVELS OF TECHNOLOGY ACCEPTANCE

Many technology enthusiasts want to blame teachers and schools as the reason technology has not had more of an impact on student achievement. They claim that teachers are mired in nineteenth-century models of instruction, and if they would embrace technology, they would see dramatic results. Numerous levels of technology integration can be identified in almost any educational institution.

Nonusers—These are "no tech" examples of instruction with teachers who do not use any digital technology applications for instruction, learning, or student work.

Beginners—These are "low tech" examples of instruction in which teachers may use computers for classroom management but not for presentation or student work.

Tryers—This level reflects instructors who are nervous about technology but are willing to try out promising applications. The initial success or failure will lead them back to beginner level or can advance them to a user level.

Users—At this level instructors confidently use technology for classroom management, presentations, and student work.

Leaders—At the leader level, instructors use technology fluently in their classrooms and promote technology use among their students and other teachers.

Early Adopters/Tech Support—Instructors at this level embrace and invent new technologies and often function as a school's technology support resource.

In almost every school, one can find a range of technology acceptance among teachers. Some younger teachers embrace technology, while others, even those who use technology outside of school, do not. There is no evidence, however, that students of teachers at higher levels of technology acceptance are higher achievers than those of teachers who do not use technology. This reinforces the realization that it is not technology or technologically savvy teachers that makes the difference in student achievement.

TECHNOLOGY TRENDS

Annually since 2002 the *Horizon Report* has identified emerging technologies and examined them for their potential impact on K–12 education (Johnson et al. 2010). The following are key trends identified in 2010:

- *Technology is increasingly a means for empowering students, a method for communication and socialization, and a ubiquitous, transparent part of their lives.* Technology is impacting all of our lives, especially the lives of students, in new and expanding ways. Once seen as an isolating influence, technology is now recognized as a primary way to stay in touch and take control of one's own learning. Multisensory, ubiquitous, and interdisciplinary technology is integrated into nearly everything we do. It gives students a public voice and a means to reach beyond the classroom for interaction and exploration.
- *Technology continues to profoundly affect the way we work, collaborate, communicate, and succeed.* Information technologies impact how people work, play, learn, socialize, and collaborate. Increasingly, technology skills are also critical to success in almost every arena, and those who are more facile with technology will advance while those without access or skills will not. The digital divide, once seen as a factor of wealth, is now seen as a factor of education. Those who have the opportunity to learn technology skills are in a better position to obtain and make use of technology than those who do not. Evolving occupations, multiple careers, and an increasingly mobile workforce contribute to this trend.

- *The perceived value of innovation and creativity is increasing.* Innovation is valued at the highest levels of business and must be embraced in schools if students are to succeed beyond their formal education. The ways we design learning experiences must reflect the growing importance of innovation and creativity as professional skills. Innovation and creativity must not be linked only to arts subjects, either; these skills are equally important in scientific inquiry, entrepreneurship, and other areas as well.
- *There is increasing interest in just-in-time, alternate, or nonformal avenues of education, such as online learning, mentoring, and independent study.* More and more, the notion of the school as the seat of educational practice is changing as students avail themselves of learning opportunities from other sources. There is a tremendous opportunity for schools to work hand-in-hand with alternate sources, to examine traditional approaches, and to reevaluate the content and experiences they are able to offer.
- *The way we think of learning environments is changing.* Traditionally, a learning environment has been a physical space, but the idea of what constitutes a learning environment is changing. The "spaces" where students learn are becoming more community driven, interdisciplinary, and supported by technologies that engage virtual communication and collaboration. This changing concept of the learning environment has clear implications for schools.

The report cites several challenges. These include that educational practices are not changing to address different students, that there is no agreement about what the new model of education might look like, and that the K–12 education establishment is resistant to profound change, including learning outside the classroom, student-directed learning, and social networking.

According to the *Horizon Report*, the technologies that will enter mainstream use in education are cloud computing (virtual servers over the Internet); collaborative environments; game-based learning; mobile computing; and augmented reality, including GPS, video and pattern recognition, and flexible displays (touch-based interfaced and flexible displays, integrated, interactive displays).

In 2010 the US Department of Education released the National Education Technology Plan. It called for five initiatives.

1. **Learning: Engage and Empower.** All learners will have engaging and empowering learning experiences both in and out of school that prepare them to be active, creative, knowledgeable, and ethical participants in our globally networked society.

2. **Assessment: Measure What Matters.** Our education system at all levels will leverage the power of technology to measure what matters and use assessment data for continuous improvement.
3. **Teaching: Prepare and Connect.** Professional educators will be supported individually and in teams by technology that connects them to data, content, resources, expertise, and learning experiences that enable and inspire more effective teaching for all learners.
4. **Infrastructure: Access and Enable.** All students and educators will have access to a comprehensive infrastructure for learning when and where they need it.
5. **Productivity: Redesign and Transform.** Our education system at all levels will redesign processes and structures to take advantage of the power of technology to improve learning outcomes while making more efficient use of time, money, and staff. (US Department of Education 2010b)

Clearly, technology will continue to transform educational practices, and there are unprecedented expectations for what it will be able to accomplish.

LIMITATIONS OF TECHNOLOGY

In counterpoint to technology enthusiasts, others have found there are many limitations to technology use.

Inadequate Training

Teachers will often cite lack of training as the reason they are not able to use technology. Although early adopters will embrace new technologies, the majority of teachers in a school desire training. "For technology to be used fully in K–12 schools, significant changes are required in teaching practices, curriculum and classroom organization" (Kleiman 2000).

A bridge is needed between the worlds of technology and classroom instruction to demonstrate how to transform pedagogy. Before any training begins, not only should the functions of the technological devices be mapped out, clear advantages for technology use and effective instructional methods should be identified to make professional development worthwhile. The training should not only demonstrate how technology works and give examples of how it is used, but also demonstrate why it is an improvement over nontechnological methods. A comprehensive transition to full effective technology implementation will take years to accomplish.

In 2011 *Education Week* summarized data regarding teacher training in technology. It found 53 percent of teachers said they spent one to eight hours in professional development for educational technology per year. Teachers reported that 78 percent of teacher training to a moderate or major extent came from independent learning and that 61 percent came from professional development activities (Technology Counts 2011). If the majority of teachers are involved in eight or fewer hours of professional development for technology, and most of that is on their own, there is a lot of work to do to achieve greater use of technology for instruction.

Limited Computers and Internet Access

Most schools have a limited number of computers in a classroom or in a school requiring teachers to coordinate schedules to make use of them. If a classroom has 25 students and five computers, access is limited to individual student work or short activities that students cycle through. In a 2011 report, 93 percent of teachers claimed that they had computers with Internet access in their classrooms with a ratio of 5.3 students to a computer (Technology Counts 2011).

If the school has a computer lab or even a mobile computer lab, teachers must coordinate with other teachers to reserve time and then must assign specific tasks or activities to maximize the access time. This certainly impedes the ability for digital technology to be a ubiquitous part of student life.

The Digital Divide

The digital divide is the gap between people who have effective access to computers and those who have limited or no access. Teachers are acutely aware of the advantage students who have computers at home have over those who don't. They will adapt assignments so that they can be completed with or without a computer. When students do not have computer access at home, schools are limited in their abilities to communicate to families. Students are at a disadvantage in accessing electronic materials such as assignments, electronic textbooks, and homework help. Parents without computer access cannot access the school data that provides important information about their children's evaluations and progress.

There is a digital divide between schools and districts as well. Some schools are well equipped with functioning, compatible, powerful classroom computers; media center online resources; and adequate bandwidth for wireless access to the Internet. Other schools have limitations on wiring, bandwidth, and at best an array of outdated computers. Students who attend schools with computer resources have a clear advantage in resource and capability than those who do not have access to those types of resources.

The digital divide will only exacerbate economic and social disadvantages with exclusion from the computer revolution.

Technical Difficulties

Teachers dread technology failures and never totally rely on technology to deliver instruction for a lesson. For technology to be successful, it must be reliable. Cuban (2001) observed that teachers, even teachers who are active users of computers at home, are reluctant to invest time in developing new teaching activities that incorporate computers in instruction. Computer use requires teachers to address logistical and technical difficulties including limited computer access, hardware crashes, software glitches, slow Internet connections, and lack of software. Cuban found that most teachers he observed found computers to be of limited utility and hard to use in their daily teaching and therefore did not use them extensively.

Lack of Tech Support

Lack of technical support when needed is a big deterrent to using technological solutions in the classroom. Many schools do not have technical support staff and must rely on the technical expertise of their teaching staff and often students to address any technical problems. Teachers cannot afford to wait on the phone for tech support while their twenty-five second graders are waiting to find out what will happen next.

Technology Evolution

Technology has changed rapidly, and it is difficult for schools to keep up. School investments in technology are only current for a limited amount of time. Before wireless technologies and the Internet, software had to be installed on every computer and data had to be collected from every computer for analysis. Upgrades were avoided because of the extensive amount of time needed to install them. This time investment made teachers demand proof that the results would be worth the effort. Teachers who may have created materials on 5 and 1/4 inch floppy disks, then converted them to 3 and 1/2 inch ones, and then to CD, may have great frustration with the introduction of cloud computing. Educators may be wary of new technologies as a result.

Fear of Inappropriate Access

A major concern has been that students would find their way into inappropriate websites and teachers would be liable. Although filtering software is widely available, this concern is still very real.

Distractions

Although there are many reasons to use computers in teaching and learning, technology, an exciting distraction for students at times, can also impede their progress and mitigate student achievement.

In Pennsylvania's Lower Merion High School, the school district gave every student a personal laptop computer, expecting teachers to improve their instruction and enable student achievement to explode. In December 2010, a survey was conducted and a total of 555 students and 71 teachers responded. The school newspaper found that when asked, "Has the 1-1 computer made you more/less likely to pay attention to teacher instruction?" 47 percent of students responding said "less likely"—compared to 11 percent who said "more likely," and 41 percent who noted "no effect."

Teachers, too, shared the students' concern, according to the survey. When asked, "Do you think students pay the majority of their attention to the material at hand when using their laptops in class?" 54 percent answered, "No, they are distracted"—compared to 27 percent who said, "Yes, they are mostly focused," and 20 percent who checked, "other."

Despite potential trouble concentrating, 73 percent of students said they were allowed to use their laptops at least 50 percent of the time in their classes, and 59 percent of teachers allow students to use the computers in an average class, according to the school survey. When teachers were asked, "Do you feel that the 1-1 laptop has changed students' work habits and time management skills?" 54 percent of teachers said, "Yes, for the worse"—compared to 20 percent answering, "Yes, for the better." Clearly, classroom use of computers has the potential to cause attention problems (Susanj 2011).

Quality Software

A huge limitation to using technology is finding software and content that meet teacher objectives. If teachers are evaluated on the basis of their students' scores on state achievement tests, then they are interested in educational materials that address the state standards. Much of the educational software developed for the home market is not linked to state standards, so teachers can't afford to spend time on it.

The research on the effect of technology in learning is emerging. Overall, across all uses in all content areas, technology does provide a small, but significant, increase in learning when implemented with fidelity. While this statistic is encouraging, the real value to the research lies in the identification of those technology interventions that get sufficiently positive results to warrant the investment. Most educators are looking for the value proposition that will significantly advance learning, teaching, and school system efficiencies. Taking advantage of these leverage points requires serious review of specific research studies that specifically address the needs and challenges of specific schools *and serious attention paid to leadership development, professional development for teachers, school culture, curricular redesign, and teacher preparation.* (Metiri Group 2006)

Whether it be a print or digital curriculum, implementing any program with fidelity is key to its success. Curriculum and educational software developers bemoan the inadequate implementation of a program, which consigns a program to failure. Thorough professional development is critical to the success of any new educational materials. This is particularly true of research-based materials whose results are dependent upon a specific type of implementation.

Incoherent Curriculum

With the ability to add, replace, supplement, or create entire curriculum using Internet sources, educators who are not trained in developing curriculum risk the possibility of spending a lot of time creating a disjointed, incoherent, inappropriate, and ineffective curriculum. In addition to the many valuable resources, there are vast amounts of untested and poor quality materials also available.

EDUCATIONAL PUBLISHERS AND TECHNOLOGY

As it did in schools, technology has revolutionized educational publishing processes. Typewriters still in use in editorial teams in the 1980s have been replaced by computers. Design teams skilled in physical camera copy paste-up, now are experts in design and page management software. Prepress filmwork, typesetting, and printing processes are all electronic. Because of electronic file transfer, much of the page production work that used to be done in the United States has moved to India because of lower costs. Technology that made the processes more efficient required employees to acquire new skill sets. But like innovations in schools, the technology revolution in educational publishing, as well as in other industries, does not have a positive effect on quality as measured in student achievement.

In addition to the investment in updating their processes, educational publishers have also made substantial investments in educational technology for classroom use. From integrated learning systems to skills software, classroom management suites, electronic books, and online digital curriculum, publishers have explored many different possibilities in search of profitable ventures. There have been three distinct strategies.

Create

When computer technology was first widely available in schools, many educational publishers established software divisions to develop software to accompany print materials. A lot of game-based software for skill practice was developed at this time, as was test preparation software. Companies that invested heavily in complete technology solutions like integrated learning systems (ILS) were envied by publishers reluctant or unable to invest in those technologies. There was deep concern that print publishers would no longer be competitive.

Educational publishers have continued to invest substantial amounts of money into hiring software developers to create educational software. Today all of the major publishers produce electronic versions of their print materials. Electronic textbooks have audio tracks, hyperlinked vocabulary words to glossary definitions, and highlight and search capabilities, as well as interactive features, such as animated science demonstrations or math solution explanations. Teacher editions have bookmarks and notes features. Teachers are able to edit publisher worksheets and tests and print them or assign them to students electronically. The most recent educational programs have options for a complete digital or print path to teach the state standards. The digital path provides a series of lessons that can be substituted for the print materials. Many of these digital lessons are not unlike the CAI and ILS systems developed in the 1980s, except they incorporate more multimedia.

License

Instead of investing in developing software, many publishers looked to license successful software from software developers. Companies like Broderbund, known for its delightful electronic books, and Davidson, known for *Math Blaster*, licensed their products to educational publishing companies. The publishing companies then correlated and bundled the software with their print programs. Other companies licensed software applications that enabled the publishing companies to create their own products.

Acquire

After initial investments in creating software products and licensing them, educational publishers began to acquire software companies that were creating interesting products. Innovative companies that had a vision for using technology to inspire and teach children, like MECC, the Minnesota Education Computing Consortium, Broderbund, and Davidson, were acquired by other companies, including educational publishers. *Oregon Trail*, one of the most popular edutainment titles developed by three student teachers in Minnesota, is one such story. "Forty years and ten iterations later, the *Oregon Trail* has sold over 65 million copies worldwide, becoming the most widely distributed educational game of all time. Market research done in 2006 found that almost 45 percent of parents with young children knew *Oregon Trail*, despite the fact that it largely disappeared from the market in the late '90s" (Lussenhop 2011).

According to Lussenhop, *Oregon Trail* disappeared from the market because its developer, MECC, was purchased by other companies looking for profit from educational products. After passing through several different companies including Mattel, which attempted to put Barbie on the Oregon Trail, the product is now owned by the Learning Company, a division of Houghton Mifflin Harcourt, one of the three big publishing companies.

Educational publishers were able to acquire many educational software assets, like *Oregon Trail* and its offshoots, that had been developed for the school market, until the 1990s when the video game business became increasingly competitive and shifted from the school to the larger home market. The emphasis on profitability rather than education prompted many software companies to abandon educational software efforts. In 2011 in reaction to this trend, some companies began developing educational problem- and simulation-based software with plans to reenter the school market.

WHAT EDUCATIONAL PUBLISHERS LEARNED ABOUT TECHNOLOGY

For all their investment and experience in educational software, educational publishers learned many lessons.

1. **Technology is a "must have."**—To be competitive, educational publishers must offer technology solutions to their customers. When schools consider educational products for purchase, the software applications are critical requirements.
2. **Major software implementations are risky.**—Most technology applications that are created by educational publishers go unused by the majority of teachers. Unless the publisher builds the cost into the purchase of the entire curriculum, schools are unwilling to commit substantial funds to complicated software that will require substantial investments in time and training. Futhermore, technology platforms have been in such flux that many schools are unlikely to have the capacity to implement new software systems.

3. **Software must be included with purchase.**—Schools and teachers expect software to be "free," embedded in the cost of a program and are not willing to pay extra for it. Educators equate software programs they can find for free on the Internet or for low cost at discount stores to be the equivalent of what educational publishers are offering for a substantial cost.

4. **Software is perceived to be less expensive than print.**—Educational publishers are faced with the same problem faced by encyclopedia publishers. Although the publisher invests the same amount of time and energy into developing content regardless of what platform it takes (print or digital), customers expect the software to be free or at least cost substantially less than the print versions.

5. **Schools and students have limited access to computers.**—Faced with different levels of access to computers in school and at home, educational publishers have constantly been forced to offer software as a supplement, or, at best, an alternative to the core curriculum. As such, the value of the software was diminished and publishers made a practice of giving the software away with the purchase of a program. A major topic of conversation in educational publishing is how many previous technologies must be supported of a new product to accommodate school capability. Few companies are producing 5 and 1/4 inch floppy and 3 and 1/2 inch disks, but schools still have working computers that use that technology. Educational publishing companies are very likely to offer online, CD, and DVD versions of the same products with the CD and DVD versions offering much less capability for recording assessments and social networking.

6. **Educational software has not been profitable.**—Few educational software products have been profitable for educational publishers. Only in the case of a state adoption that requires a technology solution have educational publishers made a profit on their technology investments.

7. **Software requires different financial models.**—Software requires maintenance, updates, and upgrades, and involves a completely different financial model than print materials.

These lessons have driven publishers to look for cost savings rather than explore additional possibilities for educational products. Once a software product is developed, the publisher will try to use the platform or at the very least correlate it to other programs to get more mileage from it. For example, if a publisher invests in writing assessment software, they will bundle it with any reading or literature program, language arts program, and even content area programs to create a technology story for each product.

Educational publishers create print alternatives for virtually all software curricula they develop. In spite of the fact that states like Florida and California have legislative proposals to push school districts to convert from print to electronic textbooks, the 100 percent technology market is very small; even with media attention, print materials remain vastly more popular than technology solutions. Some states and districts look to electronic textbooks to save money, but electronic books may be as expensive as print because the content is the same. Furthermore, schools must prepare for the investment in hardware, software, and bandwidth capacity so that when a large number of students are online at the same time, the network does not crash. Not only do these initiatives raise questions about the digital divide and opportunity to learn, questions about how younger students just learning to read will benefit from online instructional materials are unanswered.

With initiatives like Florida's and California's to move toward digital textbooks, publishers will test whether this technology will be profitable or not. And teachers will evaluate whether digital textbooks that encourage scrolling and scanning are as effective as print-based ones that encourage focused reading. On the one hand, digital textbooks will be easier to revise and update to allow for new knowledge and they will save in print, sampling, inventory, and distribution costs. On the other hand, digital open-source content resources, like "free" online content that can be modified by teachers, may begin to compete in a way they have not previously (Sewall 2010).

> While modern technology has great potential to enhance teaching and learning, turning that potential into reality on a large scale is a complex, multifaceted task. The key determinant of our success will not be the number of computers purchased or cables installed, but rather how we define educational visions, prepare and support teachers, design curriculum, address issues of equity and respond to the rapidly changing world. As is always the case in efforts to improve K–12 education, simple, short-term solutions turn out to be illusions; long-term, carefully planned commitments are required. (Kleiman 2000)

For the most part, the major educational publishers have focused their technology efforts on building ancillary components to go with their print products that create sizzle to meet requirements and sell their print products. It has been a "print first" strategy. With few exceptions, publishers have not been incentivized to explore, as for example the creators of *Oregon Trail* did, compelling applications of technology that address learning objectives and state standards. Software developers would claim that the software educational publishers develop might as well be workbook ancillaries to the textbooks.

Educational publishers and educational software is far behind development for other types of interactive media. John Geiger, president of a small innovative software company that has been commissioned to create several educational software products, describes educational publishers as being at least four—if not ten—years behind their counterparts in advertising and commercial gaming software. Most projects, he explains, that are developed by educational publishers have few advantages over printed materials with very limited user dynamics or social networking. Educational publishers are ingrained in old media, are risk averse, and debate irrelevant issues, as the world is passing them by. "Fail first" models with high risk, low investment products to test potential are common in innovative companies but are almost nonexistent in large companies that have a fear of failure (Cuban 2001). Educational software does not have to be a literal video game, but can be game-like. Assessment software should be using the techniques of advertisers to capture user interests and responses and convert them into compelling tailored responses.

By not exploring the educational possibilities of new technology, educational publishers have left the door wide open to competition from software developers who keep current (Geiger 2010). The mass-market gaming software developers have moved far beyond educational publishers in their graphics, animation, data collection, and interactivity. If these companies begin developing educational products, the educational publishers will not be able to compete.

CONCLUSION

If the existence of computers in the classroom raised student achievement, it would have been evident by now, since computers have been in classrooms in one form or another for the last thirty years.

If technology were going to revolutionize learning and education, and dramatically increase student achievement, it would have by now. Regardless of what technology enthusiasts claim, there have been substantial, numerous, and varied opportunities for technology to make an impact. Schools have tried computer labs, mobile computer carts, one-to-one computer ratios, computer assisted technology, integrated learning systems, and numerous practice programs. While technology has certainly revolutionized school processes, it has not had an effect on student achievement.

> When outcomes are considered—that is, academic achievement, college attendance, attitudes toward learning, and similar results—neither in elementary nor in high schools do researchers or practitioners offer evidence to show a moderate to strong linkage between student and teacher access and use [of computers], or between their use and outcomes. (Cuban 2001)

Using the slate to interactive whiteboard analogy, it is not difficult to see why it hasn't had the impact so many promised. Technology is a tool. A word processor is much more efficient and provides many more advantages than using a typewriter. A word processor makes writing, revising, and editing much easier, but none of that controls the quality of the writing itself. Students must still learn how to construct a sentence, organize a paragraph, and create a composition with a beginning, middle, and end. Computers and the Internet allow students to search and find information more rapidly than in prior days, but they don't motivate students to learn. Before computers, a public library allowed students to search and find information, but the availability of these resources did not in and of itself raise student achievement.

If simply having computer technology inspired students to become self-directed learners, students would have become so by now. Numerous studies show that students spend over six hours a day interacting with technology, including television, video games, and social networking in self-directed activity. Yet this does not seem to have raised student achievement. The desire of technology enthusiasts that technology will herald in an age of self-directed learners who use just-in-time learning methods to pursue meaningful projects that interest them is the same desire that advocates of student-centered learning, like John Dewey, have had for over a hundred years (Pflaum 2004). Technology will not make that happen any more than having students sit around tables instead of individual desks in rows. The battle is between teacher-centered and student-centered instruction, not traditional instruction and technology. In this battle, as Jeanne Chall concluded in her analysis of one hundred years of education, teacher-centered instruction has been shown to be more effective than student-centered instruction with or without computers.

> Traditional, teacher-centered schools, according to research and practice, are more effective than progressive, student-centered schools for the academic achievement of most children. And that approach is especially beneficial for students who come to school less well prepared for academic learning—children of less educated families, inner-city children, and those with learning difficulties at all social levels. (Chall 2000)

Educational software programs often have advantages over other means of instruction and practice, but only if the quality of the instruction and practice exercises is meaningful.

Quality curriculum and instruction are the keys. Understanding how children learn mathematics, developing incremental lessons that give them increasing challenge and insight along a learning trajectory, and checking to make sure they are making progress are examples of education regardless of whether it takes a print, a digital, or some other form.

This is not to say that technology applications should be abandoned. There is no question that technology is ubiquitous and students need to be fluent users of technology to participate in the twenty-first-century world. Like the industrial revolution, technology has made dramatic improvements in efficient processes. Technology enables educators, educational researchers, and curriculum developers to measure and analyze student learning patterns and the effects of different strategies better than ever before. It has given educators access to an enormous variety of multimedia instructional materials.

The challenge is to use technology to identify the best materials, use those in the classroom, and continue to upgrade them as new insights into learning are revealed. Secretary of Education Arne Duncan expressed these sentiments when he released the 2010 National Education Technology Plan.

> I am here today with two important messages: First, our nation's schools have yet to unleash technology's full potential to transform learning. We're at an important transition point. We're getting ready to move from a predominantly print-based classroom to a digital learning environment. We need to leverage technology's promise to improve learning. I am optimistic because states and districts are starting to lead this transformation. But we have a long way to go before we reach the goals set out in the plan we're releasing today.
>
> My second message is that technology will never replace good teachers. We all know that the most important factor in a student's success is the teacher leading the class. That will never change. The best instruction happens when a caring, skilled instructor uses every resource at his or her disposal to help students learn—including the power of technology. In today's world, technology is an essential tool. It offers teachers new ways to enrich their students' learning experiences. It offers students the ability to connect to learning opportunities anywhere, anytime.
>
> Technology empowers teachers like never before to support their personal mission of providing the best possible education to their students. But it's important to remember that technology alone isn't going to improve student achievement. The best combination is great teachers working with technology to personalize the learning experience and engage students in the pursuit of the learning they need. (Duncan 2010)

Technology is a tool. It will be as effective as the content and lessons are. Technology provides educators with tremendous opportunities to motivate students, individualize and personalize instruction, provide rich multimedia learning experiences, reach students who otherwise could not participate in learning—or not. Technology devices are simply devices, tools that give students a better opportunity to find and communicate information, but they do not replace quality teaching and curriculum. Technology cannot replace one's ability to think critically or formulate questions. Technology can provide vast amounts of information, but it cannot give students a way to navigate the information, make sense of it, and use it for learning and drawing conclusions. Simply being able to access technology, like being able to enter a library with a library card, does not make one an expert on any topic.

Curriculum developers have shown they are willing to invest in technology solutions. Through intelligent purchasing decisions, educators can incentivize them to invest in the development of digital content that will not only increase their efficiency and ability to use assessment tools to inform instruction, but provide learning experiences that will increase student achievement. Technology is not the end goal of education. It is the means to an end.

Chapter Six

Why Teacher Education and Professional Development Don't Improve Student Achievement

More than ever before, teachers are held responsible for student test score performance. Teachers and schools are punished if they do not make adequate yearly progress. Efforts such as developing systems of merit pay for teachers as opposed to step increases based on years of service are attempts to incentivize teachers to compete against their other faculty members and do more, faster, better. Yet even with all the pressure on teachers, student achievement does not dramatically advance.

> Compared with other countries, America has spent more and achieved less. If there's any good news in that, it's that we've had a chance to see what works and what doesn't. That sets the stage for a big change that everyone knows we need: building exceptional teacher personnel systems that identify great teaching, reward it and help every teacher get better. It's the thing we've been missing, and it can turn our schools around. (Gates 2011)

The Bill & Melinda Gates Foundation has been studying education to find out what makes the difference in student achievement. They have learned several things:

1. **Experience:** After the first few years, seniority seems to have no significant effect on student achievement.
2. **Advanced Degrees:** Paying teachers more money for advanced degrees has had almost no impact on student achievement.
3. **Class Size:** Having twice as many teachers per student as there were in 1960 has not affected student achievement.
4. **Smaller Schools:** After spending about $2 billion on developing a small schools initiative, the results on student achievement were disappointing.

Now the focus is on finding the "essence of effective teaching" and replicating that through professional development and incentive programs. "We know that of all the variables under a school's control, the single most decisive factor in student achievement is excellent teaching. It is astonishing what great teachers can do for their students" (Gates 2011).

According to the Bureau of Labor Statistics, in 2008 there were 3,476,200 K–12 teachers in the US workforce (Bureau of Labor Statistics 2010; Collins and Halverson 2009). The Gates Foundation has a lot of money, but educating new teachers and reeducating experienced teachers in the essence of effective teaching is a daunting task. In the end, these efforts may or may not have the desired effect on student achievement.

If teacher quality is the key to student achievement, it is logical to study the two forms of teacher education to determine if there are better ways to promote teacher quality and consequently student achievement. Both preservice education and preparation and on-the-job professional development once teachers are in the classroom have potential to impact teacher quality. A historical look at the development of teacher education programs and an analysis of standards for certification provide insight into how and why teacher education programs are structured as they are.

THE HISTORY OF TEACHER EDUCATION

Before the Civil War, as public schooling was being established, there were few prerequisites to become a teacher. A teacher simply needed to persuade a local school board of his or her moral character. By the end of the Civil War, in order to be certified to teach, most states required teachers to pass a basic skills test including US history, geography, spelling, and grammar (Ravitch 2002).

As schooling became more widespread, states designed different types of teacher education. Some states supported private academies to train teachers. Other states established *normal* schools. Normal schools were secondary schools that prepared teachers for teaching elementary school. They were not colleges. Their admission standards were low and most of their students had only an elementary school education. These schools typically offered one-year courses in basic subject matter, teaching methods, and established teaching standards, or *norms*.

Colleges and universities also developed teacher and administrator education programs. In 1900 only 4 percent of the population attended college, so these institutions saw teacher education as a way to expand enrollments. Teacher education programs in universities focused on mastery of subject matter and emphasized scholarship over practice and made their curriculums more academic and less vocational.

With the rise of high schools and competition with colleges, many normal schools raised their admission standards to require a high school diploma and extended their programs to two years for elementary and four years for high school teacher preparation. By 1930 the normal schools had become state teachers colleges and universities or had merged into existing institutions (Levine 2006).

The two avenues toward teacher education represents a dichotomy that continues to exist today, in which many colleges of education, particularly elementary education programs, are often not respected by other academic departments. Education programs that are too academic with content studies and studies of educational philosophy and theory are criticized because they do not prepare teachers for the reality of the classroom. Research on teacher education is often criticized by science and mathematics departments for its lack of rigor. Programs that emphasize classroom preparation are criticized because they do not provide teachers with content knowledge and scientific research. To address concerns, future teachers have faced more and more rigorous requirements for teacher certification.

Teacher Certification

Before the twentieth century, there were very few requirements one had to meet to become a teacher. In the twentieth century as departments of education grew, teaching became a profession and certification requirements were established in every state.

Today every state requires teachers to be certified. Typically a teacher may be certified in preK through grade 3 with an early childhood certification, in grades 1–6 with an elementary certification, and in grades 6–12 with a secondary certification. Special education and special subjects such as music and art require special certifications. Certification is active for a defined period of time, typically one to five years. Once the license expires, an educator must be recertified. To be recertified, the applicant must usually have proof of teaching experience and postgraduate course requirements. Each state has its own requirements, and although certification is not always transferrable from one state to another, there are some common requirements.

1. College degree. Applicants for elementary education certification usually have an undergraduate degree with a major or minor in education or a master's degree in education. For secondary education, a degree in a content area and an approved education program are usually required. Teachers

who teach specialized classes such as special education are required to have a master's degree.

2. Completion of an approved teacher training program either as part of a bachelor's degree or postgraduate.
3. Specific number of subject and education course credits.
4. Supervised practice teaching.
5. Most states require a passing grade on their state test or the PRAXIS exam. The PRAXIS is part of the certification process required by many states and professional licensing organizations.
6. Graduate degree. Although new K–12 teachers are not required to have a master's degree, in Ohio, New York, and Massachusetts all elementary and secondary teachers are required to complete a master's degree in education within five years of signing their first teaching contract. Many teachers are incentivized by pay increases to work toward a master's degree after teaching for a few years. Most states do require continuing education for certified teachers, which often results in the completion of a master's degree.

According to Department of Education data, over 90 percent of teachers have regular certification. More than half of the teachers have master's degrees. The majority have a degree in education with 39 percent having a bachelor's degree in a content area, which is usually a requirement for secondary 6–12 certification. Certification ensures that teachers at all levels have basic qualifications.

In 1987, in an attempt to build teacher expertise, the National Board for Professional Teaching Standards (NBPTS) was established to raise the standards for quality teaching and learning. The board developed professional teaching standards and a voluntary system to certify teachers who met the standards. To be certified, candidates must have completed portfolios of their work over the course of a year, submitted videotapes of their instruction, and taken a one-day exam that covers subject-matter knowledge and teaching methods. More than 25 percent of school districts offer financial rewards for teachers with National Board Certification and, as of 2010, more than ninety-one thousand educators are National Board Certified, representing almost 3 percent of the nation's teachers. There are five propositions for National Board Certification:

1. Teachers are committed to students and learning.
2. Teachers know the subjects they teach and how to teach those subjects.
3. Teachers are responsible for managing and monitoring student learning.
4. Teachers think systematically about their teaching practices and learn from experience.

5. Teachers are members of learning communities. (National Board for Professional Teaching Standards 2011)

In 2006 a review of twenty-one studies found "no clear pattern of effects on student achievement based on whether the teacher was Board certified" (McColskey et al. 2006). In 2008 a review of eleven studies found that "students taught by board-certified teachers had higher achievement test gains than did those taught by nonboard-certified teachers, although the differences were small and varied by state" (Hakel, Koenig, and Elliott 2008). Although there may be many benefits of National Board Certification, after more than twenty years of effort, there is minimal impact on student achievement. So once standards are met for teaching, additional certification may be beneficial for other reasons, although it has not been shown to be a solution for higher student achievement.

Preservice Education

In the United States there are more than thirteen hundred public and private colleges and universities that offer teacher preparation. Programs vary widely. The American Association of Colleges for Teacher Education (AACTE) is an alliance of eight hundred teacher preparation programs in public and private colleges and universities in every state. Its mission is to promote the learning of all students through high-quality, evidence-based preparation and continuing education for all school personnel. Its goals include developing clear statements based on evidence and professional consensus about teacher preparation in the areas of standards, curriculum, assessment, and accountability.

There is also the National Council for Accreditation of Teacher Education (NCATE) whose mission is to establish high-quality teacher preparation. In 2010 there were 656 accredited colleges of education with 70 more seeking NCATE accreditation. NCATE establishes rigorous standards for teacher education programs and holds accredited institutions accountable for meeting these standards. The six standards involve the following:

1. Candidate knowledge, skills, and professional dispositions
2. Assessment system and unit evaluation
3. Field experience and clinical practice
4. Diversity
5. Faculty qualification, performance, and development
6. Unit governance and resources (NCATE 2008)

In late 2010, NCATE and the Teacher Education Accreditation Council (TEAC) formed the Council for the Accreditation of Education Preparation (CAEP), whose mission is "raising the performance of candidates as practitioners in the nation's P–12 schools, but also raising standards for the evidence which supports claims of quality." The organizations believe the new accrediting body will add to quality, assurance, accountability, and overall teacher performance (NCATE 2010).

Despite the efforts to promote standards of accreditation among preservice teacher education programs, a study on effective teacher preparation drew these conclusions about problems with preservice education (Wilson, Floden, and Ferrini-Mundy 2001):

1. **Subject Matter Preparation.** There is a positive connection between teachers' subject matter preparation and their classroom impact, but teachers can acquire subject matter knowledge from various sources and there is little definitive research on the kinds or amount of subject matter preparation needed. Because some preservice teachers lack deep understanding, subject matter preparation is more complicated than simply requiring a major or more courses.

2. **Pedagogical Preparation.** Education in instructional methods, learning theories, foundations of education, and classroom management varies widely and although this has an effect on student achievement, there is no indication of which aspects of pedagogical preparation are most critical.

3. **Student Teaching.** Clinical experiences are a critical part of teacher preparation although duration, supervision arrangements, and settings vary dramatically. These field experiences are often disconnected with other coursework in teacher preparation. Cooperating teachers, those teachers in the school who work with student teachers serving as supervisors and mentors, can have a powerful influence on student teaching experience, but their involvement with the student teachers varies widely.

4. **Policy.** Although national accreditation, collaborative partnerships, and involvement of university faculty with K–12 education may hold promise, there is very little research on how effective these efforts are.

5. **Alternative Certification.** To address teacher shortages particularly in the areas of math and science and in urban and rural schools, most states now have alternative routes to the undergraduate program of teacher preparation but they differ significantly in their designs, although they typically involve periods of intensive academic coursework and a period of supervised on-the-job training to learn teaching skills. Supervision ranges from very little to intensive oversight and mentoring. The research comparing the quality of teachers with alternative certification and those with tra-

ditional certification is inconclusive, but the common themes that have emerged from research on effective alternative certification programs are the same as those for traditional forms of certification:

a. High standards and proper screening of candidates
b. Solid preservice academic instruction in pedagogy, subject matter, classroom management, and child development
c. Organized and comprehensive system of support from experienced, trained mentors
d. Period of observation and assistance in the classroom by an experienced teacher
e. Ongoing training, instruction, and reflection
f. Continuous monitoring, evaluation, and feedback (Legler 2002)

Teacher preparation programs have evolved over time. They are the result of what each institution perceives as necessary to prepare teachers for classroom responsibility. The fact that less than half of the programs are accredited demonstrates the independent nature of postsecondary education in the United States. Some well-respected teacher education programs are not accredited. Some schools feel that an accrediting body is not in a position to know better than their professors the best way to prepare teachers.

Unlike K–12 education, which relies on public funding and can be held accountable to state standards and assessments, postsecondary institutions are accountable to their students. Some programs emphasize pedagogy, while others emphasize student teaching. A program may graduate teachers who are effective and others who are ineffective in the classroom. Even in the same institution, one professor of education may provide a completely different educational experience than another. This is the nature of postsecondary education.

A 2006 report highly critical of teacher preparation programs outlines the problems faced by educating classroom teachers, explaining that there is no agreement on what skills and knowledge teachers need to be effective teachers and less agreement on how teachers should learn them. Analyzing teacher education programs across the country, Levine describes a curriculum in disarray with confusing standards; an imbalance between theory and practice and academic and clinical instruction; a faculty disconnected from the schools where their graduates will be placed and disconnected from the arts and sciences; insufficient quality control; low admission standards; and wide disparities among programs (Levine 2006). This is evidenced in teaching experiences as described below:

No professional feels completely prepared on her first day of work, but while a new lawyer might work under the tutelage of a seasoned partner, a first-year

teacher usually takes charge of her classroom from the very first day. One sur-
vivor of this trial by fire is Amy Treadwell, a teacher for 10 years who received
her master's degree in education from DePaul University, one of the largest
private universities in the Chicago area. She took courses in children's literature
and on "Race, Culture and Class"; one on the history of education, another on
research, several on teaching methods. She even spent one semester as a student
teacher at a Chicago elementary school. But when she walked into her first job,
teaching first graders on the city's South Side, she discovered a major shortcom-
ing: She had no idea how to teach children to read. "I was certified and stamped
with a mark of approval, and I couldn't teach them the one thing they most
needed to know how to do," she told me. (Green 2010)

With no consistency among education programs, and little research to
assess the effectiveness of these programs, Levine's study offered a nine-
point template for judging the quality of teacher education programs. These
included explicit purpose, curricular coherence, curricular balance, faculty
composition, admissions criteria, degrees awarded, research, finances, and
self-assessment. The recommendations include transforming schools of education into schools focused on classroom practice, with a focus on student
achievement as the primary measure of teacher education program success.
The study also recommends making five-year teacher education programs
the norm and establishing effective mechanisms for teacher education quality
control.

In 2010, Levine reported that in three states—Indiana, Michigan, and
Ohio—universities working with the Woodrow Wilson Foundation had begun to move from an on-campus to a clinical program in which preservice
teachers spent most of their time in schools observing and being supervised
by master teachers. He argued for working to improve university-based
teacher education programs, rather than replacing them (Levine 2010).

Even when the keys to teacher effectiveness are identified and widely
accepted, it would be a massive undertaking to transform the teacher
preparation programs in thirteen hundred colleges and universities, each
with its own program. In September 2010, the AACTE and the Partnership
for 21st Century Skills issued a report that outlined their shared vision for
integrating twenty-first-century skills into educator preparation. It includes
aligning twenty-first-century knowledge and skills initiatives in both P–12
schools and educator preparation programs (Partnership for 21st Century
Skills and AACTE 2010). The report includes instructional models and examples of how AACTE members are addressing twenty-first-century skills.
In this case the twenty-first-century skills have been established and are
incorporated into the Common Core Standards and this vision is a massive
undertaking.

Although there are teacher education programs that graduate highly capable teachers, coordinating the efforts of teacher preservice programs to promote higher student achievement, if and when those efforts could be identified, would be very difficult to accomplish.

THE ART OF TEACHING

Teaching involves a combination of elements that result in student achievement. None of these elements by itself guarantees a teacher's effectiveness, but the absence of any one diminishes student achievement. These elements include content knowledge so that teachers can present information and respond to student questions. The art of teaching also involves classroom management skills that include effective discipline, organization, and being able to relate to students. Another element of teaching is the ability to plan lessons so that the lesson progression and materials facilitate learning. Employing effective teaching methods at the appropriate times, including cooperative learning, hands-on experiences, grouping, and direct instruction is important to the art of teaching, so is an understanding of how children learn so that lessons and learning experiences build upon one another.

Depth of Content Knowledge

The most obvious element a teacher appears to need is content knowledge. Of course, math teachers should know the math they are teaching. Science teachers should know the science they are teaching. Some people may think that is all teachers need to be able to teach. Teachers need to know what they are teaching, and there is no better way to learn something than to be required to teach it. Because we have all been students, we assume that teachers know everything. Yet, if you graduate with a degree in education and achieve a preK–6 teaching certificate, there is a very good chance that you do not have a content foundation in any subject area. For example, very few teachers have a solid understanding of mathematics, science, or social studies. Many will readily admit they don't like to teach science or math because they were never good at it. Some primary teachers don't want to teach the intermediate grades because they don't feel confident that they could even *do* the math at a fifth grade level. Education courses that focus on theories of learning and methods classes are typically devoid of content. Even secondary teachers at the 6–12 level often find themselves teaching a subject for which they are not certified because of the needs of the school where they are employed.

Teachers' knowledge of content is a huge concern particularly in the areas of math and science. Some argue that engineers and mathematicians should be called upon to teach or that teachers be required to take more content courses in college. As Deborah Ball points out, however, teaching mathematics is different from being able to *do* mathematics.

> We will miss the mark if we specify necessary professional qualifications—and the recommended education needed to attain those qualifications—based solely on the content of the school curriculum. Teaching is a professional practice that demands knowledge and skill beyond what is visible from an examination of the curriculum. An adequate portrait of the mathematical knowledge needed for effective instruction depends on an analysis of the work of teaching. What do teachers do with mathematics in the course of their work? In what sorts of mathematical reasoning do they engage regularly? What kinds of mathematical problems do they regularly face? Without such examination of the mathematical demands of teaching, ideas about what teachers need to know are likely to underestimate and misestimate what is entailed.
>
> Knowing how to multiply 0.3×0.7, and being able to produce efficiently the answer of 0.21, is not sufficient to explain and justify the algorithm to students. In teaching fifth graders, a student will likely ask why, in multiplication, you count the number of decimal places in the numbers you are multiplying and "count over" the same number of places in the product to place the decimal point correctly. The student may point out that when you add two decimals, you simply line the numbers up:
>
> $$0.3 \times 0.7 = 0.21$$
> $$0.3 + 0.7 = 1.0$$
>
> Being able to do the calculations oneself is insufficient for being able to respond well. Even understanding the procedure in the formal terms that one might learn in a mathematics course may not equip one to explain it in ways that are both mathematically valid and accessible to fifth graders. The capacity to do this is a form of mathematical work that has been overlooked in the current discussions of improving teaching quality.
>
> Knowing mathematics for teaching includes knowing and being able to do the mathematics that we would want any competent adult to know. But knowing mathematics for teaching also requires more, and this "more" is not merely skill in teaching the material. (Ball 2003)

Content knowledge is important for teachers, but it is a specialized knowledge. It is one thing to know how to divide fractions, for example. It is a very different knowledge that is needed to teach someone else how to divide fractions so that they understand why the result is a larger number than the divisor or the dividend. Many teachers are nervous about straying too far from the textbook when teaching subjects in which they are not confident. For example, if a wrong answer is included in a teacher's edition of a math program, teachers may mark correct student answers incorrect. Furthermore, without content knowledge, teachers may not be able to address student questions adequately or inspire gifted students to explore content beyond the textbook. Of course, to be effective, a teacher needs content knowledge, but even if a teacher is a subject matter expert he or she will be ineffective if classroom management, planning, or other teaching skills are missing.

Effective Classroom Control, Management, Discipline, and Technique

The major shock that new teachers routinely have is how important classroom management is to learning. It is quite difficult to explain how a class of first graders can get out of control and intimidate an adult, but classroom management and control are the primary concerns of most new teachers and can remain a problem for teachers with years of experience. Doug Lemov's book *Teach Like a Champion* outlines forty-nine techniques that have nothing to do with content or preparation but have to do with lesson delivery and interacting with students. "I believe in content-based professional development, obviously," he told the *New York Times*. "But I feel like it's insufficient. . . . It doesn't matter what questions you're asking if the kids are running the classroom" (Green 2010).

Lemov maintains that the use of specific, concrete, and actionable techniques can make mediocre teachers into exceptional teachers. Mastering and practicing the techniques will raise academic and behavioral expectations and improve student achievement. Techniques such as not allowing a student to opt out of answering a question, or setting and defending high standards of correctness, establish consistent standards that students know will be enforced no matter what. "One of the problems with teaching is that there's a temptation to evaluate what we do in the classroom based on how clever it is, how it aligns with a larger philosophy, or even how gratifying it is to use, not necessarily how effective it is in driving student achievement" (Lemov 2010).

Teachers who are inconsistent and have poor classroom management, even if they are knowledgeable content experts, will not be effective in promoting student achievement. Managing a classroom efficiently and getting along with students will not improve student performance, however, if the ability to prepare lessons and use effective teaching methods is lacking.

Comprehensive Lesson Preparation

A significant element of teacher quality is the ability to prepare for lessons. Having the materials ready, a plan for what the lesson objective is, and how you will introduce, practice, and check for understanding are key to effective and efficient instruction. Teachers who don't have the right materials ready waste valuable time assembling them as students grow impatient. Teachers who haven't identified the lesson objective or know where the lesson is going leave it up to chance that students will get anything out of the lesson.

In their work *Understanding by Design*, Wiggins and McTighe consider lesson planning so important they advocate a lesson planning procedure that works backward, beginning with identifying the desired outcomes, then determining acceptable evidence or what the students will produce to show they have achieved the desired outcomes, and then planning the learning experiences and instruction that will result in the acceptable evidence that demonstrates the desired outcomes (Wiggins and McTighe 1998).

> Many teachers *begin* with textbooks, favored lessons, and time-honored activities rather than deriving those tools from targets, goals, or standards. We are advocating the reverse: One starts with the end—the desired results (goals or standards)—and then derives the curriculum from the evidence of learning—(performances) called for by the standard and the teaching needed to equip students to perform. (8)

Effective lesson planning is a critical aspect of teaching. But without classroom management or content knowledge, instruction is likely to be ineffective. Furthermore, many teachers are able to plan what they think will be dynamic engaging lessons only to have them fail because they use inappropriate teaching methods.

Effective Teaching Methods

Teaching methods are the different ways that teachers teach. Common teaching methods include lecturing and having students take notes, having students work on a task in a small group, having students demonstrate concepts using concrete manipulatives or in hands-on science activities. The Socratic method, named for the classical Greek philosopher Socrates, involves asking and answering questions to stimulate debate and critical thinking. Some methods include multiple exposures or senses. For example, some methods advocate visualizing a concept, declaring the concept, and then demonstrating the concept (See It, Say It, Do It). Others involve a progression from teacher modeling to guided practice to independent practice (I Do, We Do, You Do).

Stigler and Hiebert in their analysis of the international comparison of mathematics teaching methods maintain that the methods that a teacher uses significantly impact student achievement.

> Americans focus on the competence of teachers. They decry the quality of applicants for teaching positions and criticize the talent of the current teaching

corps. . . . Although variability in competence is certainly visible . . . such differences are dwarfed by the differences in *teaching methods* that we see across cultures. . . . We have watched many examples of good teachers employing limited methods that, no matter how competently they are executed, could not lead to high levels of student achievement. Although there are teachers using extraordinary methods in all cultures, the extraordinary is not what defines most students' classroom experiences. Students' day-to-day experiences are mainly determined by the methods most commonly used by teachers within a culture. (Stigler and Hiebert 1999)

A teacher can be a content expert and have planning and classroom management down, but may not be using the most effective methods to promote student achievement. Even if a teacher is able to use a variety of methods, unless he or she understands how children learn, student performance will suffer.

Understanding Children's Learning Trajectories

An understanding of how children develop understanding of concepts in each subject area is a critical element in effective teaching.

Children follow natural developmental progressions in learning and development. As a simple example, children first learn to crawl, which is followed by walking, running, skipping, and jumping with increased speed and dexterity. Similarly, they follow natural developmental progressions in learning math; they learn mathematical ideas and skills in their own way. When educators understand these developmental progressions, and sequence activities based on them, they can build mathematically enriched learning environments that are developmentally appropriate and effective. These developmental paths are a main component of a *learning trajectory*. (Clements and Sarama 2009a)

Each level of thinking along the trajectory is more sophisticated than the last. The trajectory, or developmental progression, describes a typical path children follow in developing understanding and skill about a concept such as counting or a skill such as reading. The art of teaching involves understanding that these incremental steps are important in learning and do not assume that students see things in the same way that adults do. To teach a child to read, for example, is very different from reading to a child. Recognizing that a child may not recognize that words are made of individual sounds or that letters correspond to sounds and teaching those vital early reading skills makes teaching challenging and rewarding.

When teachers understand children's learning trajectories, they know what objectives need to be set, where to start with instruction, where to go next, and how to get there. Without an understanding of children's developmental progressions, teachers may repeat concepts that students have already mastered and bore students. Alternatively they may also take giant leaps from one concept to the next and lose students. Without understanding how children learn, they may never be able to reach students who are above or below average.

TEACHER EFFECTIVENESS

A major issue is what the focus of professional development should be. Many people look at standardized test scores to measure teacher effectiveness. Teachers themselves, 92 percent, measure effectiveness first and foremost by whether students are engaged in their coursework, then 72 percent by how much students are learning compared with students in other schools, and 71 percent based on feedback from administrators. Only 56 percent say they measure performance on how well their students perform on standardized tests (Coggshal, Ott, and Lasanga 2010). So the measure that the public is using to evaluate teacher effectiveness is not the same as the measure teachers use themselves.

A teacher's description of a great class rarely has anything to do with test scores.

> I remember my best class; it still makes me smile. In fact, it gets better with age. I was teaching history and, as the kids walked into the classroom, one student asked me if I'd see the recent news about violence in the Middle East. (I always thought it a sign of success that my students took an active interest in the world around them.) I prompted an elaboration and the next thing I knew a discussion had erupted. . . . The kids keep going, and I was loving it. I listened. I arbitrated. I corrected. I offered an occasional prompt or question. Then the bell rang, but they didn't move, didn't jump up to meet their friends in the hall between classes! They weren't finished talking. I had to urge them out the door, and as they left they were still going at it. . . . Then the next morning I get a call from a parent. At first I'm nervous—did she find out her kid hasn't memorized the pharaohs? But it's a good call. . . . She says, "Something strange happened last night. . . . He came home, read the newspaper, watched the news on TV and wanted to talk about what was going on in the world. He mentioned something about what happened in class . . ." (Dockterman 1997)

If teachers want to do a good job and measure their effectiveness on how engaged students are, they are likely to look for curriculum and professional development experiences that will excite students, and be fun, without regard to how effective they are. Many educational experiences, including games and puzzles and a lot of computer software, are primarily designed to be motivating without a lot of concern about learning and standards. This is a significant disconnect between the goal of classroom activities and student achievement. There is no reason that activities cannot be motivating *and* promote student achievement, but many do not.

In the United States, we assume teachers are competent once they have completed their teacher-training programs and are certified. These are quantitative measures of teacher competence. Yet many teachers are unprepared for the challenges of the classroom and face the fear of not being able to measure up. Many people assume you are either cut out to be a teacher or you are not. Many teachers are afraid to ask for help because they are afraid of appearing weak or unable to control the classroom.

If a teacher does not have adequate content knowledge, is struggling with classroom management issues, does not know how to prepare for lessons, is not using effective teaching methods, or does not understand how children learn, that teacher needs help, as most new teachers do. Observations of struggling teachers and low performing schools can often identify the element that needs attention. In this example, classroom management is a critical problem:

> But when it came to actual teaching, the daily task of getting students to learn, the school floundered. Students disobeyed teachers' instructions, and class discussions veered away from the lesson plans. In one class Lemov observed, the teacher spent several minutes debating a student about why he didn't have a pencil. Another divided her students into two groups to practice multiplication together, only to watch them turn to the more interesting work of chatting. A single quiet student soldiered on with the problems. As Lemov drove from Syracuse back to his home in Albany, he tried to figure out what he could do to help. He knew how to advise schools to adopt a better curriculum or raise standards or develop better communication channels between teachers and principals. But he realized that he had no clue how to advise schools about their main event: how to teach. (Green 2010)

Because teachers most often work in isolation from other teachers, it may be very difficult for them to ask for help or to acknowledge that they are having problems. Professional development offers some hope for them.

Professional/Staff Development

The term *professional development* means "a comprehensive, sustained, and intensive approach to improving teachers' and principals' effectiveness in raising student achievement" (National Staff Development Council 2001). Professional development is the ongoing education teachers engage in after they graduate from college. Professional development can take the form of online college classes, graduate-level courses, conferences, and educational consultant presentations. Many states require demonstration of professional development in the form of continuing education credits or work toward advanced degrees.

> For the nearly 75% of the educators working in schools today beyond their novice years, professional development is the single most important strategy for extending and refining their knowledge, skills, dispositions, and practices throughout their careers. For those who are new to positions, strong preparation programs establish the foundation for success. (Jaquith et al. 2010)

The National Staff Development Council has established standards for staff development, which schools and districts can use to learn whether their staff development programs are aligned to enable a faculty to draw conclusions and make recommendations in planning quality professional learning. These include the following:

Context Standards

- Organize adults into learning communities whose goals are aligned with those of the school and district. (Learning Communities)
- Require skillful school and district leaders who guide continuous instructional improvement. (Leadership)
- Require resources to support adult learning and collaboration. (Resources)

Process Standards

- Use disaggregated student data to determine learning priorities, monitor progress, and help sustain continuous improvement. (Data-Driven)
- Use multiple sources of information to guide improvement and demonstrate its impact. (Evaluation)
- Prepare educators to apply research to decision making. (Research-Based)
- Use learning strategies appropriate to the intended goal. (Design)
- Apply knowledge about human learning and change. (Learning)
- Provide educators with the knowledge and skills to collaborate. (Collaboration)

Content Standards

- Prepare educators to understand and appreciate all students, create safe, orderly and supportive learning environments, and hold high expectations for their academic achievement. (Equity)
- Deepen educators' content knowledge, provide them with research-based instructional strategies to assist students in meeting rigorous academic

standards, and prepare them to use various types of classroom assessments appropriately. (Quality Teaching)
• Provide educators with knowledge and skills to involve families and other stakeholders appropriately. (Family Involvement)

These standards are admirable, but they are not often reflected in actual practice.

Models for Professional Development

With the new focus on academic standards, technology, and increasing diversity in schools, and with the emphasis in legislation on improving teacher quality, it would seem that continuing education and professional development would be the keys to improved academic achievement. Yet models of professional development have been largely ineffective and have resulted in an antipathy toward professional development among school faculty.

In-Service Workshops—In this model the district or school contracts with an outside consultant to give the faculty a one-time training on a particular topic or area. These "sit and get" sessions may occur after school or during an all-day staff development day. Even when the presenter is interesting and energetic, these workshops rarely result in any meaningful application. They often are unconnected to classroom experience and have little continuity with other professional development.

Conference Attendance—Many schools pay for teachers to attend professional conferences such as National Council of Teachers of Mathematics (NCTM), International Reading Association (IRA), or Association of Supervisors and Curriculum Developers (ASCD). These conferences offer numerous workshops on a variety of topics. Teachers attend these sessions and often earn continuing education credits toward recertification, but it is not clear how relevant or effective they are in promoting student achievement. Teachers may learn something new, but it is likely disconnected from their classroom context. They may or may not share what they learned from the conference with other teachers.

Community Practice/Lesson Study—Lesson Study is a model borrowed from Japan in which a group of teachers work together to define a problem related to a learning goal, plan a lesson to solve it, teach the lesson, observe the lesson, evaluate the lesson, reflect on its effect, revise the lesson, teach the revised lesson, and share the results. The idea is that the most effective way to improve teaching is in the context of a lesson. The challenge is how to identify the kinds of changes that will improve student learning and share the knowledge with other teachers. The group then comes together to discuss their observations of the lesson. They may then revise and reteach the lesson and produce a report of what the study lesson has taught them.

Although 67 percent of teachers and 78 percent of principals surveyed think that greater collaboration would have a major impact on improving student achievement, collaboration efforts in schools vary widely. The most frequent types of collaboration are teachers meeting in teams to learn how to promote student achievement, school leaders sharing responsibility with teachers, and mentoring. The least frequent is teachers observing each other and providing feedback. Collaboration is much more common at the elementary than the secondary level (MetLife 2010).

Coaching/Mentoring—In some schools new teachers are assigned a coach or mentor within the school. The mentor can provide one-on-one assistance. This has the potential to be quite effective and lend needed support to new teachers, although there is little data beyond anecdotal evidence that supports this approach.

Online Courses—Continuing education webinars and online courses are widely available, but there is little data about their effectiveness in promoting student achievement.

Reflective Evaluation—In this model an administrator or another teacher observes a teacher and provides feedback. This has the potential to be very powerful, but it is not widely practiced. Because teachers usually work alone, many are intimidated by others who might be critical. Administrators who only enter the classroom when it is time for evaluation create a stressful environment rather than a supportive one.

Problems with Professional Development

One would think that teachers would embrace opportunities for professional development. Unfortunately there have been so many ineffective professional development efforts that teachers are suspicious. Useless staff development programs have been described as "soul killing." Professional development days are often filled with other types of announcements or comprise admonitions about procedural infractions such as grade and attendance reports. In many cases professional development may be focused on instructional problems that affect only a limited number of teachers. Too often professional development has little impact on teachers or their students.

> Bombarding teachers with waves of ineffective reforms can have another downside: Teachers can grow weary. They are asked over and over to change the way they do x, y, or z. Even when they try to accommodate the reformers and adopt a new feature or two, nothing much happens. They do not notice much improvement in students' learning. Although it might feel to teachers that they

are changing, the basic system is running essentially as it did before. Always changing, and yet staying the same, is a discouraging state of affairs. It can lead to a defeatist kind of cynicism. Quick fixes that focus on changing individual features leave behind a skeptical teaching corps. (Stigler and Hiebert 1999)

There are a host of problems with models of professional development that are currently in use. Relevance, coherence, and lack of commitment are reasons many professional development efforts fall short.

Relevance—Professional development that does not focus on what teachers are facing in the classroom will not have relevance to them. Music teachers, for example, who sit through sessions on mathematics strategies usually feel they are wasting their time. Instead of active learning strategies that good teachers use with their students, much professional development, especially district wide, uses a passive lecture format in which an expert relays what teachers should or should not be doing. Even the most positive teachers can begin to feel that the expert does not understand the realities of the classroom.

Coherence—Much of what passes for professional development, particularly conference workshops and isolated workshops, has no coherence with other professional development initiatives. Effective educational experiences develop a coherent scope and sequence of skills and concepts. Learning even a good strategy in isolation from practice without a context of where it fits into the curriculum often ensures that it will not become classroom practice.

Commitment—Commitment and accountability are often absent on the part of the administration. Even after a series of coherent professional development experiences, if there is no follow-up, no assessment, and no further interest on the part of the administration, teachers are unlikely to embrace the new learning. Teachers work alone for the most part and make their own choices in the classroom. Without follow-up, there is no way of knowing if the new learning was interpreted correctly or implemented with fidelity. Professional development is a commitment to improved practice. For professional development to be effective, estimates are that there should be twenty or more hours of contact time to reinforce learning and to determine the effects (Desimone 2011).

Professors and Teachers

Another difficulty in improving teacher quality through continuing education and professional development has to do with the disconnect between educators at the college level and those in preK–12 education. Spend any time discussing teaching strategies with college and K–12 educators and it won't take long to realize they operate in very different worlds. The two camps do not communicate well.

College instructors design their own courses, choose their own textbooks, and deliver the material in any way they see fit. Their audience is in large part paying to attend and is motivated to learn and to do well. College instructors are experts in their discipline and can critique instructional materials based on their merits and content coverage. College instructors may have two or three classes a day and have office hours to meet with students individually and prepare the next class. To get tenure, they are expected to devote a substantial portion of their time conducting their own research and guiding students in their own research.

PreK–12 teachers are given a set of guidelines, often a school-adopted text, and students of all ability levels are assigned to them. These students by and large have varying degrees of interest, motivation, background knowledge, and attention span. K–6 teachers may teach all subjects (reading, math, science, social studies, health, art, and physical education). It is inconceivable that they would be experts in every subject.

A college professor may find it difficult to understand why preK–12 teachers don't spend time designing their own courses and why they don't use a host of different resources they have garnered from innovative sources. It is easy for them to assume that preK–12 teachers are content experts as they are.

A major complaint among preK–12 teachers is that their college experience did not prepare them for the reality of the classroom. This is true on many levels, but mainly it is the stark reality of dealing with discipline and organization issues, which is so very different in a college environment. First year teachers are confronted with extreme issues such as abusive parents, teen pregnancy, gangs, bullying, and suicide as well as the mundane issues of motivation, organization, and paperwork. For first year teachers, concept development and the effectiveness of strategies often are lower priorities than classroom management and discipline they need to survive. The stark reality of K–12 teaching often causes a sense of mistrust of the college experience and a confirmation that professors are out of touch with preK–12 classroom realities. This mutual disrespect is a cause of concern.

This gap between basic research in cognitive psychology and the practice of teaching has negative consequences for each side. In their distrust of basic science, teachers miss an opportunity to improve their students' learning by applying their expertise on relevant dimensions of learning. In allowing this distrust to exist, scientists undermine the public's trust in the value of the basic science to understanding human behavior. Just as the science of medicine need not undermine the expertise of a doctor, the science of psychology need not invalidate practice-based knowledge, but rather supplement it with general information about theories of the mind and learning, without direct prescriptions for what to do in a certain classroom situation. In order to repair this distrust, scientists must first summarize our findings for audiences outside of our community, with an eye toward informing educational practice. In doing so, we need to describe our basic science findings as theories of how the mind works, not straightforward recipes for educational reform. (Riener 2010)

College professors value accuracy, research, precision, and knowledge. PreK–12 teachers value organization, motivation, discipline, and humor. Academics often write in scholarly journals. Teachers are most likely to read teaching magazines filled with fun ideas and classroom management tips. A math professor may enjoy spending time discussing and refining a math term definition. A preK–12 teacher may recognize that the nuances of a definition will be lost on most students struggling with math. Professors have difficulty understanding why a preK–12 teacher does not care about developments in pedagogy and instructional design. preK–12 teachers see educational researchers as ivory tower types who have no idea what it's like in a public school classroom. Professors do not attend teacher conferences and teachers do not attend educational research conferences such as that of the American Educational Research Association (AERA). Interestingly, NCTM holds a research presession before the national conference. Many educational researchers attend and present to each other and then leave when the convention starts.

With this dichotomy it's no wonder that a professor would become irate over censorship in textbooks and the preK–12 teachers and administrators would appreciate the filter because they wouldn't have the lesson descend into giggling or deal with the wrath of an unhappy parent. When selecting artwork for a fine arts program, teachers asked that the publisher not include any signs of tobacco use because they wanted to be able to discuss artwork, not the hazards of smoking. Of course, there would be no tolerance of nudes in a K–12 fine arts program. Art professors might find these concerns absurd.

As a result of the conflict in values, instead of mutual respect, the two groups often have mutual disdain and distrust for each other. Yet, in the final analysis, to promote education the two groups need to communicate. It is the academics who engage in educational research and should be offering valuable insights into learning, pedagogy, and curriculum, but unless academics understand the realities of the classroom and engage with preK–12 teachers, they will not be able to make realistic recommendations. The continuing gulf between these groups of educators helps to ensure the status quo will continue to rule.

TEACHER EDUCATION AND EDUCATIONAL MATERIALS

A source of professional development that is all but overlooked is in the training and use of educational materials. Rarely do colleges of education teach preservice teachers how to use educational materials or how to evaluate them. Yet when new teachers begin their careers, they are equipped with the educational materials the school, district, and or state has selected for them, in addition to any materials they choose or create for themselves. State and national standards may identify the topics that teachers are required to teach, but the educational materials provide the daily lessons, scope and sequence, activities, and content that teachers use to teach.

If you ask teachers, however, the vast majority would say curricular materials like textbooks are used only as one of many resources. Teachers will claim they know best what their students need and pick the most appropriate resources to meet those needs. Many pride themselves that they don't use textbooks and that textbooks may only be needed for "new" teachers. Statistics, however, tell a different story.

> A 2002 survey of elementary and high school teachers found that about 80 percent use textbooks in their classrooms. Nearly half of student class time was spent using textbooks. And those numbers, from a survey sponsored by the National Education Association and the Association of American Publishers, most likely *understate* teachers' and students' true dependence on textbooks. Shadow studies, which track teachers' activities during the school day, suggest that 80 to 90 percent of classroom and homework assignments are textbook-driven or textbook-centered. History and social studies teachers, for example, often rely almost exclusively on textbooks, instead of requiring students to review primary sources and read trade books by top historians. (Whitman 2004)

The use of educational materials, whether they are adopted by the school or selected by the teacher, provides significant opportunities for professional development.

Professional Development with New Curriculum

The professional development that supported advances in reading instruction over the past twenty years is a good example of how new materials can provide teacher education after teachers have begun teaching. The whole language movement that swept into education in the 1980s and 1990s promoted this antitextbook perspective. During this time textbook bashing was a popular activity. Textbooks were seen as boring, with drill-and-kill skill activities that replaced authentic experience, stifled teachers, and inhibited quality instruction. Children would be motivated to learn to read and write holistically if they were surrounded by quality print and supportive teachers. This romantic movement led by educators like Ken and Yetta Goodman sought to empower teachers to design their own curriculums. The movement put many teachers at odds with textbooks.

When tests in California showed that children were not learning how to read, and at alarming levels, and research showed that children did need a solid foundation in phonemic awareness and phonics, the whole language movement began to lose steam. Instead of every teacher becoming trained in these skills and creating his or her own curriculum, standards in many states were changed to reflect the new skills and standards, and publishers addressed them in new educational materials.

Following the Reading First initiative in 2001 (National Institute for Literacy 2001), which provided financial assistance to states and districts to establish scientifically based reading programs in grades P–3, many teachers participated in professional development to learn to teach the new programs that had been developed. To qualify for Reading First grant applications, reading programs made a dramatic shift from whole language to a focus on the five pillars of Reading First: phonemic awareness, phonics, fluency, vocabulary, and comprehension. The Reading First grants included funding for professional development to ensure that all teachers had the skills they needed to teach these programs effectively. Teachers not only learned how to use the new materials, many also learned how to teach phonemic awareness, sound and letter correspondences, phonics, and comprehension skills using explicit instruction.

When new basal reading programs are adopted and purchased, publishers often provide professional development or in-service training to use the features and strategies to their best advantage. In some cases, these sessions can also include education on content, teaching methods, and lesson planning in conjunction with the new program. This training can take the form of one session or a series of sessions. Often professional development related to the implementation of a new curriculum involves the trainer model in which individual teachers are trained on using the new curriculum and they in turn train their colleagues.

In the case of the Reading First initiative, publishers developed new educational materials and many teachers were trained to use them, effectively learning to teach early reading skills. Although long-term trends in reading have remained relatively flat, the decline evidenced from 1980 to 1990 among nine-year-olds has been reversed (IES National Center for Education Statistics 2008).

Making widespread improvements in educational practices so they have an effect on teacher quality and student performance in this case involved researchers who identified skills students need and effective instructional methods to teach them. It also involved setting higher standards and developing new curricular materials that include the skills and methods and address the new standards. All of this would have been worthless unless teachers were engaged in professional development that taught them how to effectively implement the new materials.

Teacher Education using Educational Materials

Some subject area textbooks are employed more intensively than others, depending in large part on teacher confidence. Teachers are less confident about math and science and are much more likely to use textbooks in those subjects than they are in reading or language arts. Using these educational materials provides a level of teacher education in these subjects that many teachers would not otherwise have.

> Not only are curriculum materials well-positioned to influence individual teachers' work but, unlike many other innovations, textbooks are already "scaled up" and part of the routine of schools. They have "reach" in the system. At the local level, text adoptions are the primary routine in most districts for updating the curriculum every five to seven years (Carus 1990). In our fragmented school system, textbooks are also one way that educators strive for a common curriculum across diverse settings. Despite their central role in the instructional system, however, curriculum materials have played an uneven role in practice. (Ball and Cohen 1996)

Mathematics

Math is the second largest curriculum area, it is tested nationally, and it is not easily integrated into reading, so teaching math is a high priority. Because elementary teachers typically have little confidence in their math knowledge, they tend to rely on textbooks more than they do in other subjects. Because of increases in complexity in middle school and high school, math teachers at those levels tend to rely on textbooks, too. Without math textbooks, many teachers would be at a serious loss in how to approach mathematics instruction.

In math, the majority of teachers teach from the student textbook pages, presenting individual skills and concepts and worked examples, followed by practice exercises. Elementary teachers tend to believe they are successful in teaching mathematics if their students have learned the basic operational facts (addition, subtraction, multiplication, and division). Although math manipulatives are strongly encouraged to make math concepts concrete and most basal math programs include comprehensive manipulative kits at the elementary levels, there is little evidence that these materials are widely used. Although teachers often make textbook selections based on how many math manipulatives come with the program, particularly at the primary levels, most teachers rarely use them effectively. For one thing they are noisy and messy. Secondly, teachers who do not understand the math concepts themselves and do not have professional development in mathematics have difficulty demonstrating those concepts with manipulatives. So many teachers allow students to play with manipulatives in the name of teaching hands-on math, but without underlying concept development. This practice can go on throughout elementary school, even after the majority of students have grasped the concepts.

The math wars that rage between people who believe that mastering the basic facts and learning math skills based on formulas or algorithms (step-by-step procedures) is the goal of instruction and those who believe that math fluency involves conceptual understanding in number sense, reasoning, and problem solving are played out in the different types of math programs available. The most popular and widely sold programs are the step-by-step basals with periodic word problems. Less popular among teachers although more popular among math supervisors are the inquiry-based, conceptual development programs. These types of programs require intensive professional development for teachers to realize the benefits from them.

The Math Panel modeled after the National Reading Panel that promoted the Reading First initiative called for an end to the math wars: "Conceptual understanding, computational and procedural fluency, and problem solving skills are equally important and mutually reinforce each other. Debates regarding the relative importance of each of these components of mathematics are misguided" (US Department of Education 2008). Whereas the Reading First initiative inspired dramatic changes in basal reading programs because the funding relied on "scientifically based" reading programs, which meant inclusion of sound phonemic awareness and phonics instruction, the Math Panel has not had the same clout. For one thing, many reading programs in the 1990s had abandoned phonics, so its inclusion changed the way reading instruction was presented. In math, even skill-based programs include word problems, so a publisher could claim to be addressing a balance of skills and conceptual understanding without changing the program substantively.

Furthermore, teachers, particularly elementary teachers, have much less confidence in their knowledge of mathematics than reading and have little critical judgement when it comes to math instruction. They expect that students will not like math and many will not understand more complex concepts, because teachers themselves may not. This would be an unacceptable assumption in reading instruction. So many teachers learned to memorize basic facts and how to mulitiply and divide (yours is not to wonder why, just invert and multiply) without understanding how and why algorithms work that they expect this in their students. Many teachers are afraid of student questions in mathematics because they themselves may not know the answers. If a math textbook poses questions, teachers want the suggested answers to be included for them because they often don't know enough math to figure it out themselves.

Math textbooks provide teachers with a foundation in mathematics, but if increased student achievement is desired, teachers need intensive professional development in mathematics to improve the quality of mathematics teaching.

Science

If elementary teachers are unconfident about math, they are even less confident about science (earth, life, and physical science). At least in math, teachers feel they can "do" elementary math. But unlike math, the stakes are not as high because the subject is not tested as seriously as mathematics, so many teachers feel good if they incorporate science readings into their reading program or make cross-curricular connections to science in mathematics.

> Fewer than one-third of elementary teachers reported feeling very well qualified to teach each of the science disciplines. More grade K–5 teachers stated feeling very well qualified to teach life science and earth science than physical science, which is consistent with teacher reports of their college coursework.
>
> It is clear that elementary school teachers do not feel equally qualified to teach all academic subjects, with preparedness to teach science paling in comparison to mathematics, language arts, and social studies. Where fewer than 3 in 10 elementary teachers reported feeling well prepared to teach the sciences, 77 percent indicated that they were very well qualified to teach reading/language arts. Large percentages of teachers reported the same high level of qualification to teach mathematics (66 percent) and social studies (52 percent). (Fulp 2002)

Without science educational materials, many teachers would be lost with trying to create an effective science program that includes the recommendations from science educators, including inquiry-based instruction or guided inquiry in which questions are posed and students use scientific methods and materials to answer them. As reading and math have taken priority in preK–12 education because of testing and adequate yearly progress, science has become much less of a priority to the relief of many teachers. In many schools, science has been integrated into reading with nonfiction science-based reading materials.

> Professional development is key to supporting effective science instruction. We call for a dramatic departure from current professional development practice, both in scope and kind. Teachers need opportunities to deepen their knowledge of the science content of the K–8 curriculum. They also need opportunities to learn how students learn science and how to teach it. They need to know how children's understanding of core ideas in science builds across K–8, not just at a given grade or grade band. They need to learn about the conceptual ideas that students have in the earliest grades and their ideas about science itself. They need to learn how to assess children's developing ideas over time and how

to interpret and respond (instructionally) to the results of assessment. In sum, teachers need opportunities to learn how to teach science as an integrated body of knowledge and practice—to teach for scientific proficiency. They need to learn how to teach science to diverse student populations, to provide adequate opportunities for all students to learn science. These needs represent a significant change from what virtually all active teachers learned in college and what most colleges teach aspiring teachers today. (Committee on Science Learning, Kindergarten Through Eighth Grade 2007)

Using educational materials in different subject areas gives teachers support in four of the elements of teaching: a basic level of content knowledge, lesson preparation, teaching methods, and an organized scope and sequence of skills. Educational materials that meet current standards and are grounded in content area and learning theory research have the potential to provide substantive professional development for teachers and improvements in teacher quality and student achievement.

CONCLUSION

One of the very few things that everyone can agree on about education is that improving teacher quality is a promising solution to increasing student achievement. There is, however, very little agreement on how to do that. Some focus on colleges of education to improve preservice teacher education. Some focus on certification. Some focus on different forms of professional development believing that teachers will improve if they participate in professional development programs. Some focus on incentivizing teachers to improve on their own with merit pay. Unfortunately, none of these has been a clear solution.

But what makes a good teacher? There have been many quests for the one essential trait, and they have all come up empty-handed. Among the factors that do not predict whether a teacher will succeed: a graduate-school degree, a high score on the SAT, an extroverted personality, politeness, confidence, warmth, enthusiasm and having passed the teacher-certification exam on the first try. (Green 2010)

In the past fifty years there has been an increasing effort to define and quantify teacher effectiveness with certifications, degrees, years of experience, and postgraduate education credits. Instead of student test scores or other measures, teacher quality has been defined by the quality of a teacher's education program, credentials held, educational attainment, and certification status. Educators have been incentivized and rewarded for their efforts to continue their education with financial reimbursements for additional course-work. Some schools even pay teachers to attend professional development sessions. In many schools, teachers receive salary increases when they earn advanced degrees or National Board Certification. Unfortunately, these efforts do not necessarily lead to increased student achievement.

Measurements of teacher quality include classroom observations by principals, accumulated continuing education credits, and subject matter knowledge. There are tests, such as the PRAXIS exam, that are intended to assess teacher competence. Efforts are under way to establish a Teacher Performance Assessment, which would document teaching and learning in three- to five-day learning segments (Amercian Association of Colleges for Teacher Education 2011). This would be in addition to the *U.S. News & World Report* and National Council on Teacher Quality efforts to rate the quality of teacher education programs around the United States.

> The study found that, while there had been clear progress in some areas—for example, a steady increase in access to instruction and mentoring for beginning teachers—most teachers continue to have limited opportunities for sustained, ongoing forms of professional development. Indeed, by 2008, fewer teachers had access to intensive professional learning opportunities on most topics than was true several years earlier. Furthermore, only 15% of teachers reported being in collaborative work settings, half as many as a decade earlier. This study also found, however, that opportunities for professional learning vary widely across states, and that some appear to support more available and intensive professional development than others. (Jaquith et al. 2010)

In most cases preK–12 teachers do not have relationships with colleges of education after they begin teaching, so there is minimal sharing and testing of new ideas and methods. Educational materials provide teachers with some relevant professional development and teacher education, but that is only as effective as the materials themselves. After years of experience with continuing education and professional development initiatives, it is clear that no one has been able to identify the keys to increasing student achievement. So many promising initiatives have proved ineffective. Asking individual teachers to make it happen on their own with carrot-and-stick incentives seems doomed to failure, as if teachers have been holding back on doing the best job they can waiting for incentives.

Although there is some evidence that teaching experience has a positive effect on reading and math outcomes, most forms of professional development and advanced certification, including having an advanced degree, do not show significant effects on student achievement. As a result of not finding a way to provide effective professional development, there is no agreement about how to attract and retain effective teachers. Some believe that standards must be raised; at the same time others suggest that certification requirements be eliminated so subject matter experts can enter the classroom. "The United States is always reforming but not always improving. The most alarming aspect of classroom teaching in the United States is not how we are teaching now but that we have no mechanism for getting better" (Stigler and Hiebert 1999).

The best that can be said is that when "professional development is focused on academic content and curriculum that is aligned with standards-based reform, teaching practice and student achievement are *likely* to improve" (Whitehurst 2002). With all the efforts that have been made, if teacher education and professional development alone were the key to improved student achievement, it would have been obvious by now.

Chapter Seven

Rising above the Plateau

In a letter to his friend James Madison in 1787, reflecting on the new Constitution, Thomas Jefferson wrote, "Above all things I hope the education of the common people will be attended to; convinced that on their good sense we may rely with the most security for the preservation of a due degree of liberty." Jefferson's hopes are still reflected today.

> Education is the key to America's economic growth and prosperity and to our ability to compete in the global economy. It is the path to good jobs and higher earning power for Americans. It is necessary for our democracy to work. It fosters the cross-border, cross-cultural collaboration required to solve the most challenging problems of our time. (US Department of Education 2010a)

Our challenge is to build upon the educational system we have to move above the current plateau of student achievement.

WHERE WE ARE

We have a public education system that has been developing for more than two hundred years. It has served the country well throughout much of the nation's history, helping the United States to become a world power. Because the United States offered free public high school education, the nation had the best educated workforce in the world. If we implemented our system as is, even with all its flaws, in a country that does not have compulsory education, it would, to use an automobile analogy, propel that nation from 0 to 60 miles per hour in a few short years. Yet we have reached a point in our development where our educational system works to perpetuate the status quo instead of continual improvement. We can't seem to get above 60.

We have an enormous corpus of standards, but our institutions of higher education, our professional development, our curriculum and its selection process all work to keep our nation in a holding pattern of advancement. This would be fine, except that in order to keep pace with other countries that have caught up with or surpassed us in many areas, we need to find ways to improve our educational system so that it is dynamic, works on continually improving student achievement, and prepares our children for the future.

In the quest for solutions in the name of reform, we have gone from tree to tree looking for and embracing educational fads and initiatives to find *the* solution to all our problems: longer school year, longer school day, merit teacher pay, more testing, different kinds of testing, identifying and firing incompetent teachers, professional development, charter schools, school vouchers, school choice, technology solutions, small schools, smaller class sizes, differentiated instruction, even 3D multimedia. We've looked to innovations like technology to be the silver bullet, the simple solution that will magically cause our students' test scores to start rising. Unsurprisingly, none of these solutions is the answer.

It is as if we have been trying and trying unsuccessfully to lose weight. We try one quick weight loss diet after another only to find that we have to change the patterns and methods of the simple choices we make every single day to break out of our plateau.

California is a good example of the frustration of reform efforts. It has tried all kinds of reforms, targeting almost every part of the school system, including new standards, financial incentives, and new assessments. Yet none of these had any substantive effect on student achievement. The Brookings Brown Center 2009 report on American education explains that "the science of turnarounds is weak and devoid of practical, effective strategies for educators to employ. Examples of large-scale, system-wide turnarounds are nonexistent. A lot of work needs to be done before the odds of turning around failing schools begin to tip in a favorable direction" (Loveless 2010).

Because everyone has been to school, it is easy to believe that each of us understands how schools work and how best to solve the problems. It's easy to focus on one piece of the puzzle and try to fix it. Yet even if we could do one thing, such as identifying all the "bad" teachers and firing them, without a lot of other changes, it would not, and has not, had much effect on promoting student achievement.

Public education is very complicated, intertwined with millions of variables including family issues (home life, parental support, early childhood experiences, socioeconomic factors), student ability issues (learning ability, desire to learn, student efficacy), teacher factors (qualifications, professional development, management capability, discipline, content knowledge), social issues (student/teacher personality conflicts, student social adjustment), and school issues (environment, administration support, curriculum resources). Any one of these can be a reason for an educational experience to be less than adequate. Any one of these factors, as well as many others, can have a dramatic positive or negative effect on a child's educational achievement.

Lest we bury ourselves under a mountain of despair, one can take heart that the system does work for many people. The majority of children start school at ages five or six and graduate at seventeen or eighteen. The system is operated by intelligent, dedicated people who have been licensed by their states and screened by their employers—people who want to make a difference in the lives of children. From teachers and teachers' aides, to principals and superintendents, to editors and salespeople at educational publishers, to educational product suppliers, to politicians involved in educational priorities, everyone is attempting to do the best possible job that can be done within the system. Of course, some are more effective than others, but you don't stay in education if you don't care about improving lives.

I have personally known salespeople and consultants in educational publishing who believe in a particular curriculum so fervently that they will not sell other products even if doing so would be to their financial benefit. I knew a pressman at Von Hoffman, a huge printing company in Missouri, who held up a printing job so that he could call the publisher because he found a math error in a textbook. People at Tracermedia, a software developer in Ohio, would much rather work on educational products than advertising because it gives them a sense of purpose. When I was teaching, I'll never forget seeing a special needs student in the school office who begged me to get his teacher. "Miss Rubin, call Mr. Bricker. I'm in big trouble." People who are in education in whatever capacity feel a sense of purpose and responsibility. The system is not failing, but neither is it improving.

How can we move beyond the status quo and above the plateau in American education? How can we improve instruction and curriculum to result in improved student achievement so that American children can maximize their future potential and contribute to the nation's future health and prosperity? In identifying the priorities in the process of developing textbooks, recounting the development of educational standards, exploring educational technology initiatives, and examining teacher education, many clues are revealed.

CURRICULUM *IS* A KEY

At the same time that so many of our educational reform efforts have focused on higher standards, testing, professional development, school choice, or technology, curriculum has been ignored. As a typical example of this oversight, in spring of 2011 a webinar for educators on implementing the Common Core Standards presented the effort as requiring each and every one of the 6.2 million teachers in the United States to personally interpret the Common Core Standards, review his or her practices, and revise or rewrite the curriculum. There was no mention of how to identify effective coverage of the Common Core Standards in curricular materials. The one mention of published materials was that the materials might be labeled as meeting the standards but would not really do so. Teachers were on their own to identify appropriate materials and implement the standards.

Quality curriculum taught by quality teachers has the most potential to improve student achievement. Research supports this. In a summary of the effects of different influences in education, charter schools and state standards had no effect and merit pay for teachers had an insignificant effect on student achievement. But more effective math, preschool, and reading curricula had significant effects (Whitehurst 2009).

In a meta-analysis conducted by Robert Marzano of the factors that have the most impact on student achievement, a *guaranteed and viable curriculum* was number one. Of those elements that a school can control, the opportunity to learn content sequenced in an effective manner was more effective than any other factor, including challenging goals and effective feedback, parent and community involvement, a safe and orderly environment, and collegiality and professionalism (Marzano 2003).

> I want to be as emphatic as possible: the impact of the actual, taught curriculum on school quality, on student learning, is indescribably important. Robert Marzano did a meta-analysis of in-school factors that affect student achievement. Coming in at the top—first place—is *what gets taught*, what he calls a "guaranteed and viable curriculum." That is, if teachers can lay out a sound—a viable— set of standards and can then guarantee (more or less) that these standards actually get taught, we can raise levels of achievement immensely. (Schmoker 2006)

Educational reform efforts have by and large ignored this reality. Curriculum has been ignored in the United States for a variety of reasons. One is the lack of understanding of what a curriculum is or how effective curricula are created. Curriculum refers to "the systematic study of language and literature, science and mathematics, history, the arts, and foreign languages that convey important knowledge and skills, cultivate aesthetic imagination and teach students to think critically and reflectively about the world in which they live" (Ravitch 2000).

Without this understanding it is very easy to discount its importance. If teachers are expected to develop their own curriculums, then it must not be that difficult since they are supposed to be able to do this at the same time they are working with students and meeting all the other school responsibilities. With this perspective, published materials are simply a resource, and might be incorporated into the teacher lesson plans or not, depending on teacher choice, regardless of any curriculum scope and sequence. A worksheet, an activity, a chapter might be used or not. The quality of the materials or how they meet the standards is not all that important.

In addition to seeing curriculum materials as supplemental resources, the fact that curriculum in the United States is primarily developed by for-profit publishers makes it appear to many educators to be too commercial and have questionable motives. In addition, government entities are reluctant to promote one curriculum over another, interfering with the free market. There is abhorrence, also, to promoting a national curriculum. The free market through competition is supposed to inspire publishers to create the most effective curriculum at affordable costs.

What has happened, however, is that without informed consumers, the free market has incentivized publishers to compete on superfluous features and consolidate so much so that all of the major curriculums in each subject are virtually the same. In effect, we have a national curriculum that emphasizes design, an overwhelming number of components and pages, and current educational trends and fads. Even when excellent, effective resources are built into curricular materials, they are hidden or unrealized by consumers.

The importance of curriculum is not a recent revelation. In 1983, *A Nation at Risk* made the following recommendations that have yet to be realized:

1. Textbooks and other tools of learning and teaching should be upgraded and updated to assure more rigorous content. We call upon university scientists, scholars, and members of professional societies, in collaboration with master teachers, to help in this task, as they did in the post-*Sputnik* era. They should assist willing publishers in developing the products or publish their own alternatives where there are persistent inadequacies.
2. In considering textbooks for adoption, states and school districts should (a) evaluate texts and other materials on their ability to present rigorous and challenging material clearly; and (b) require publishers to furnish evaluation data on the material's effectiveness.
3. Because no textbook in any subject can be geared to the needs of all students, funds should be made available to support text development in "thin-market" areas, such as those for disadvantaged students, the learning disabled, and the gifted and talented.
4. To assure quality, all publishers should furnish evidence of the quality and appropriateness of textbooks, based on results from field trials and credible

evaluation. In view of the enormous numbers and varieties of texts available, more widespread consumer information services for purchasers are badly needed.

5. New instructional materials should reflect the most current applications of technology in appropriate curriculum areas, the best scholarship in each discipline, and research in learning and teaching. (National Commission on Excellence in Education 1983)

Instead of concentrating efforts on improving these critical elements, school reforms have focused on structure and management issues like competition between charter schools and public schools, merit pay, raising teaching credentials, raising standards, or increased use of technology. As evidenced from the stagnant NAEP test scores these efforts have not had the desired effects.

At the same time that educational reformers have been busy writing standards, funding small schools initiatives, changing legislation to inspire more charter schools, the curriculum that the majority of schools use from the major textbook providers has not improved over the years. Because the consumers of curricular materials do not recognize qualitative differences, and once standards have been addressed, believe all curriculum is equally effective, publishers have focused their energies on the elements that consumers do differentiate: design and graphics, technology applications, and the inclusion of more pages and components.

> A reason we have fallen behind so many of our international peers is perhaps that we have been pursuing the peripheral while they have been pursuing the fundamental. While we have been dabbling in pedagogical, management, and accountability fads, they have written common core curricula—and that has made all the difference. A common core curriculum is not just a piece of paper that guides the teacher; it is a living document that guides and brings coherence to the whole educational endeavor. (American Educator 2011)

While all these reform efforts have been under way, people just assume that teachers will be incentivized by merit pay or threatened by not making adequate yearly progress to improve curriculum on their own. Teacher expertise, however, is centered on content knowledge, classroom management, lesson planning, teaching methods, and understanding how children learn, not curriculum development. Quality curriculum development is a very different art form. Standards, even rigorous, high-quality standards, are not a curriculum. Quality curriculum presents thorough and accurate content that has been carefully reviewed. Quality curriculum translates standards into lesson objectives, organizes the lessons into a logical sequence that supports how students learn, and provides lesson plans, activities, and materials with concept introduction, development, practice, and assessments using effective practices.

To expect every teacher to create a complete curriculum for every subject defies logic. Even high school teachers devoted to one subject would have to spend years studying the subject to make sure it was comprehensive, reviewing educational research to identify the best teaching methods and how children learn, and then actually writing the materials in a coherent way. An elementary teacher teaches multiple subjects. The idea that they just know all the content as well as the most effective methods for teaching it and then can create all the materials to do so is absurd. It places totally unrealistic overwhelming expectations on teachers and completely devalues the contribution that curriculum developers make.

I suggest that student achievement is stagnant in large part because curriculum has been stagnant. And curriculum has been stagnant because customers have not purchased or implemented curricular materials that really can make a difference in student achievement. This is not to say that there are not some wonderful things in textbooks, but that those wonderful things are not the elements that affect student achievement or are not promoted and implemented with fidelity.

A solid curriculum that is systematically upgraded with updated content, improved teaching methods, and new tools as they are discovered, and then implemented with fidelity by experienced teachers can slowly but surely improve student achievement. Focusing reform efforts on incentivizing the development of quality curriculum and building teacher expertise to be able to recognize and implement effective curriculum will positively impact what teachers and students do *every day*.

Amazingly, the two elements—curriculum and teacher expertise—that have the most potential to have the greatest effect on student achievement have been the most mysterious and least studied. Merit pay incentives or fear of not making adequate yearly progress are supposed to somehow magically cause improvements in curriculum and teaching. If, however, schools can't identify what they need to do to impact student achievement, they are unlikely to do it.

It is clear that the desired results are interdependent. To advance student achievement, improved teaching methods and improved curriculum are necessary. If curricula were systematically revised based on educational research to bring the most effective methods to the classroom, and teachers used the curricula to continually develop expertise, student achievement would be positively affected. As teachers develop expertise, they will be much more capable of identifying and implementing the most effective curriculum. Examining the relationship between teachers and textbooks helps to explain underlying causes.

TEACHERS AND TEXTBOOKS:
THE DYSFUNCTIONAL RELATIONSHIP

Walk into almost any school and you will see an array of curricular materials: textbooks, workbooks, math manipulatives such as counting rods and pattern blocks, educational software, flash cards, posters, and countless other tools intended to support instruction. Schools purchase textbook series and educational materials to deliver curriculum. Teachers spend a lot of their own money on supplemental materials, as well. Yet these materials are used and not used in vastly different ways from teacher to teacher, school to school, and subject to subject, resulting in what has been called "curricular chaos" (Schmoker 2006). This virtually ensures stagnant student achievement.

Because teachers are most insecure about their content knowledge in math and because math is a measure of adequate yearly progress, mathematics textbooks are used most religiously. On the other extreme, very few language arts textbooks are used in this manner. In language arts, including writing, grammar, usage, mechanics, and spelling, worksheets and implementing the writing process have turned many former language arts textbooks into handbooks. Handbooks provide information but not curriculum. Science and social studies textbooks, which require significant amounts of reading, have been relegated to second class status because they are not tested nationally in the same way as reading and mathematics. As a result, teachers use curriculum haphazardly.

> In most schools, even the most talented, hard-working teachers do not typically follow a common curriculum. Despite slight improvements here, teachers continue to enter a system that allows them to teach largely what they want, regardless of importance or priority, at variance with any kind of coherent or agreed-upon curriculum. (Schmoker 2006)

Without a curriculum in place, there is no consistency from class to class, let alone from grade to grade, or school to school. In one third grade class, for example, the teacher may decide to emphasize writing, while in another, the teacher emphasizes grammar and mechanics. When students are in fourth grade, one group will be at a disadvantage.

Using a particular curriculum, however, even with fidelity, does not ensure greater student achievement. The free market nature of the textbook adoption and purchase process has resulted in materials that are almost guaranteed to promote the status quo. The highest selling materials year after year are those that supposedly make teachers' lives easier. They require little change from what teachers had been doing and include texts that are easier to read and include multimedia explanations and more options, such as supplemental technology, note-taking lessons, extra practice workbooks, and assessment and presentation software. They do not provide any innovation or insights in new teaching methods or how children learn. Those types of materials do not sell because they look like too much work. When innovative elements are included in curricular materials, they are often buried deep and many educators do not realize they are there. Unless teachers understand the importance of implementing specific methods in particular sequences, they have no incentive to incorporate changes into their methods.

It is not difficult to understand why this situation exists. Colleges of education that prepare teachers for the classroom virtually ignore curriculum. They teach their students about educational philosophy, some teaching methods, and how to plan lessons. When panicked new teachers enter the classroom, they often have the impression that they are required to create the entire curriculum and all the materials themselves. They may be relieved to have educational materials to use, but quickly get the impression that textbooks are inferior to what a really good teacher should do. With a background in lesson planning but without a background in curriculum development, it is easy to see that this would make sense.

This attitude is reinforced for the most part in popular media and in most professional development outlets, including teacher conferences and teaching magazines. In popular media, the only news about textbooks or curricula that emerges is related to a particular controversy. The popular media is devoid of any information about effective curriculum. If and when a school adopts a curriculum and experiences increased student achievement, any good news rarely if ever considers the new curriculum as a cause. Professional development, teacher conferences, and popular teaching magazines focus on lesson planning, specific strategies or teaching methods, or trends. If they do mention educational materials, they focus on teacher created or supplemental materials that address a particular skill or lesson, not curricular materials.

The impression that all textbooks and published curricula are inferior is further reinforced by many in the academic community who publish blanket condemnations of textbooks.

> Sit down and read a textbook in any subject. Read the boring, abbreviated pap in the history textbooks that reduces stirring events, colorful personalities, and riveting controversies to a dull page or a few leaden paragraphs. Read the literature textbooks with their heavy overlay of pedagogical jargon and their meager representation of any significant literature. (Ravitch 2010)

With no background in curriculum and such negative press, it is no wonder that teachers would not expect any published curriculum to be any good and would hide the fact that they use it.

In fact, publishers go to extraordinary lengths to create meaningful curriculum that will meet the standards and appeal to teachers. Publishers of basal reading programs and high school literature anthologies spend millions of dollars securing permissions to reproduce authentic literature and countless hours selecting works that are in an appropriate reading range so children can read them, fitting themes to build comprehension, and representing a wide range of authors.

Open any current history textbook and in addition to efforts to write an accurate and engaging narrative, you will find short biographies of key figures in history, history through art features, an analysis of political cartoons, point/counterpoint arguments about historical issues, and historical controversies that are still debated today.

The criticism that textbooks are boring is completely subjective. A typical student would condemn *any* history or science text, no matter how riveting or boring, simply because it represents schoolwork. Publishers have included suggested trade literature to read in addition to the text that supposedly is engaging prose, but by and large those books, too, are "boring" to students. Reading a textbook or even watching a historical documentary or what many would call an exciting science program will not engage typical students. The majority of children would not choose to participate in these activities unless they were assigned. This is where the teaching comes into play. It is the teacher's use of the material, the assignments, discussions, and activities that are necessary to teach a subject and build understanding. Only the most self-motivated students are interested enough in all topics and have the perseverance to teach themselves.

All students will not be riveted by every lesson, even with great teachers. Some students will not be riveted by any school lesson. The goal of public education is to *educate* students not to entertain them. If students are entertained by learning or while learning, so much the better, but the pursuit of entertainment too often sends classrooms down the wrong path. The best teachers motivate students to work to develop skills and understandings, even when students are uninterested. The best curricular materials provide a comprehensive development of concepts, a survey of a course that builds along student learning trajectories and is supported with meaningful activities, appropriate readings, practice, and assessments to monitor understanding. It is the building of skills and the understanding of concepts that creates excitement and engagement in school.

Like adults, students are motivated by autonomy, being able to do something by themselves; mastery, being really good at something; and purpose, learning things that are worthwhile (Pink 2009). The familiar statements "Let me do it myself!" and "Why do I have to know this?" are reflections of these motivations.

Teachers and textbooks have the same goal: to educate students and promote student achievement. But they do not get along well enough to accomplish this goal. Teachers do not appreciate what curriculum can do to help them in their efforts; textbooks, in their desire to be selected, downplay their value and promote the superfluous. One cannot do an effective job without the other, however. Teachers cannot create the entire curriculum by themselves and without teachers textbooks are worthless for the vast majority of students, who are not able to teach themselves.

PreK–12 schools are responsible to the public to develop children's abilities to read and write and understand and use mathematics. Schools are responsible for exposing students to science, social studies, art and music that they would not otherwise encounter to help them become informed and productive citizens. PreK–12 schooling is centered on agreed upon standards of learning that identify what students should know and be able to do at specific grade levels. This makes preK–12 education significantly different from postsecondary and adult education. It takes teachers using curriculum to accomplish this.

Teaching reading is not a question of looking up a bit of information on the Internet. It requires explicit instruction and practice in identifying sounds and relating them to letters and words and then building comprehension. Education is not about giving students a choice of whether they want to learn how to add and subtract. To lay out the careful skill and concept development in the most efficient and effective way requires a good curriculum and to present it requires a good teacher.

Good educational standards are carefully constructed to identify skills *and* applications of skills in meaningful contexts. But it is serious skill and concept development that happens in schools. A high school student reading on a first grade level is not going to learn how to read "just in time." No third grader, or even a ninth grader, knows what the future will hold for them. Public school education is about equipping students with the foundational skills and understandings, the tools that will best prepare them for an unknown future and that will enable them to be successful in any endeavor.

> An education is an enlightening and enriching experience that results in a body of knowledge and skill—both academic and social—that enables one to be a responsible and productive citizen. What is fundamental to an education is the specific body of knowledge and skill, and the best means of acquiring it; what is peripheral is everything else. (American Educator 2011)

This is not an endorsement of one curriculum or a national curriculum. Because education is constantly evolving and there is such diversity in the student and faculty populations, it is highly advantageous to have a variety of highly effective materials that are systematically upgraded as new information becomes available. Materials that are effective for a group of struggling students may not be as effective for advanced students or even average students. Unfortunately, with the consolidation of the textbook industry, there are few choices. If, however, publishers begin to target their efforts and resources on creating effective materials for different populations of students because effectiveness is the most competitive focus, the free market should allow for a new generation of effective materials that address the needs of different populations of students.

Using the best curriculum, strategies, and methods to teach the agreed upon state and national standards is what should guide educators. It is irresponsible to do otherwise.

To improve student achievement will take the continual improvement of the teaching arts (content knowledge, teaching methods, lesson planning abilities, understanding of how children learn, and classroom management skills). These arts of teaching can be developed and supported by using improved curricular materials with understanding and fidelity. The dysfunctional relationship in which teachers try to create all of their own curriculum, disregard the materials they have available to use, and have such low expectations for the effectiveness of published materials has resulted in stagnant student achievement levels. The two things that matter—teacher expertise and a viable curriculum—should be the focus of all reform efforts.

The following recommendations are suggestions for advancing student achievement by focusing on the education elements that matter. These suggestions involve the principles of effective professional development:

- Focuses on teachers as central to student learning, yet includes all other members of the school community;
- Focuses on individual, collegial, and organizational improvement;
- Respects and nurtures the intellectual and leadership capacity of teachers, principals, and others in the school community;
- Reflects best available research and practice in teaching, learning, and leadership;
- Enables teachers to develop further expertise in subject content, teaching strategies, uses of technologies, and other essential elements in teaching to high standards;
- Promotes continuous inquiry and improvement embedded in the daily life of schools;
- Is planned collaboratively by those who will participate in and facilitate that development;

- Requires substantial time and other resources;
- Is driven by a coherent long-term plan;
- Is evaluated ultimately on the basis of its impact on teacher effectiveness and student learning; and this assessment guides subsequent development efforts. (WestEd 2000)

The recommendations are focused on three goals designed to build and improve the arts of teaching and select and implement the best available curriculum to support teachers with the ultimate goal of improving student achievement.

1. Build personal teacher expertise in understanding and recognizing guaranteed and viable curriculum, which will also improve teacher understanding of and expertise in content knowledge, teaching methods, children's learning trajectories, and lesson planning.
2. Carefully evaluate and select the best available curriculum to not only make the best curriculum available to teachers and students but to incentivize curriculum developers to prioritize effectiveness in curriculum development.
3. Implement improved curriculum with fidelity across all grades and in every classroom.

BUILDING TEACHER EXPERTISE

Teachers come in as many shapes and sizes as students do. One teacher may inspire one child and cripple another. There is no one winning style that works for all children. When asked to write about their most influential teacher, a group of graduate students identified teachers from a range of teaching styles, from teachers who let students guide their own instruction to teachers who demand students follow a specific path (Dockterman 1997). Teaching style does not dictate teacher quality. All of these people would be considered "good" teachers.

Teaching is the cumulative effect of the choices teachers make every day. The choices in lesson planning, classroom management, and teaching methods all have an impact on student achievement. A teacher may choose to use cooperative grouping for one part of a lesson to build communication skills or use whole class grouping. A teacher may choose to ignore a student infraction so as not to derail a lesson or may choose to address it. A teacher may choose to go to the computer lab on one day to have students conduct their project research on the Internet. A group of teachers chooses one curriculum over another. These are all choices that are within the power of teachers to make.

Teachers' choices are informed by many influences, including their own experience as students, their preservice education, their experience in the classroom, what they learn from other teachers, the curriculum they use, and professional development. Better teachers make better choices in each of the arts of teaching: content knowledge, classroom management, lesson planning, teaching methods, and understanding how children learn. The best professional development is that which focuses on helping teachers understand and make better choices in the classroom.

> Let's look at just one teacher to see the full power of good instruction. As a high school English instructor, Sean Connors took a position in the poorest, lowest-achieving high school in his community, where writing scores were the lowest in town and well below the state average. I watched him teach. He was clear, organized, and effective. But more to the point, he did nothing unusual—nothing any teacher couldn't do or hasn't already learned. He was clear about which writing standards he expected students to learn on any particular day. He showed them samples of the kind of work he expected, and had students analyze and discuss the samples. He explained and modeled each specific skill—with students' involvement—on his overhead projector. He had students practice the new skills briefly in pairs, then individually while he circulated. He called on students randomly to share, so he could see if they were learning. Some educators call this a "check for understanding."
>
> When Connors felt that students were ready, he assessed how well they had learned the new skill. There's nothing exotic in this approach. This simple lesson structure could be effectively repeated or varied for an endless number of standards, eventually saving precious preparation time. (Schmoker 2006)

Increasing teacher expertise will not only improve student experiences in the classroom, the more teachers know about content, classroom management, lesson planning, how children learn, and effective teaching methods, the better they will be able to identify, select, and implement the most effective curriculum and make intelligent adjustments for poor curriculum. Being discriminating consumers of curriculum will incentivize publishers to compete to create more effective materials.

Understanding teacher expertise and implementing strategies to develop it are critical steps in improving curriculum and student achievement.

Understanding Teacher Expertise

Schools need expert educators. The difference between experts and nonexperts is not that one does things well and the other does things badly. Rather, the experts address problems and continually expand their knowledge base and competence, whereas nonexperts carry out practiced routines. It is when routines fail, as they do when student achievement remains static, that the difference between experts and nonexperts shows itself.

> The career of the expert is one of progressively advancing on the problems constituting a field of work, whereas the career of the nonexpert is one of gradually constricting the field of work so that it more closely conforms to the routines the nonexpert is prepared to execute. Study and practice build up the knowledge that makes one an expert. (Bereiter and Scardamalia 1993)

According to Bereiter and Scardamalia, experts are not smarter or innately more talented. They are better at solving problems in their domains because of the knowledge they can draw on, knowledge that is so effective that it enables experts to get by with *less* thinking than nonexperts. Their depth of knowledge allows them to focus on the important, relevant considerations. Expert doctors don't reinvent a new technique or procedure for each new patient. Through their experience, they can identify and solve most problems that relate to their areas of expertise. They begin by using the standard techniques and procedures based on their own experience and the experience of other doctors over the years. When they encounter something they don't recognize, they expand their competence to learn about it and try different remedies.

It takes a great deal of time to become an expert. Some estimate as much as ten thousand hours, which would be equivalent to a minimum of two years of teaching. Beginning teachers go through a novice stage in which they are starving for help and support and curriculum to give them lessons and strategies to use. As they gain confidence, they add more to their repertoire. After more experience, they become competent and apply goal-directed plans and strategies. When a teacher has accumulated enough experience, he or she can quickly assess and recognize what needs to be done and has less need for planning and problem solving. As teachers become experts, a lot of decision making becomes unnecessary and, like expert craftspeople, they naturally do the right thing without having to think much about it.

Experts choose opportunities to learn as much as they can about their craft. For example, they read magazines related to their field and seek out experiences that will enrich their knowledge. Nonexperts minimize their opportunities for growth. Given the same unique problem, experts will work harder and do a great deal more thinking because they want to figure it out to learn more. Expert teachers are not going to change for the sake of change or follow fads that will not materialize into student achievement. But they will seek more knowledge and problem solve to invent new processes and methods when the old ones are not working.

When researchers ran the numbers in dozens of different studies, every factor under a school's control produced just a tiny impact, except for one: which teacher the student had been assigned to. Some teachers could regularly lift their students' test scores above the average for children of the same race, class and ability level. Others' students left with below-average results year after year. William Sanders, a statistician studying Tennessee teachers with a colleague, found that a student with a weak teacher for three straight years would score, on average, 50 percentile points behind a similar student with a strong teacher for those years. Teachers working in the same building, teaching the same grade, produced very different outcomes. And the gaps were huge. Eric Hanushek, a Stanford economist, found that while the top 5 percent of teachers were able to impart a year and a half's worth of learning to students in one school year, as judged by standardized tests, the weakest 5 percent advanced their students only half a year of material each year. (Green 2010)

There are expert educators in every school. Some are content experts. Some are expert planners. Some are expert technicians, knowing how to manage a classroom. Some are expert at identifying the most effective teaching methods.

An education system that develops and recognizes expertise, learns from it, shares knowledge, and encourages experts to tackle and solve problems and lay the foundation for continual improvement will have improved student achievement.

Identifying Teacher Experts

In every school, there are teachers who have strengths in the different teaching arts. Some may be content experts, even if they are not strong in classroom management. Others may have great relationships with students and have good classroom management, but struggle with lesson planning.

The first step is to have teachers identify their own and each other's strengths by conducting an anonymous survey that rates all teachers in the school on each area of teaching. Curriculum specialists, principals, department heads, or lead teachers could conduct the survey and record the results. For example, using table 7.1, each teacher in the school could be rated 1–5 in each of the areas of expertise with 1 being a weakness and 5 being a strength.

Following the survey, teachers with a 4 or 5 rating in a category would be asked to conduct a ten to fifteen minute training session in which they describe what they do in their area of expertise and how they developed their methods. They would then answer questions and serve as a resource for other teachers.

These sessions could be scheduled during staff meetings or arranged at their own time to provide ongoing, relevant, and coherent professional development in the art of teaching.

Table 7.1. Sample Teacher Rating Survey

Teacher Name	Depth of Content Knowledge	Effective Classroom Control, Management, Discipline, and Technique	Comprehensive Lesson Preparation	Effective Teaching Methods	Understanding Children's Learning Trajectories
Florence Masters	1 2 ③ 4 5	1 2 3 4 ⑤	1 2 3 ④ 5	1 2 ③ 4 5	1 ② 3 4 5
	1 2 3 4 5	1 2 3 4 5	1 2 3 4 5	1 2 3 4 5	1 2 3 4 5
	1 2 3 4 5	1 2 3 4 5	1 2 3 4 5	1 2 3 4 5	1 2 3 4 5
	1 2 3 4 5	1 2 3 4 5	1 2 3 4 5	1 2 3 4 5	1 2 3 4 5
	1 2 3 4 5	1 2 3 4 5	1 2 3 4 5	1 2 3 4 5	1 2 3 4 5
	1 2 3 4 5	1 2 3 4 5	1 2 3 4 5	1 2 3 4 5	1 2 3 4 5
	1 2 3 4 5	1 2 3 4 5	1 2 3 4 5	1 2 3 4 5	1 2 3 4 5
	1 2 3 4 5	1 2 3 4 5	1 2 3 4 5	1 2 3 4 5	1 2 3 4 5
	1 2 3 4 5	1 2 3 4 5	1 2 3 4 5	1 2 3 4 5	1 2 3 4 5
	1 2 3 4 5	1 2 3 4 5	1 2 3 4 5	1 2 3 4 5	1 2 3 4 5
	1 2 3 4 5	1 2 3 4 5	1 2 3 4 5	1 2 3 4 5	1 2 3 4 5

Rate teachers in each category from Low (1) to High (5).

Weekly or biweekly teacher meetings that focus on discussing a standard, what it means, what methods are most effective for achieving it, and whether the school's curriculum needs support is a simple way to promote professional development, provide new teachers with needed support, and allow expert teachers to share their knowledge.

Incentivizing Teachers to Develop Expertise

Merit pay and bonuses don't motivate teachers. In his book *Drive,* Daniel Pink reports that not only have there been instances of cheating to receive merit pay, but even when teachers were offered up to $15,000 in bonuses for good test scores, the incentives had zero impact on student performance (Pink 2009). Monetary incentives don't even motivate a lot of people in business. Furthermore, merit pay inspires competition among teachers. Pitting teachers against one another hoping that it will inspire them to perform better rarely works and destroys self-motivation. Successful schools build teams of teachers who collaborate and cooperate to promote student achievement.

Teaching isn't about money. No one goes into teaching to earn bonuses. Of course, a teacher wants to earn a respectable living, but like other professionals, teachers tend to divorce themselves from salary considerations and focus on managing their classrooms and working with students. Few teachers bother to calculate their hourly rate, and the predictable pay structure based on years of service encourages them not to. Several studies have shown that experiments with merit pay are not effective. One experiment tested whether rewarding teachers for improved student test scores would cause scores to rise. It was left up to the teacher to determine what he or she needed to do to raise the scores. The hypothesis was that incentivizing teachers would improve test scores.

> By and large, results did not confirm this hypothesis. While the general trend in middle school mathematics performance was upward over the period of the project, students of teachers randomly assigned to the treatment group (eligible for bonuses) did not outperform students whose teachers were assigned to the control group (not eligible for bonuses). (Springer et al. 2010)

Teachers are driven by the things that have been shown to motivate the vast majority of people: autonomy, the desire to direct our own lives; mastery, the urge to make progress and get better at something that matters; and purpose, the yearning to do what we do in the service of something larger than ourselves (Pink 2009). Teachers may be more driven by purpose than other people. The greatest reward a teacher ever receives is an emotional one. It's having students come back to see them and tell them what a difference they made in their lives. Testimonials like, "You were my favorite teacher." "You taught me how to read . . . or write . . . or love science . . . or math." "I'm glad you made me work hard." "You made me believe in myself." This is what motivates teachers. Pulitzer Prize–winner Kathleen Parker's tribute to her eleventh grade English teacher is the kind of testament that motivates teachers to inspire their students and make a difference in their lives. No monetary award could come anywhere close to matching this bonus. It makes me cry every time I read it.

> The teacher was mine for only three months, but he changed my life in a flicker of light. I thought of him Monday when—if you'll grant me this small indulgence—I was awarded the Pulitzer Prize for commentary. . . .
>
> Every living soul knows the feeling of helplessness when a crowd of peers awaits the answer you do not know. Whatever I said was utterly ridiculous, I suppose, because my classmates erupted in peals of laughter.
>
> I have not forgotten that moment, or the next, during all these years. As I was trying to figure out how to hurl myself under my desk, Mr. Gasque tossed me a sugarcoated, tangerine-colored lifesaver from the good ship lollipop.
>
> He whirled. No perfectly executed pirouette can top the spin executed by Mr. Gasque that day. Suddenly facing the class, he flushed crimson and his voice trembled with rage.
>
> "Don't. You. Ever. Laugh. At her. Again," he said. "She can out-write every one of you any day of the week."
>
> It is not possible to describe my gratitude. Time suspended and I dangled languorously from a fluff of cloud while my colleagues drowned in stunned silence. I dangle even now, like those silly participles I eventually got to know. Probably no one but me remembers Mr. Gasque's act of paternal chivalry, but I basked in those words and in the thought that what he said might be true. I started that day to try to write as well as he said I could. I am still trying. (Parker 2010)

Too often educators work in isolation. When they work together effectively and learn from and share with each other, they promote student achievement. Identifying and recognizing teachers with strengths in the arts of teaching and having them share their strategies with others is one way to reward and incentivize teachers to develop expertise. This acknowledges teacher autonomy and recognizes mastery in a purposeful mission.

Promoting opportunities to learn and work together and providing the tools, resources, and strategies to help each teacher become memorable will not only improve teacher competence but also promote student achievement.

Expertise and Respect

Education is a noble endeavor. People who are willing to commit their energies to educating others in whatever capacity deserve respect. Denigrating teachers, principals, superintendents, boards of education, schools of education, publishers, and politicians is not just a waste of time, it defeats the goal of improving the system and sets us back. Yet some people advocate starting over, firing the teachers, throwing out the curriculum, or even waiting for a new crop of students to come in (Dillon 2010).

Respect for educators is a characteristic of countries with the highest student achievement. A 2011 study found that "international comparisons show that in the countries with the highest performance, teachers are typically paid better relative to others, education credentials are valued more, and a higher share of educational spending is devoted to instructional services than is the case in the United States" (Paine and Schleicher 2011). Furthermore, Sue Szachowicz, the principal of Brockton High in Massachusetts, which saw the most improvement in student achievement of any school in the state, demonstrated that student achievement can be improved by changing methods, not personnel.

> I think the concept of "turnaround" is the most deceptive word that you can use because it implies people from the outside leaping into the school to turn everything. And, in fact, our turnaround was dramatic in terms of the success of the students, but it's been about 10 years of hard work. The key to our success has been adult learning. If you don't change how someone does something, of course you're not going to get different results. So we did not fire all the teachers. We did work with the team that we had and we've had some pretty dramatic results. (Szachowicz 2011)

Firing all experienced teachers and replacing them with Teach for America recruits will not solve our student achievement stagnation problem, and it disrespects the incredible amount of knowledge that experienced teachers have accumulated. Ignoring all the work that has gone into developing curriculum ensures that the same mistakes will be repeated due to the failure to learn from history. Such an action also shows a callous lack of respect for the knowledge and experience that curriculum developers have to offer. We need to start with what we have and improve it. All participants now and in the past have contributed to the education knowledge base through their successes and their failures. As Newton said, "If I have seen further, it is only by standing on the shoulders of giants."

Instead of wasting time looking for someone to blame for the plateau in student achievement, we should respect the knowledge gained by the trials of others and mobilize our current resources to improve our system to move beyond the plateau and prepare our students for the future.

DEVELOPING THE ARTS OF TEACHING

Developing teacher expertise in each of the five arts of teaching will improve classroom experience and develop more informed consumers of curriculum. To improve teacher quality and consequently student achievement, each of these five areas should be addressed.

1. Depth of Content Knowledge
2. Effective Classroom Control, Management, Discipline, and Technique
3. Comprehensive Lesson Preparation
4. Effective Teaching Methods
5. Understanding Children's Learning Trajectories

One way to develop teacher expertise is in preservice teacher education. There is no question that efforts to improve the quality of preservice education by making it more rigorous and relevant are important. For the vast majority of practicing teachers, however, in-service education and professional development are required.

The most effective in-service education is conducted by teachers, addressing relevance, coherence, and commitment to continuous improvement. What could be more relevant than building content knowledge, lesson planning, and teaching method expertise in the service of teaching a quality curriculum that teaches to rigorous standards and follows children's learning trajectories? Instead of distracting efforts in fads, new technologies, or writing curriculum, building expertise in what teachers do every day in the classroom after choosing the most effective curriculum based on research has great potential for increasing student achievement.

The suggestions for developing the arts of teaching are intended to be initial steps to building teacher expertise that can be accomplished within the confines of the school community.

Developing Depth of Content Knowledge

Although content knowledge alone does not make an effective teacher, it is a critical element of teacher expertise. Whatever curriculum is being used is a source of content knowledge, and as teacher expertise develops, teachers will be able to recognize the differences in the quality of the content in different curriculums. In addition to recognizing and promoting genuine interest in content, schools can help to develop teachers' content knowledge in the following ways.

Collaborate on Studying the Standards

Purpose: To provide collaborative efforts to understand teaching objectives, improve teaching methods, and establish a leadership group to promote ongoing professional development.

Schools are responsible for meeting the agreed-upon state or national standards. Curriculum materials may provide pathways to teaching toward the standards but without teacher understanding and knowledge of the standards, it is very easy for schools to miss the mark. Weekly or biweekly teacher meetings that focus on discussing a standard, what it means, what methods are most effective for achieving it, and whether the school's curriculum needs support is a simple way to promote professional development, provide new teachers with needed support, and allow expert teachers to share their knowledge.

These meetings of grade level or subject area teachers could have a standing agenda: read the standard, discuss what it means, plot the concepts that lead to the standard, evaluate the curriculum being used to see if the concepts are developed, and determine the most effective methods for developing the standard. These sessions could not only help to educate new teachers, they also could encourage all teachers to reevaluate their own methods. Standards discussions could be repeated year after year as new methods are tested and new teachers and ideas come into the school.

Studying the standards would also educate faculty about the standards and make them better evaluators of curriculum. If teachers agree on what the standards require, they can more easily evaluate whether a curriculum will help them achieve the standards or whether they are on their own. These meetings could develop expertise among the faculty and, when they are ready to invest in a new curriculum, incentivize publishers to produce more effective materials.

Use Existing Curriculum for Content Development

Purpose: To develop faculty expertise using relevant materials and strategies.

Whatever curriculum is being used in a school can provide the lessons for ongoing professional development. In professional development sessions, teachers can analyze the teaching methods, the lesson progressions, and the content to identify strengths and weaknesses. Teachers using the same curriculum can compare the way they implement the curriculum and determine if and how the implementation choices impact student achievement. Curriculum is primarily for teachers and if "it has any effect on pupils, it will have it by virtue of having had an effect on teachers" (Bruner 1977).

If a curriculum has been adopted based on its incorporation of sound practices and the quality of the development of standards along learning trajectories, then educating the faculty on using the curriculum is a very effective form of professional development. A new reading curriculum can teach faculty about the most effective strategies for teaching phonemic awareness, phonics, decoding skills, and comprehension. Science and mathematics curricula with intentional background information for teachers can give them the foundation in these subjects they may have missed in their formal education. Training in a new effective curriculum can help break away from the status quo of student achievement.

Curriculum has the advantage of being relevant to the day-to-day classroom experience.

> Conversations around the curriculum and about some of the adaptations teachers may need or want to make can help them think through facets of the subject matter, as well as the consequences of instructional decisions for student learning. The goal of conversations around curriculum materials is not to make teachers technicians, but to help them understand that curriculum materials are professional tools, tools that when used thoughtfully and well can help them with their job. (Grossman et al. 2000)

Even an inadequate curriculum provides effective professional development. Expert educators can explain why a series of lessons or methods is inadequate and demonstrate more effective practices. This gives new faculty a chance to learn the most effective practices, expert teachers an opportunity to share their knowledge, and schools to provide consistent and coherent educational experiences for their students.

Developing Effective Classroom Control, Management, Discipline, and Technique

Without effective classroom management, teachers cannot hope to accomplish much in the classroom. Good classroom management involves relating to students, motivating them, and maintaining order so that students have the opportunity to learn.

Focus on Building Relationships with Students

Purpose: To promote student engagement and achievement.

A May 2011 report shows that it is the quality of relationships between staff and students and between staff and parents that most strongly defines safe schools. The study showed that students in disadvantaged schools in high poverty environments that had high-quality relationships actually felt safer than students in advantaged schools with low-quality relationships. The report analyzed the internal and external conditions that matter for feelings of safety and then the extent to which factors under the control of the schools mediate those external influences and how the strongest determinant of safety is the degree to which the school enrolls high-achieving students (Steinberg, Allensworth, and Johnson 2011). The quality of relationships between staff and students is important in a school's sense of safety and also in student achievement.

To increase student achievement, instead of diverting resources and energy so that a few may benefit, it seems that efforts would more effectively be focused on developing relationships within the school. This would improve school quality across the board, ensuring that all schools across the nation meet standards for safety, teacher quality, and access to resources so that they can meet the needs of the diverse populations of students in each community.

Recognize That Learning Is Work

Purpose: To set realistic expectations for learning.

Students excel in the same way experts become experts. They work at it, and it is a long, developmental process. Some students appear to just know how to add and subtract but the secret is that for some students math is not work so they get a lot of practice through play. For some children reading is such a pleasure that they can't stop reading. Of course, with more practice these children are going to be better at math and reading. There's no magic to it.

Education involves learning skills and then applying them in purposeful activities. Students learn the alphabet, how letters correspond to sounds, how to spell words, the structure of a sentence, a paragraph, and a composition in order to apply those skills in meaningful writing. Students learn the number system, how to count, add, subtract, multiply, and divide so that they can apply those skills in understanding how mathematics helps make sense of the world.

Children do gain a lot of information and knowledge incidentally from their environment, but very few children are going to learn to read, develop a strong vocabulary, learn advanced mathematics, history, government, or the complex ideas of science without formal schooling.

Students who are behind their peers need more work, more instruction, and more practice. Identifying and grouping students with those who are on the same levels on learning trajectories and providing additional support and alternative ways of teaching concepts during afterschool hours or summer school to meet grade level standards are answers to addressing the needs of struggling students.

Learning to read, write, calculate, and understand the principles of science and social studies takes years of work and is not a function of a child's particular interest, talent, or inheritance. Acknowledging this can inspire new curriculum materials and methods that will likely provide more focused, efficient, and effective learning opportunities.

Build Student Engagement through Student Achievement

Purpose: To prioritize student achievement above all other concerns.

Student engagement is typically defined as the willingness of a student to make a psychological investment in learning. It is a rare child who doesn't come to kindergarten willing to make an investment in learning. They want to learn to read. They want to learn what school has to offer. If a child achieves some success in school and begins to gain meaningful skills and knowledge, he or she is likely to remain engaged. Promoting student engagement is not the same as entertaining students. Identifying the appropriate place a child is on the learning trajectory, allowing them to have a chance to achieve understanding, is critical to promoting student engagement. Students can be entertained without learning or achieving anything. It is working, learning, and achieving with purpose that is most engaging.

In Daniel Pink's work *Drive,* he identifies the three motivators that engage people: autonomy, the desire to direct our own lives; mastery, the urge to make progress and get better at something that matters; and purpose, the yearning to do what we do in the service of something larger than ourselves (Pink 2009). Children are no different. Pink asserts that instead of challenging students into engagement, we are bribing them into compliance with mediocre results. Offering to pay children for grades, punishing them for lack of effort, or rewarding them for doing nothing are all disincentives to student engagement.

The age-old question that students ask, "Why do I have to learn this?" is an inkling of their need for purpose. When school is focused on student achievement of the standards that have been developed to provide a meaningful education for productive citizens, purpose is evident.

Unfortunately many professional development efforts and assessments have focused not on student achievement but on inconsequential elements.

Reforms in the United States often are tied to particular theories of teaching or to educational fads instead of specific learning outcomes. Because of this, success often is measured by the degree to which teachers implement recommended practices. Someone is marked as a good teacher because he or she uses

cooperative groups or concrete manipulatives, instead of on the basis of his or
her students' successful learning. (Stigler and Hiebert 1999)

Countless articles about educational technology argue that technology will
promote student engagement, and studies show that student engagement
is the main way that teachers measure their success (Coggshal, Ott, and
Lasanga 2010). But student engagement does not always equate to student
achievement. By prioritizing student achievement in everything schools do,
educators can provide engaging activities that have the purpose of promoting
student achievement. At first, this can be as simple as identifying the learning
objective behind every activity and how it relates to the standards. It can also
be accomplished by analyzing what the best tool for each learning objective
is. As this becomes second nature, it can be realized by identifying, planning,
and sequencing activities that develop from one to another.

A new initiative was launched in April 2011 between the Pearson Foundation and the Bill & Melinda Gates Foundation to fund an instructional system
and twenty-four online courses covering K–12 English language arts and
K–10 math. This initiative, developed with the intent to widen access and
spur innovation around the Common Core Standards, is designed to "engage
and motivate" students and to incorporate social networking, gaming, video,
and simulation, coupled with assessment and teacher professional development, both online and blended (Nagel 2011).

The fact that the program is primarily focused on student engagement
rather than student achievement is troublesome. Publishers, Pearson included,
have been developing materials designed to "engage and motivate" students
around the standards for at least fifty years. While the goals are lofty and are
filled with promise with the two foundations behind them, it would seem
that it should succeed. But prioritizing student engagement and focusing on
technologies instead of the most effective instruction, content, and methods to
increase student achievement has resulted in disappointing results regardless
of how much time, energy, and money is spent.

There are so many people shouting in education that it is very confusing to
stay focused on what matters. Schools are responsible for educating children
and promoting student achievement. As a result of the confusion, there are
many, many methods and products being used that take up a great deal of
valuable time but don't promote or support student achievement. Educational
software should be motivating but it should primarily have an educational
purpose that ties into the larger curriculum.

> While having a wide variety of tools at the disposal of teachers and students
> is a laudable goal, in making these purchases, it seems like the learning objec-
> tives are secondary to acquiring the tools. . . . While districts look for as many

ways as possible to use the digital technology in which they have invested, educators and parents must ask whether digital technology is always the best route to learning. In many cases, it might not be. We need to ask what criteria should be used when deciding whether to incorporate digital technology into a lesson. What lessons will be enhanced by digital technology and which could best be accomplished using other tools? These questions reflect the complexity of teaching and demonstrate that no one method, such as the integration of digital technology, is superior in all instances. I am not suggesting a complete dismissal of digital technology, but I do suggest re-examining our priorities. (Bess 2011)

This is not to say that student engagement is irrelevant, that technology should never be used in schools, or that there should never be a pizza party. Technology should be used in the service of the most effective methods to advance student achievement. Having students use word processors to produce writing assignments has demonstrated benefits for high school writing over handwritten assignments. Certainly a continual assessment of new technologies and software to evaluate their potential for improving student achievement over mechanical methods is warranted. But taking valuable time to use technology because it is available, even if it is not a proven method to increase student achievement, is a disservice.

Developing Lesson Preparation Skills

Lesson preparation is the ability to identify lesson objectives, prepare materials that will develop those objectives, and organize the introduction, practice, and assessment of concepts in a way to maximize student understanding. When teachers develop expertise in lesson planning, they not only become more effective teachers, they can discriminate between effective and ineffective strategies in different curriculum materials.

Use Existing Curriculum to Develop Lesson Planning Expertise

Purpose: To develop faculty expertise using relevant materials and strategies.

In professional development sessions, teachers can analyze the strengths and weakness of the teaching methods and the lesson progressions in the curriculum. They can participate in lesson study sessions in which they go through a specific lesson and discuss whether the objectives are sound and the introduction, practice, and assessment of concepts will promote student understanding. Experienced teachers can help newer teachers identify more effective planning techniques. Newer teachers may be able to provide innovative insights or questions about established practices. Both can develop their critical analysis skills.

The value of analyzing the existing curriculum, regardless of how effective it is, is that it is immediately relevant. If it is not as effective as it could be, teachers can identify and implement more effective practices. If it is effective, they can confirm and improve their implementation.

Recruit Retired Teachers to Volunteer as Mentors to New Teachers

Purpose: To communicate valuable experience to new teachers.

New teachers are particularly vulnerable and need a great deal of support, but they are not likely to ask for it. To support professional development efforts in the school, retired teachers have a wealth of knowledge and an empathetic ear that can be a godsend to new teachers. Retired teachers can be particularly valuable in identifying effective lesson preparation strategies. Instead of losing the knowledge and requiring each new generation of teachers to start from scratch, recruiting retired teachers to mentor new teachers would provide ongoing relevant professional development. Meeting with a mentor once a week or even once a month to discuss concerns and issues can also help new teachers avoid repeating mistakes and help them evaluate curricular materials that will support their teaching.

Developing Effective Teaching Methods

What the teacher does with students day in and day out—how they group students, develop lessons to link one concept to another, introduce a concept, inspire critical thinking and problem solving, provide appropriate practice, check for understanding, and reteach when necessary—is little understood but critical to improved student achievement. It is not the use of technology or any particular tool, or any one particular lesson or project that promotes student achievement. It is the effective instructional choices in the methods that a teacher makes every day.

> Long-term improvement in teaching will depend more on the development of effective *methods for teaching* than on the identification and recruitment of talented individuals into the profession. . . . Recruiting highly qualified teachers will not result in steady improvement as long as they continue to use the same scripts. It is the scripts that must be improved. (Stigler and Hiebert 1999)

Educational researchers study the effectiveness of teaching methods. Every month, magazines like *Kappan* and *Educational Leadership* and organizations like AERA (American Educational Research Association) as well as other professional organizations are publishing more articles and studies revealing more about how children learn and what strategies are most effective.

When teachers develop expertise in teaching methods, they are not only more effective in the classroom, but more informed as consumers of curriculum and through their curriculum choices incentivize curriculum developers to continually upgrade their materials with the most effective methods.

Recognize Education Is Evolving

Purpose: To open the door to continuous, ongoing improvement.

Recognizing that education is evolving is a small but significant change for teachers to make. It is small because it can happen inside each person's head. It is significant because it can have wide implications and lead to individuals making very different educational choices. For teachers that could involve a continual reevaluation of their lessons and methods to make sure they are the most effective. It could involve sharing effective methods with other teachers to improve their teaching.

It is comforting to think you know what you are doing and to convince yourself that you are being the most effective. After the first few years of struggle, most teachers who stay in education have developed a bank of lesson plans that seem to work and helped them achieve a modicum of success. After a few years, teachers have systems established for classroom management and organizational strategies. Many teachers begin to breathe easier at this point. They have paid their dues.

But the world of knowledge is not treading water. Recognizing that education is evolving provides the basis for a long-term continuous improvement model that can produce small, incremental improvements in teaching over long periods of time.

Education should continually be *upgraded*, not continually *reinvented* and reformed. Experience does matter. Imagine that instead of upgrading cell phones, they were continually reinvented and certain necessary functions were replaced with superfluous features that never really worked.

The idea that a fifty-year-old teacher would still be using the exact same materials and approaches he or she developed twenty-five years earlier seems inconceivable, but it happens. It's as if you would still be using the first cell phone you got in the mid-1980s and never upgraded. On the other hand, the expectation that a teacher who spends an exhausting day in the classroom would be able to keep up with all the newest information about education year after year is unrealistic. Consider elementary school teachers who teach all the subject areas. Keeping up with the upgrades in one subject is a full-time job, let alone keeping up with all subjects.

Teachers on their own are not going to be able to keep up with all the relevant educational research. Nor should it be expected that they do. Curriculum supervisors in schools and curriculum developers do have the potential to keep current because their focus and time is not spent working with students in the classroom. Many curriculum supervisors do exactly that. Improving the flow of new educational understandings from research and translating them into curriculum for use in the classroom contribute to the continuous improvement of educational practices. This has the potential to significantly improve student achievement.

Empower Curriculum Specialists

Purpose: To promote professional development and provide ongoing teacher evaluation and feedback on the essential elements that promote student achievement.

Curriculum specialists typically serve in an advisory capacity in a school or in a district. They may come into a class to demonstrate a lesson, but too often the classroom teacher uses that occasion as a free period to grade papers or attend to other concerns. Curriculum specialists could be empowered to observe classroom teachers' lessons on a regular schedule and evaluate how effectively they are using teaching methods or implementing a new curriculum. They could then submit their evaluations as part of each teacher's performance review. This could go a long way to promoting ongoing relevant professional development with continuous improvement and consequently improve student achievement. If a district does not have curriculum specialists, expert teachers could be assigned or retired teachers could be recruited as volunteers to provide the same service.

Establish a Research Culture in Schools

Purpose: To avoid fads and learn from experience.

This is another simple change that can happen in one's head. In a research culture, people simply ask for evidence to explain why changes should be implemented and follow up on how things turned out. In a research culture, parents, teachers, and administrators would ask about the impact of different methods and programs on student achievement. On an individual basis, if one teacher tries a new method, he or she would test it to see how effective it was in comparison to other methods. If a school implemented a new curriculum, it would be analyzed to see how it was being implemented and what effects it had on student achievement. Staff meetings and reports could be generated to identify strengths and weaknesses in the curriculum and adapt.

A 2009 conference report by the Achievement Gap Initiative at Harvard University explained how teams of administrators and faculty members from fifteen different high schools accepted responsibility for improving student achievement and focused on research and improved instruction. The main lesson was that student achievement rose when core groups of leaders in each school took responsibility for focusing thoughtfully and relentlessly on improving the quality of instruction.

> Leadership teams succeeded initially because they used their positional authority effectively to jump-start the change process. Then they built trust. More specifically, they demonstrated commitment through hard work and long hours; they studied research-based literature to expand their knowledge and competence; they persevered to follow through on the promises they made; and they found ways to remain respectful of peers, even when asking them to improve their performance. In these ways, leadership teams earned the respect of their colleagues and the authority to push people outside their comfort zones. With cultivated competence and earned authority, they were able to help their colleagues overcome the types of fear and resistance that so often prevent effective reforms in American high schools. All these schools remain works in progress, but they are not typical. Their stories convey critically important principles, processes, and practices that can help high schools across the nation raise achievement and close gaps. (Achievement Gap Initiative at Harvard University 2009)

A research culture is based in evidence rather than anecdotes and politics. A research culture respects fair tests and draws conclusions from them. A research culture can challenge the status quo and root out teaching methods that may be popular but are not effective.

Understanding Children's Learning Trajectories

Purpose: Reconceive instruction to support how students learn.

Exciting revelations are emerging from educational researchers into how children learn in each subject. These revelations confirm commonsensical observations of how children learn. Many experienced teachers may already intuitively know this. In mathematics, professors Douglas Clements and Julie Sarama at the University of Buffalo have identified the learning progressions in different strands of mathematics (Clements and Sarama 2009a, 2009b; Daro, Mosher, and Corcoran 2011). In the 1970s under Edmund Henderson at the University of Virginia, educational researchers discovered how children learned to spell (Henderson 1981). Other works chronicle how children learn to read (Spear-Swerling and Sternberg 1996) and develop informational writing abilities (Donovan and Smolkin 2011). Other work is being done to identify learning trajectories in science (Corcoran, Mosher, and Rogat 2009). These learning trajectories show that learning is incremental, building on previously acquired skills and concepts. It is not that a child is just magically talented in math or reading or music. A student may have achieved different levels in a subject area quickly, but the levels were there nonetheless.

The identification of how children learn has profound implications for the way curriculum is organized. For example, math curriculum is typically organized by chapters: addition, geometry, subtraction, and multiplication. Organizing a curriculum based on learning trajectories would not be traditional but it could be very effective. It could help to smooth out the disjointed leaps from one topic to another and make the curriculum more coherent. A curriculum organized by learning trajectories would be based on the logic of the discipline and close attention to students' thinking and how it develops. So instead of, for example, a chapter on addition followed by a chapter on subtraction, lessons would build on children's basic understanding of counting and adding and subtracting to small collections. According to Clements and Sarama this would be followed by adding small collections by counting all items, then introducing subtraction in solving take-away problems (Clements and Sarama 2009b). Lessons would build from there by counting on and finding missing addends (the numbers added together). Later the lessons would focus on problem solving using flexible strategies. Around age seven, lessons would involve multidigit addition and subtraction.

Lesson sequences based on learning trajectories is *learning-centered* instruction. It would not be organized by the subdivisions in a discipline. Nor would it be student-centered instruction in the sense that children determine what they want to learn and when they want to learn it. It is, however, individualized with students at different places along the trajectory.

Teachers' understanding of how children learn particular concepts in conjunction with curriculum organized by learning trajectories would provide significant scaffolding for student achievement.

EVALUATE AND SELECT THE
BEST AVAILABLE CURRICULUM

Developing teacher expertise is a critical step in improving the quality of instruction and also improving teachers' abilities to identify, adopt, and implement effective curriculum. With informed and intelligent consumers, publishers will be incentivized to prioritize effectiveness in the development of curricular materials.

Teaching tools including the latest technologies will affect student achievement only in the service of implementing a quality curriculum by quality teachers. Tools and new technologies should be continually evaluated for their potential to improve teaching efficiency and effectiveness. Diverting efforts from the implementation of a quality curriculum to using technology for technology's sake focuses on the wrong priorities.

Using ineffective tools and ineffective curriculum because of poor choices is teaching with a major disadvantage. Purchasing inferior tools does nothing to incentivize curriculum developers to improve instruction or student achievement.

A direct, efficient, and effective way to increase student achievement is to select and implement a curriculum that addresses rigorous standards of learning, sequences concepts along children's learning trajectories, employs the most effective teaching methods identified by research, and presents in-depth, important, accurate, age-appropriate content, concepts, and skills.

To identify and select the most effective curriculum, the school's adoption committee should develop expertise in subject area content, research-based teaching methods, and the science of how children learn so that they can evaluate the quality of each of these elements in competing materials. Improving these areas of expertise can be the basis of ongoing professional development so that teachers are ready to implement improved curriculum.

Educational publishers, who are in the best position to develop curriculum, have not been incentivized to prioritize effectiveness. With an informed curriculum selection process, instead of teachers creating new curriculum, schools can take advantage of the free market to inspire a new age of improved materials.

Understand the Power of a Strong Curriculum

Purpose: To distinguish a well-designed curriculum that can have significant effects on student achievement and improved instruction from mediocre curricula.

With the emphasis on setting state and national standards since 1990, the nation has a choice of content and performance standards to evaluate. The value of standards is in the objectives they provide quality teachers and curriculum developers. Instead of focusing efforts on creating more standards in order to increase student achievement, efforts should be focused on creating effective curriculum that teaches the standards and increasing teacher expertise in implementing the curriculum.

A curriculum is not a set of standards, nor is it a set of lessons, although it includes both. Standards are global statements that describe what students should be learning at different grade levels but they do not provide the materials, instruction, practice activities, or assessments. A curriculum is not one teaching method but incorporates different teaching methods to teach concepts in an organized way. A curriculum is the set of daily lesson plans, activities, supporting resources, and assessments organized in a way to develop student skills and understandings in a subject area. It is not a hodgepodge of engaging fun activities. It is a set of lessons that can be engaging but is carefully planned to develop specific understandings that are expressed in the standards.

Developing a quality curriculum, even after high-quality rigorous standards are in place, takes time. Developing a quality curriculum involves research in how children learn and the most effective methods and strategies to facilitate learning. It involves sequencing skills and concepts to facilitate learning; developing activities, strategies, and methods to introduce and develop and assess understanding; and providing effective reteaching strategies if students are not progressing. Testing the curriculum to make sure that it works, revising it, and testing it again take even more time.

Following is an illustration of the process of effective curriculum development. It begins with a standard, the desired result of instruction, but it takes into consideration the related standards at kindergarten and second grade. It also incorporates the research in the understanding of mathematical learning trajectories. The standard is one of the twenty-one Common Core Mathematics standards at grade 1. The Common Core Standards related to counting at the kindergarten level are much more involved, so the major instruction for learning to count falls on the kindergarten teachers.

Number and Operations in Base 10 Strand

TEXTBOX 7.1. EXTENDING THE COUNTING SEQUENCE

- 1.NBT.1. Count to 120, starting at any number less than 120. In this range, read and write numerals and represent a number of objects with a written numeral.

Know number names and the count sequence.
- K.CC.1. Count to 100 by ones and by tens.
- K.CC.2. Count forward beginning from a given number within the known sequence (instead of having to begin at 1).
- K.CC.3. Write numbers from 0 to 20. Represent a number of objects with a written numeral 0–20 (with 0 representing a count of no objects).

Count to tell the number of objects.
- K.CC.4. Understand the relationship between numbers and quantities; connect counting to cardinality.
  - When counting objects, say the number names in the standard order, pairing each object with one and only one number name and each number name with one and only one object.

○ Understand that the last number name said tells the number of objects counted. The number of objects is the same regardless of their arrangement or the order in which they were counted.

○ Understand that each successive number name refers to a quantity that is one larger.

- K.CC.5. Count to answer "how many?" questions about as many as 20 things arranged in a line, a rectangular array, or a circle, or as many as 10 things in a scattered configuration; given a number from 1–20, count out that many objects.

Compare numbers.

- K.CC.6. Identify whether the number of objects in one group is greater than, less than, or equal to the number of objects in another group, for example, by using matching and counting strategies.
- K.CC.7. Compare two numbers between 1 and 10 presented as written numerals.

The grade 2 Common Core Standards related to counting involve a growing understanding of place value, or knowing what the difference is between the 1s, 10s, 100s, and 1000s in a number.

TEXTBOX 7.2. UNDERSTANDING PLACE VALUE

- 2.NBT.1. Understand that the three digits of a three-digit number represent amounts of hundreds, tens, and ones; for example, 706 equals 7 hundreds, 0 tens, and 6 ones. Understand the following as special cases:
  ○ 100 can be thought of as a bundle of ten tens—called a "hundred."
  ○ The numbers 100, 200, 300, 400, 500, 600, 700, 800, 900 refer to one, two, three, four, five, six, seven, eight, or nine hundreds (and 0 tens and 0 ones).
- 2.NBT.2. Count within 1000; skip-count by 5s, 10s, and 100s.
- 2.NBT.3. Read and write numbers to 1000 using base-ten numerals, number names, and expanded form.
- 2.NBT.4. Compare two three-digit numbers based on meanings of the hundreds, tens, and ones digits, using >, =, and < symbols to record the results of comparisons. (Common Core State Standards Initiative 2010a)

For an adult, counting to 120 is a simple, tedious task, and it is easy to discount the conceptual understandings that are required in order to count to 120. Clements and Sarama have identified eighteen levels on the mathematics counting learning trajectory that children must achieve before they are able

Table 7.2. Counting Learning Trajectory

1	Pre-Counter	No verbal counting.
2	Chanter	*Verbal.* Chants "sing-song" or sometimes indistinguishable number words.
3	Reciter	*Verbal.* Verbally counts with separate words, not necessarily in the correct order. Puts objects, actions, and words in many-to-one (age 1–8) or overly rigid one-to-one (age 1) correspondence (age 2–6).
4	Reciter (10)	*Verbal.* Verbally counts to ten, with *some* correspondence with objects, but may either continue an overly rigid correspondence or exhibit performance errors (e.g., skipping, double-counting). Producing, may give desired number.
5	Corresponder	Keeps one-to-one correspondence between counting words and objects (one word for each object), at least for small groups of objects laid in a line. May answer a "how many?" question by re-counting the objects, or violate 1-1 or word order to make the last number word be the desired or predicted word.
6	Counter (Small Numbers)	Accurately counts objects in a line to 5 and answers the "how many" question with the last number counted. When objects are visible, and especially with small numbers, begins to understand cardinality.
7	Counter (10)	Counts arrangements of objects to 10. May be able to write or draw to represent 1–10. May be able to tell the number just after or just before another number, but only by counting up from 1. Verbal counting to 20 is developing.
8	Producer (Small Numbers)	Counts out objects to 5. Recognizes that counting is relevant to situations in which a certain number must be placed.
9	Counter and Producer (10+)	Counts and counts out objects accurately to 10 then beyond (to about 30). Has explicit understanding of cardinality (how numbers tell how many). Keeps track of objects that have and have not been counted, even in different arrangements. Writes or draws to represent 1 to 10 (then 20, then 30). Gives next number (usually to 20s or 30s). Separates the decade and the ones part of a number word, and begins to relate each part of a number word/numeral to the quantity to which it refers. Recognizes errors in others' counting and can eliminate most errors in own counting (point-object) if asked to try hard.
10	Counter Backward from 10	*Verbal and Object.* Counts backward from 10 to 1, verbally, or when removing objects from a group.

11	Counter from N (N+1, N−1)	*Verbal and Object.* Counts verbally and with objects from numbers other than 1 (but does not yet keep track of number of counts). Determines numbers just after or just before immediately.
12	Skip Counter by 10s to 100	*Verbal and Object.* Skip counts by tens up to 100 or beyond with understanding: e.g., "sees" groups of 10 within a quantity and counts those groups by 10 (this relates to multiplication and algebraic thinking).
13	Counter to 100	*Verbal.* Counts to 100. Makes decade transition (e.g., from 29 to 30) starting at any number.
14	Counter on Using Patterns	*Strategy.* Keeps track of a few counting acts, but only by using numerical pattern (spatial, auditory or rhythmic).
15	Skip Counter	*Verbal and Object.* Counts by fives and twos with understanding.
16	Counter of Imagined Items	*Strategy.* Counts mental images of hidden objects.
17	Counter on Keeping Track	*Strategy.* Keeps track of counting acts numerically, first with objects, then by "counting counts." Counts up 1 to 4 *more* from a given number.
18	Counter of Quantitative Units/Place Value	Understands the base-ten numeration system and place-value concepts, including ideas of counting in units and multiples of hundreds, tens, and ones. When counting groups of 10, can decompose into 10 ones if that is useful. Understands value of a digit according to the place of the digit within a number. Counts unusual units, such as "wholes," when shown combinations of wholes and parts.

Source: Adapted from "Learning Trajectories in Early Mathematics," Clements and Sarama 2009b.

to count to 120 (2009b). Although you can see many levels of the trajectory leading up to counting to 120 reflected in the Common Core Standards, you can also see that the standards are not in the order of the learning trajectory (see table 7.2).

If you are writing an effective curriculum to teach the Count to 120 Common Core Standard, you would need to develop each of the following:

1. Provide an assessment strategy so the teacher can determine where the majority of the students in the class are on the learning trajectory. It may very well be that many children have not met the kindergarten Common Core Standards, especially considering that many states have only half-day kindergarten and that reading takes priority over mathematics in kindergarten.
2. Plan a series of review lessons with lesson objectives to review the kindergarten mathematics standards. Even if students "covered" the content in kindergarten, many children will not remember from the previous year. Studies show that over a summer break students who do not engage in reading and math activities lose a substantial amount of the progress they made the previous year.
3. The review lessons should get students to level 14 on the learning trajectory because the kindergarten standards include counting to 100 by ones and tens. Plan a series of lessons and lesson objectives for levels 14–18 on the learning trajectory.
4. Write the review lessons and the new lessons. Each lesson should follow a lesson plan and include teaching methods that will facilitate learning.
   a. **Lesson Plans.** Typical lesson plans in mathematics include methods for each of the following:
      i. Previous skill maintenance warm-up
      ii. Activating prior knowledge
      iii. Concept introduction
      iv. Teaching
      v. Guided practice
      vi. Checking for understanding
      vii. Independent practice
      viii. Reflection and assessment
   b. **Methods.** The most effective methods used will differ depending on the concept being introduced. Possible methods for teaching a concept in first grade mathematics may include items i through xi below. Different methods may be used in different parts of the lesson. For example, the skill maintenance could be a game-like activity, the concept introduction

could be an exploration, the teaching could be modeling, and the guided practice could involve collaboration.

    i. Game-like activity
    ii. Exploration using concrete manipulatives
    iii. Direct instruction
    iv. Modeling
    v. Demonstration
    vi. Asking questions
    vii. Role playing
    viii. Teacher explanation
    ix. Peer to peer explanation
    x. Collaborating—working in groups
    xi. Storytelling

5. Review and test each lesson. This step will help to ensure the lesson will be effective. The following questions should be addressed.
   a. Do the lesson methods and activities address the lesson objective? Often lessons include fun and engaging activities but they have nothing to do with the lesson objective.
   b. Are the activities on level? Sometimes the activities are too easy or too difficult and students will not be able to grasp the lesson objective.
   c. Are there additional methods that will more effectively teach the concept? This is where a review of educational research and input from experienced teachers can be very helpful.
6. Revise each lesson based on the feedback from the review.
7. Write reteaching activities for students who did not achieve the lesson objective.

This is a process for developing a series of lessons to address one of the twenty-one Common Core Standards in a first grade mathematics program. Missing here is the integration of other mathematics standards, such as standards relating to addition and subtraction, which are related.

Stigler and Hiebert explain that a good curriculum is like a well-formed story. A story has a beginning that introduces the story, a middle with a sequence of events that fit together to tell the story, and a conclusion. When a story or a series of lessons switches from topic to topic without coherence, concepts are not comprehensible (1999).

A good curriculum has coherence so that each lesson connects and builds on previous lessons. Using a quality curriculum with fidelity does make a difference in student achievement. "U.S. students encounter less-challenging mathematics, and because it is presented in a less-coherent way, they must work harder to make sense of it than their peers in Germany and Japan [who perform at higher levels in mathematics]" (Stigler and Hiebert 1999).

Curriculum advertisements always claim that new educational materials meet the appropriate standards. Upon examination however, in most cases reviewers will find that new materials are redesigned older materials that are simply correlated to new standards. That is the most cost-effective development procedure. Publishers frequently base even brand-new materials on older materials or patterns of organization on competitive programs. New programs are not likely to have been developed from the new standards or from understanding of developmental sequences of children's learning trajectories. If the people selecting the new materials are not equipped or neglect to identify the developmental sequences for each of the standards and select the programs based on correlations, the curriculum will likely not help them rise above the status quo.

> A strong curriculum brings clarity to a school's endeavor; it has practical, intellectual, and philosophical benefits. It gives shape to the subjects, helps ensure consistency within and among schools, makes room for first-rate books and tests, and leaves teachers room for professional judgment and creativity. It can be a gift to a community as well as a school; it can become the foundation for a school's cultural life. It is never perfect, but that is part of its vitality. It challenges us to think through it and beyond it. It does not solve a school's problems, but it offers good working material and a clear perspective. (Senechal 2011)

A quality curriculum takes knowledge, research, and time to develop. It is unrealistic to expect every teacher or every school or school district to develop its own curriculum for every subject. Teachers are rarely educated in curriculum development and do not have expertise in it. Teachers should be responsible for distinguishing between an effective and ineffective curriculum and for adapting a curriculum to meet the needs of the particular students in the school district. Furthermore, a curriculum's effectiveness cannot be judged on the number of components or features it has. A quality curriculum will incorporate effective and research-based strategies, lessons, and methods to meet the agreed-upon standards. An effective curriculum will have been tested in real classroom situations.

Recognize the Effect That Improved Teaching Methods Have on Student Achievement

Purpose: To distinguish effective teaching methods that promote student achievement and employ them.

A major key to learning and student achievement is the identification of the significant concepts related to the development of a learning standard. Once the developmental progressions are identified, employing the most effective *teaching methods* to facilitate learning of each concept opens the door to student understanding and achievement. It is the teacher's methods of delivering of a solid curriculum day after day that truly make the difference in student achievement.

An example of the effect of curriculum and teaching methods is the transformation Brockton High School in Massachusetts made from a low performing to a high performing school after its students scored very poorly on the Massachusetts Comprehensive Assessment System (MCAS). The poor test scores made the faculty ask, "What were we teaching? How were we teaching it? And most importantly, how did we know the kids were learning it?" Before the MCAS came along, the Brockton High School principal, Sue Szachowicz, acknowledged that academics were not the main priority of the school. At first they tried to outguess the test but when that didn't work they identified the skills that were needed to pass the test and developed specific strategies and methods for teaching those skills (Szachowicz 2011).

An example from Stigler and Hiebert's analysis of the international comparison of typical mathematics teaching demonstrates the importance of daily strategies (1999). They found that in the typical American classroom teachers present a mathematics problem and demonstrate how to solve it, and then students practice solving a number of similar problems. When American teachers do pose problems for students to solve, typically at the first hint of struggle, teachers demonstrate or have a student demonstrate how to solve it, focusing on memorizing terms and practicing procedures, rather than sense making or problem solving. Many students, even capable students, do not engage in problem solving and simply wait until someone shows them what to do. Then because they have not engaged in the problem-solving process, they are lucky to remember the procedures until the chapter test. The curriculum materials, in the name of helping students understand procedures and making it easy to use for teachers, are complicit in these methods. Some teachers, like high school math teacher Dan Meyer, recognize that the methods employed to teach math using the curricula in the United States all but ensures that students won't retain it (Meyer 2010).

In contrast, in a typical Japanese math lesson the teacher poses a problem that is somewhat more difficult than the problems presented previously and leaves the problem solving up to the students. Everyone is expected to struggle through the problem. The Japanese teachers also routinely link together the parts of the lesson. Instead of using the overhead projector, they use the blackboard, beginning at the left-hand side. As they develop the lesson, they work across the board so that everyone can see the development of thought. These teaching *methods* promote understanding and likely result in higher mathematics achievement among Japanese students.

Teaching is a *system*. It is not a loose mixture of individual features thrown together by the teacher. It works more like a machine, with the parts operating together and reinforcing one another, driving the vehicle forward. . . . When we watched a Japanese lesson, for example, we noticed that the teacher presents a problem to the students without first demonstrating how to solve the problem. We realized that U.S. teachers almost never do this. (Stigler and Hiebert 1999)

In reading, effective teaching includes the recognition that children need to develop phonemic awareness before they can read. Phonemic awareness is the recognition that words comprise different sounds. Playful instruction and practice that focuses on segmenting and blending sounds are effective methods for the development of phonemic awareness. Although some children seem to intuitively have phonemic awareness, most children need that explicit instruction (Adams 1994).

In early mathematics, effective teaching methods involve playing simple math games. These provide the explicit instruction that shows students that numbers on a line are the same quantity representations as numbers on a dial, on a thermometer, in a group, and on a die. This is critical to developing early number sense, the foundation of all mathematics understanding (Griffin 2004).

A good curriculum identifies the incremental concepts and steps that develop understanding of a learning standard and provide effective teaching methods to convey each concept. Expert teachers use effective methods. If teachers are open to it, they will be continually trying different methods to teach specific concepts. Teachers can find methods in the curriculum they are using and from sharing with other teachers. Regardless of class sizes, merit pay, or school vouchers, if teachers use ineffective methods the chances that students will achieve are limited.

Reevaluating teaching *methods* and strategies, even those methods that are baked into American education, could promote significant student achievement. Research, discussions, and comparisons of different methods for teaching the same concepts provide opportunities to improve practices and consequently student achievement.

Focus Teacher Efforts on Implementing a Quality Curriculum Rather Than Writing One

Purpose: To maximize teacher energies in improving instruction and promoting student achievement.

It is really easy for teachers, parents, and other interested parties to determine that they have to write their own curriculum instead of using published curricula.

Now that the Common Core Standards are in place, there are initiatives to write new curriculum to teach the standards. Countless webinars and professional development sessions provide introductions to the Common Core Standards and never mention curriculum, as if each individual teacher will have to create or adapt the materials they have to teach the Common Core. These efforts ignore all the curricula that has been carefully developed by nonprofit and for-profit companies. Teachers are set up to *implement curriculum* and work with students. Writing curriculum is a completely different knowledge and skill set.

> When there is no curriculum, teachers are kept busy but not necessarily in the best ways. After selecting what to teach, chasing after the materials, and putting together lessons, teachers have little time to think about the chosen topic, to consider different ways of teaching it, or to respond to students' insights and difficulties. (Senechal 2011)

This is not to say that curriculum cannot be improved, but educators can improve curriculum by carefully evaluating the available curricula and selecting the one that will best promote student achievement in their school, thereby incentivizing publishers to focus on the priority of developing effective curriculum. Schools do not even need to design the curriculum and spell out what they need. They simply need to use the free market system to identify and purchase the most effective curriculum. "Materials could be designed to place teachers in the center of curriculum construction and make teachers' learning central to efforts to improve education, without requiring heroic assumptions about each teacher's capacities as an original designer of curriculum" (Ball and Cohen 1996).

The advantages to using the free market system to select and thereby incentivize publishers to create more effective curriculum are profound. Publishers have resources that no teacher or school has. They have editors who can contact experts in each discipline and tap them to create developmental sequences that promote student understanding. They have access to the whole team of players: editors, production editors, designers, and sales and marketing people who can make the curriculum appealing and available to a wide market.

No curriculum will be perfect, and marketing and the profit motive can obscure both strengths and weaknesses in a curriculum. Publishers, however, are well positioned to keep current with educational research and tap the brightest minds. They have the resources to develop comprehensive materials. Working with authors and researchers, they also have the potential to be innovative in a way that would be incredibly difficult for teachers working in the classroom to achieve.

Educators have the power of the purse. They can use the free market system to force the creation of materials that will promote student achievement instead of the status quo.

If publishers were incentivized to create the most effective curriculum they would do the following:

1. Study all the available research on effective teaching practices in the discipline and incorporate it into program plans
2. Study the history of each discipline to identify the most effective practices and avoid pitfalls
3. Carefully involve authors and educational experts in designing the curriculum
4. Seriously test materials in schools to ensure they promote student achievement
5. Identify and demonstrate why the program will be more effective than other programs in the sales presentations and other sales materials
6. Include, as part of the business plan, information about how a product will promote academic achievement and document how such a goal is to be achieved

Establish Curriculum Evaluation Teams

Purpose: To break the cycle of adopting curricular materials that will perpetuate the status quo.

When it is time to adopt a new curriculum in a subject area, establish an adoption committee comprising a curriculum specialist or supervisor, a new teacher, and a retired teacher. If it is possible, give the employees a sabbatical to research the curriculum choices. The curriculum specialist would be responsible for making sure the curriculum is up to date and reflects the current understandings of the most effective practices in teaching. The new teacher will be responsible for making sure the curriculum is useful and can be implemented. This will also help new teachers build an understanding of their new profession.

> New teachers need opportunities to analyze and critique curriculum materials in their early years, in the company of more experienced colleagues. Such curricular conversations become opportunities for teachers to deepen their own understanding of the subject matter. . . . Such curricular conversations are helpful to all but especially to new teachers who tend to latch on uncritically to whatever curriculum they are handed. (Grossman and Thompson 2004)

The retired teacher will be responsible for making sure the curriculum is practical and is not a rehash of a previously failed curriculum. Once the evaluation team makes a selection, it should be prepared to prove to the rest of the faculty that the curriculum will be effective and will be worth changing the seemingly tried and true methods of experienced teachers. Not leaving the curriculum purchase decisions up to teachers who are likely to recommend a curriculum that is the same as the current one improves the potential of moving beyond the status quo.

Establish Curriculum Evaluation Criteria

Purpose: To evaluate curriculum based on the quality of the features that will support instruction and promote student achievement.

Establishing curriculum criteria that focus on the essential elements of a good curriculum will make it much more likely that an ineffectual curriculum, even if it comprises titillating technology and flashy components and reflects all the new trends and labels, will not be adopted. The curriculum evaluation team should spend weeks if not months on the following activities.

1. **Teaching Methods Are Based on Effective Research and Experience**
    a. Identify research-based teaching methods that have been shown to have the greatest effect on student achievement.
    b. Show how these methods are or are not incorporated in the program. An inferior curriculum may have the correct labels but not the most effective practices.
2. **Student Learning Trajectories Are the Foundation of the Development of Lessons and Concepts**
    a. Identify the learning trajectories for each standard to be addressed at each grade level.
    b. Show how the curriculum is organized along learning trajectories so that concepts are developed in a developmental progression. In an inadequate curriculum, an entire standard may just be referenced in one lesson and not developed at all.
3. **Content Is Accurate and Comprehensive and Meets Curriculum Standards**
    a. Identify the content and concepts that need to be taught at each grade level.
    b. Show how each concept is introduced, developed, practiced, and assessed in the curriculum.
    c. Verify the content is comprehensive and accurate.
    d. Identify the skills that students need to build at each grade level.
    e. Show how each skill is introduced, developed, practiced, and assessed.
4. **Curriculum Effectiveness Can Be Verified**
    a. Visit other schools where the curriculum has been implemented.
    b. Interview teachers about its strengths and weaknesses.

No curriculum will be perfect but there are curricula that are much more in-structionally effective than others. If publishers understood that their materials would be evaluated and selected based on these criteria, it would not take very long for major publishers to begin producing materials that reflected them.

Use Alternative Assessments to Evaluate Potential Curriculum

Purpose: To select the best available curriculum for the needs of a school.

Once evaluation criteria and a curriculum evaluation team is in place, the work of evaluating curriculum for selection should involve multiple assess-ments. Just as one test cannot determine a student's potential, one test or per-spective does not determine how effective a curriculum may be. By providing alternative assessments, a school can avoid the mistake of selecting curricu-lum, which has the greatest potential to improve student achievement, on the basis of superfluous or superficial features such as cover design, page count, publisher incentives or relationships, extra components, or one person's pref-erences. Below are different ways to evaluate curriculum.

1. Evaluate each new curriculum based on the evaluation criteria to assess the content, teaching methods, lesson planning, and concept development.
2. Establish a list of the shortcomings of the existing curriculum and com-pare each potential new curriculum to see if it addresses the shortcomings.
3. Identify student weaknesses. Evaluate potential curricula based on how well it will address student weaknesses.
4. Develop a list of goals for the new curriculum and ask curriculum devel-opers to demonstrate how their curriculum will meet the goals. Following all presentations, evaluate the responses and verify that the claims are true.
5. Itemize the differences between the existing curriculum or practices and those in a proposed new curriculum. Verify that the changes are improve-ments.
6. Compare the proposed curriculum by having teachers teach specific les-sons strictly following the lesson plans. Then compare and contrast the instruction, methods, assessments, and materials from each curriculum and compare to current practices to identify differences, advantages, and disadvantages.
7. Pilot test a multiweek chapter or unit from each proposed curriculum and compare instructional methods and student responses to determine which curriculum is most effective.
8. Establish teams of educators who each evaluate and test one curriculum over the course of a month. Then have the teams compare curricula and debate the advantages and disadvantages of each.

Select the Most Effective Curriculum

No curriculum will be perfect, but after rigorous evaluations, schools should be able to identify a curriculum that best meets their needs. Selecting the curriculum, explaining the reasons for the selection to the winners and losers, is critical to incentivizing publishers to focus on those elements that will promote student achievement. If a publisher wins an adoption because it was considered to be most effective and another loses because it was considered ineffective, it will not take long for publishers to prioritize those elements that make curriculum effective. As more and more schools do this, the next time a school that establishes high standards for curriculum is in the market for a new program, the selections will be markedly better.

Furthermore, if the selected curriculum has been rigorously tested and the evaluation committee has ample evidence of its quality and superiority over other curricula, the faculty will be more amenable to making the changes in their practices that the new curricula should require.

IMPLEMENT CURRICULUM WITH FIDELITY

Once a curriculum has been selected, if teachers engage in ongoing in-service professional development to build expertise in content knowledge, teaching methods, lesson planning, and understanding how children learn, they will be able to maximize the potential of the new curriculum.

If a school has chosen and invested in a new curriculum based on rigorous criteria, having every teacher implement it with fidelity will maximize its potential benefit to students. Studies show that good curriculum implemented with fidelity has a positive effect on student achievement as shown in this study (See figure 7.1).

Three schools in Pittsburgh that were weak implementers of a standards-based math curriculum were compared with three schools with similar demographics that were strong implementers. Note that racial differences were eliminated in the strong implementation schools, and that performance soared. There is no reason to believe that any of the individual differences in teachers previously described, such as cognitive ability or education, differed among the weak implementation schools versus the strong implementation schools. Yet the teachers in the strong implementation schools were dramatically more effective than teachers in the weak implementation schools. Thus a main effect of curriculum implementation swamped the effects of individual differences in background among teachers. (Whitehurst 2002)

Too often, however, a school invests in a new curriculum and nothing changes. Teachers continue to use the older curricular materials.

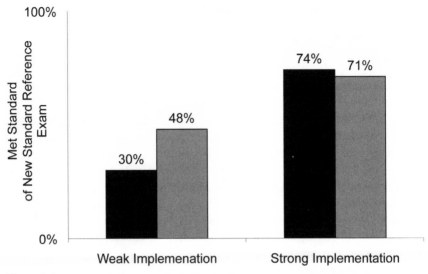

Figure 7.1.

The existing instructional system adapts to the new curriculum in predictable ways. Teachers can regard the new curriculum as a foreign invasion into their regular teaching practices, and try to fit it in with those practices. Even with professional development and monitoring, most teachers know that once in their classrooms, they can teach as they please. (Collins and Halverson 2009; Bereiter and Scardamalia 1993)

If a school invests time and energy into adopting a new curriculum, the school owes it to their community to implement it with fidelity, even if it means substantial changes. New curriculum can be the impetus for upgrading teaching methods and patterns to promote student achievement.

Publisher In-Service Training

Purpose: To realize the value of a new curriculum by maximizing the potential of the features that will support instruction and promote student achievement.

To implement a new curriculum with fidelity, every educator in the school needs to understand how the curriculum is organized and how it is intended to be used to promote student understanding and achievement. Too often the very best features are ignored or the carefully crafted scope and sequence of a program is abandoned because teachers do not understand the value to students or reasoning behind the curriculum. Curriculum developers want their materials to be successful and most offer teacher in-service or training sessions with the purchase. Schools can take full advantage of these and request a customized focus. Schools may request follow-up sessions.

To optimize the in-service sessions for the implementation of a new curriculum, schools might consider the following requests to the curriculum developer. Without specific requests, many publishers will simply give a component overview if they do provide in-service training.

1. **How Children Learn.** Explain the significance of the concept development and organization of the curriculum and its advantages and how it supports student learning trajectories. This will give teachers the rationale for following or adjusting the order of the program and will build their expertise in understanding how children learn.
2. **Lesson Planning.** Explain the basic lesson plan and how it affects student understanding and achievement. Teachers should understand how the curriculum supports the introduction of concepts, checking for understanding, assigning effective activities that will develop understanding, providing practice opportunities, and assessing student understanding. This will give teachers the rationale for following or adjusting the lesson plan and will build their expertise in lesson planning.
3. **Teaching Methods.** Explain program features and methods that may or may not be part of the typical lesson plan that are supported by research so that teachers know why they should use particular methods. This will help to develop teacher expertise in teaching methods.
4. **Content Development.** Explain the program philosophy of content development so that it is understood how concepts are connected and build upon one another.
5. **Model a Lesson.** Having a consultant model a lesson from each grade level of the curriculum is an excellent way for teachers to see how procedures and methods may be different from what they have been doing. The lesson modeling will give teachers an opportunity to ask questions about the curriculum and methods.

Following the initial in-service, schools can negotiate to have the publisher return periodically to answer questions and to work with teachers to implement the curriculum effectively. In follow-up sessions, schools may request these types of services.

1. Publisher representatives observe teachers presenting lessons and provide constructive feedback for implementation.
2. Teachers collect questions and problems they have had with methods and have publisher representatives provide feedback.
3. Publisher representatives model lessons teachers have taught. These models are used as a lesson study in which teachers critique the lesson, compare and contrast different approaches to it, discuss methods, and develop understanding of the curriculum.

4. Publisher representatives model use of program components that have not yet been implemented.

Continue Ongoing Standards and Curriculum Discussions

Purpose: To provide collaborative efforts to understand teaching objectives, improve teaching methods, and establish a leadership group to promote ongoing professional development.

Once a new curriculum has been selected and is in use, teachers using the same materials could meet weekly or biweekly to discuss how to address a standard, an upcoming lesson and how to approach it, or how specific elements of the new curriculum continue to promote professional development; these are simple ways to provide new teachers with needed support and allow expert teachers to share their knowledge.

The meetings can have a standing agenda: identify the specific topic (standards, method, or lesson), ask one faculty member with expertise to present his or her approach to it, and promote discussion and questions. These sessions could not only help to educate new teachers, they could also encourage all teachers to reevaluate their own methods. These types of discussions could even be repeated year after year as new methods are tested and new teachers and ideas come into the school.

Monitor Curriculum Effects

Purpose: To reinforce effective practices and develop faculty expertise using relevant materials and strategies.

If a research culture has been established in a school, then teacher researchers will look for ways to test whether the new curriculum is effective. By testing specifics, such as particular methods, development of concepts, or lesson organization, teachers will accumulate data about how effective the new curriculum is or if some aspects are more effective than others. If the faculty determines that something is not working as it should, they can make adjustments as a staff and test those effects. In this way, changes to the curriculum will be implemented school-wide.

FEAR OF CHANGE

Change inspires fear. Ronald Ferguson, director of the Achievement Gap Initiative at Harvard, outlines six fears that must be overcome if change is to occur.

1. Fear of wasting time and energy. Leaders might not follow through on new agendas, or the ideas embedded in those agendas might not be worth pursuing.
2. Fear of losing autonomy. New agendas might require activities, materials, or methods that differ from what the teacher prefers or is accustomed to.
3. Fear of experiencing incompetence when trying new things. The new agendas might require learning new skills or behaviors that seem difficult to master.
4. Fear of becoming socially isolated. Cooperating with new agendas might require behaviors that valued colleagues would object to. For example, colleagues might accuse cooperative teachers of selling out or breaking solidarity by "sucking up to the principal."
5. Fear of unpleasant surprises. New agendas might increase uncertainty for people who like stability and predictability.
6. Fear of more work. Complying with new agendas might require more work than people feel inclined to undertake. (Achievement Gap Initiative at Harvard University 2009)

These fears can pervade a culture at a school or among curriculum developers and result in paralysis. This is where leadership teams must intercede and overcome fear with clearly stated motives concerning the goals of the work, their growing competence as organizational and instructional leaders based on their expertise, their unwavering reliability in keeping commitments, and the constant collegiality and respect (Achievement Gap Initiative 2009). Fear of change is not inconsequential, but the status quo is not acceptable. If the education community works toward the same goal—increasing student achievement—then change will have credibility and acceptance.

Unless significant changes that can impact the effectiveness of teachers and curriculum are made in our educational system, student achievement will remain static. Using the same teaching methods and types of curriculum that have been in schools will ensure that student achievement remains static.

CONCLUSION

"Insanity: doing the same thing over and over again and expecting different results." This saying, attributed to Albert Einstein, US (German-born) physicist (1879–1955), speaks to the need to implement real change in education to promote student achievement. Moving beyond the plateau and breaking out of the status quo of educational practice and student achievement are awesome tasks. They require acknowledgment of certain truths about education and making some fundamental changes. Ron Ferguson continues with five steps that lead to high schools becoming exemplary:

> Small but expanding alliances of leaders in these high schools undertook the following *five steps to becoming exemplary*. They
>
> I. Accepted their responsibility to lead the change process.
> II. Declared the purposes of the work in mission statements that focused on a few key ideas and priorities that stakeholders could understand and embrace.
> III. Designed strategies, plans, capacity, and incentives for broadly inclusive adult learning.
> IV. Developed and refined quality standards for judging teacher and student work.
> V. Skillfully and relentlessly implemented plans, monitored quality, and provided appropriate supports and incentives.
>
> These *five steps to becoming exemplary* can be understood as a cycle that repeats as a school's conception of "the problem to be solved" evolves. (Achievement Gap Initiative 2009)

Of course school improvements can be achieved without the help of curriculum developers, but efforts toward student achievement could certainly be supported by effective curriculum. Currently educational publishers are incentivized to deliver the same types of materials they have in the past. The best-selling programs are ones that experienced educators select because they make it easier to do what they are currently doing. The best sellers, even if they identify where standards are covered, have not substantially revised their curriculum to reflect the conceptual development of each standard, the most recent research in understanding how children learn, or the most effective methods for teaching the concepts that develop the standards. All of that would require significant change, and currently significant change does not sell.

Without curricular materials to assist them in increasing student achievement, schools are left to their own devices and seem to try one get-rich-quick scheme after another, all to no avail. As a result, a fragmented system with all kinds of competing initiatives can emerge with teachers who are suspicious of any new reform, frustrated administrators, angry parents, and politicians searching for silver bullets to implement before the next election.

The free market system is not working to ensure the cream of curriculum is rising to the top because many of the people purchasing curriculum and incentivizing publishers to produce it are not trained with specific knowledge of the critical elements that make one curriculum more effective than others.

The free market system *could* be incredibly productive in inspiring publishers to innovate and compete to create the most effective materials. If the curriculum selection process were revised and updated to encourage and support the adoption of the most *effective* curricula on the market, schools could use them to promote professional development, help teachers understand and make meaningful changes in their teaching methods, improve the coherence of conceptual development of lessons, and assist the educational processes in America to move beyond the plateau of student achievement.

With the publication and adoption of the Common Core Standards, American education has a new opportunity to make effective changes.

> In part we must break the vicious cycle in which we find ourselves—where the weak U.S. future teachers are getting weak training mathematically, and are just not prepared to teach the demanding mathematics curriculum we need especially for middle schools if we hope to compete internationally. This is especially true given that 48 of the states are currently considering the adoption of the more rigorous "Common Core" standards. K–12 mathematics curriculum taught by teachers with an inadequate mathematics background produces high school graduates who are similarly weak. Some of them then become future teachers who are not given a strong preparation in mathematics and then they teach and the cycle continues. Perhaps the force is with us at this moment in time to begin to break the cycle. The "Common Core" standards are more challenging and the study gives evidence of how teacher education might be shaped differently. The challenge is now with the states who set the certification policies and the universities and colleges that interpret them. (Center for Research in Math and Science Education 2010)

American education has spent the last several decades developing standards and focusing on inconsequential reforms that have only served to perpetuate the status quo. By building teacher expertise, selecting the most effective curricula available, and implementing the curricula with fidelity, schools will greatly improve their chances of making meaningful changes that will lead to improved student achievement.

As the proverb says, "The best time to plant a tree is twenty years ago. The second best time is now."

Chronology

Major Initiatives in Standards Development

1983: *A NATION AT RISK*

The National Commission on Excellence in Education's 1983 report, *A Nation at Risk,* started the modern standards movement. It maintained that America had "squandered" its *Sputnik* moment and found that an alarming number of Americans were functionally illiterate. It also explained that standardized test scores had declined and international comparisons were poor, and it documented the increase in remedial courses in mathematics, reading, and writing. The report also argued that high school curricula was "homogenized, diluted, and diffused to the point that they no longer have a central purpose." *A Nation at Risk* got people's attention.

The recommendations included strengthening high school graduation requirements, setting more rigorous standards and higher expectations, and making serious attempts to help students meet the higher expectations by devoting significantly more time to instruction with a longer school day and year and improving teacher preparation.

1989: NATIONAL EDUCATION SUMMIT

In 1989 President George H. W. Bush and the nation's governors held an Education Summit conference and established six goals to address the issues raised in *A Nation at Risk.* Bill Clinton, then governor of Arkansas, attended the conference. The report they issued emphasized developing standards that would increase student performance by the year 2000, including being first in the world in science and mathematics achievement, which could be measured on the international comparison Trends in International Mathematics and Science Study (TIMSS) test. Two groups were established to implement the new educational goals: the National Education Goals Panel (NEGP) and the National Council on Education Standards and Testing (NCEST). Later Congress adopted eight educational goals and provided funding for the development of standards in each of the major academic disciplines.

1989: NCTM STANDARDS

In 1989 the National Council of Teachers of Mathematics (NCTM) released its *Curriculum and Evaluation Standards for School Mathematics*. The NCTM standards were a first attempt by a professional organization to develop standards and expectations for educators. They identified what students should understand and be able to do mathematically at different benchmarks. The math standards included number and operations, algebra, geometry, measurement, data analysis and probability, problem solving, reasoning and proof, communication, connections, and representation. NCTM followed the content standards with *Professional Standards for Teaching Mathematics* (1991) and *Assessment Standards for School Mathematics* (1995) and subsequently revised the 1989 standards with a 2000 edition of *Principles and Standards for School Mathematics*. These standards were written for different grade spans: preK–2, 3–5, 6–8, and 9–12. In 2006, NCTM published *Curriculum Focal Points*, which articulated the concepts and skills in each of the mathematics topics to be addressed at each grade level.

The NCTM standards were the first of the professional organization standards and had a tremendous impact on the creation of state mathematics standards, as well as standards in other disciplines. Educational materials reflected both state standards and the NCTM standards.

1991: THE SCANS REPORT

In 1991 the Secretary's Commission on Achieving Necessary Skills (SCANS), appointed by the Secretary of Labor, issued a report that identified the skills people need to succeed in the working world. Its purpose was to help educators understand how curriculum and instruction should change to ensure that these skills were addressed. The skills included basic skills (reading, writing, arithmetic, listening, speaking), thinking skills (creative thinking, decision making, problem solving, and seeing things in the mind's eye, knowing how to learn, and reasoning), and personal qualities (responsibility, self-esteem, sociability, self-management, and integrity/honesty). It also outlined five workplace competencies: managing resources, working with others, acquiring and using information, understanding complex systems, and technology (Secretary's Commission on Achieving Necessary Skills 1991). After the SCANS report these skills began appearing in state standards, and subsequently, educational materials.

1993: *BENCHMARKS FOR SCIENCE LITERACY,* PROJECT 2061

In 1993 the American Association for the Advancement of Science published a set of standards, which included the nature of science, mathematics, and technology; the physical setting, the living environment, the human organism, human society, the designed world, the mathematical world, human perspectives, common themes, and habits of mind (American Association for the Advancement of Science 1993). These standards were in the grade spans K–2, 3–5, 6–8, and 9–12. *Benchmarks* was a comprehensive, authoritative set of standards, including science, technology, engineering, and mathematics (STEM) and became a resource for state standards committees.

1994: GOALS 2000

In 1994 President Clinton signed the Goals 2000: Educate America Act. This act was intended to advance national education standards and assessments and spurred subject matter organizations to establish standards in their disciplines. Many organizations used the NCTM standards as a guideline. Goals 2000 created a council to certify national and state content and performance standards and state assessments. Because the goals focused on improving student achievement in challenging subject matter, it was imperative that the knowledge, skills, and understandings were identified. Only one set of content standards was certified in each subject area. Many sets of standards, funded by the Department of Education, followed this legislation. All of these standards, however, were voluntary and served only as references to state departments of education.

1994: NATIONAL STANDARDS FOR CIVICS AND GOVERNMENT

The *National Standards for Civics and Government* were developed in 1994 for grade spans K–4, 6–8, and 9–12. They involve such questions as, what is government and what should it do; what are the basic values, foundations, and principles of American democracy; how does the government embody

American democracy; what is the relationship of the United States to other nations; and what are the roles of citizens in American democracy (Center for Civic Education 1994).

1994: NATIONAL GEOGRAPHY STANDARDS

The National Council for Geographic Education published *Geography for Life: National Geography Standards* in 1994. These standards include eighteen national standards and six essential elements: the world in spatial terms, places and regions, physical systems, human systems, environment and society, and the uses of geography (National Council for Geographic Education 1994).

1994: NATIONAL STANDARDS FOR ARTS EDUCATION

The Consortium of National Arts Education Associations developed the national arts standards that included the review of state-level arts education frameworks, international standards, and national forums. The standards were developed in spans K–4, 5–8, and 9–12 and cover visual arts, dance, music, and theater. Each discipline includes standards for creating, evaluating, using and understanding techniques, history and culture, and connections among the arts and other disciplines (Consortium of National Arts Education Associations 1994).

1996: READING STANDARDS

The Standards Project for the English Language Arts (SPELA) was codirected by the International Reading Association (IRA), the National Council of Teachers of English (NCTE), and the Center for the Study of Reading at the University of Illinois. The standards took four years to develop and were widely reviewed. They include twelve standards relating to a wide range of reading and literature strategies, listening, speaking, visual skills, writing, language convention, using resources, using technology, and English language learning (International Reading Association and National Council of Teachers of English 1996).

1996: NATIONAL SCIENCE EDUCATION STANDARDS

In 1996 the *National Science Education Standards* were published. The National Research Council relied heavily on *Benchmarks*, Project 2061 in drafting its science content standards. They included content standards, professional standards, and assessment standards. These standards were produced by the National Research Council and were the result of four years of work by twenty-two scientific and science education societies and over eighteen thousand individual contributors. The content standards included unifying concepts and processes in science; science as inquiry; physical, life, earth, and space science; science and technology; science in personal and social perspectives; and the history and nature of science (National Research Council 1996).

1996: NATIONAL STANDARDS FOR HISTORY

Under the guidance of the National Council for History Standards, the National Center for History in the Schools published the *National Standards for History Basic Edition* in 1996. The standards covered the spans K–4 and 5–12 and included chronological thinking, historical comprehension, historical analysis and interpretation, research capabilities, and issues analysis and decision making. They also included topics for K–4 involving living and working together in families and communities, now and long ago; state and regional history; US history; and the history of peoples of many cultures around the world. For the 5–8 span the standards involved US and world history (National Center for History in the Schools 1996).

1996: STANDARDS FOR FOREIGN LANGUAGE LEARNING

First published in 1996 the *Standards for Foreign Language Learning: Preparing for the 21st Century* represented a consensus among business leaders, educators, government, and the community on the role of foreign language instruction. The standards for benchmark grades 4, 8, and 12 involved the five Cs: communication, connections, comparisons, communities, and cultures (American Council on the Teaching of Foreign Languages 1996).

1997: NATIONAL CONTENT STANDARDS IN ECONOMICS

The Council for Economic Education published the *Voluntary National Content Standards in Economics* in 1997. There were twenty economics content standards, each an essential principle of economics that economically literate students should know and be able to do at grades 4, 8, and 12. A second edition was published in 2010. The standards include concepts of scarcity, decision making, allocation, incentives, trade, specialization, markets and prices, role of prices, competition and market structure, institutions, money and inflation, interest rates, income, entrepreneurship, economic growth, role of government and market failure, government failure, economic fluctuations, unemployment and inflation, and fiscal and monetary policy (Council for Economic Education 2010).

1997: NATIONAL STANDARDS FOR PHYSICAL EDUCATION

Moving into the Future: National Standards for Physical Education was originally published in 1997 and now appears in a second edition. The standards include competency in motor skills, understanding of movement concepts as they apply to physical activities, participation in physical activity, health, responsibility, and values of physical activity (American Alliance for Health, Physical Education, Recreation and Dance 1997).

1998: TECHNOLOGY FOUNDATION STANDARDS FOR STUDENTS

In 1998 the *National Educational Technology Standards for Students* (NETS) was published by the International Society for Technology in Education (ISTE) and came to be known as the ISTE/NETS. These standards included basic operations and concepts; social, ethical and human issues; and technology productivity, communications, research, problem-solving and decision-making tools. The standards were revised in 2007 to include standards for creativity and innovation, communication and collaboration, research and information fluency, critical thinking, problem solving and decision making, digital citizenship, and technology operations and concepts (International Society for Technology in Education 1998).

2002: NO CHILD LEFT BEHIND (NCLB) REAUTHORIZATION OF THE FEDERAL ELEMENTARY AND SECONDARY EDUCATION ACT (ESEA)

In January 2002, President George W. Bush signed the No Child Left Behind Act into law. It contained the most sweeping changes to the ESEA since it was first enacted in 1965. There were four pillars of NCLB: stronger accountability for results, more freedom for states and communities, proven education methods, and more choices for parents. As a result of NCLB, all fifty states had to submit state education standards for approval and make accommodations for testing to ensure that schools made adequate yearly progress. NCLB also put emphasis on incorporating practices and programs that had been proven effective through rigorous scientific research. NCLB launched another round of state standards writing and test creation (US Department of Education 2002).

2004: 21ST CENTURY SKILLS

In 2004 the Partnership for 21st Century Skills launched the Framework for 21st Century Learning. The partnership is a national organization that advocates for twenty-first-century readiness, providing tools and resources to promote student achievement by promoting the academic subjects with critical thinking, problem solving, communication, collaboration, creativity, and innovation. Founded in 2002 by the US Department of Education and several large corporations, fifteen states have developed 21st Century Learning initiatives and leading educational companies, including the major publishers, have become members of the partnership. The 21st Century Skills include learning and innovation skills (critical thinking, communication collaboration, creativity); life and career skills; information, media and technology skills; and core subjects with twenty-first-century themes (Partnership for 21st Century Skills 2009). The 21st Century Skills are now reflected in many state standards and curriculum.

2010: COMMON CORE STATE STANDARDS INITIATIVE

The debate between local and federal control of schools has been waged since the earliest days of public education in America. In the last thirty years the debate intensified as national organizations took on the task of creating voluntary standards and then states re-created their standards to comply with No Child Left Behind. Throughout the nineteenth and twentieth centuries it was up to the states to create their own standards.

Other countries, including England, Japan, and China, have national standards and most countries include their national standards in their curriculum guides. Some countries have a national curriculum for all schools to follow. In the United States the idea of national standards, let alone a national curriculum, has been hotly debated.

National Standards—not federal standards—managed by the federal government—are a necessity in an advanced society operating in a highly interdependent, competitive global economy. The United States is one nation, not fifty independent states. It makes little sense for each state to have markedly different standards in mathematics, science, English, and other important subjects. . . . In the most important subjects, schools throughout the country use textbooks that are so similar in content as to be indistinguishable from each other. The same is true of tests. This informal national curriculum is usually geared to minimal competencies, and expectations about what students should learn are consistently low and unchallenging. (Ravitch 1995)

In 2010, the Common Core State Standards initiative, a state-led effort coordinated by the National Governors Association Center for Best Practices and the Council of Chief State School Officers, developed a set of standards for English and mathematics. Content experts, educators, students, and civic organizations developed the standards. The development team reviewed standards from states, professional organizations, and countries around the world. They were opened for public comment and garnered over ten thousand responses. The Common Core Standards are voluntary, but by 2011, forty-two states had formally adopted them to replace their own English/reading/language arts and mathematics standards (Council of Chief State School Officers and the National Governors Association 2010). New assessments will be created to align with the Common Core Standards.

References

AAP School Division. "AAP School Division Adoption Schedule." American Association of Publishers, 2009.

Aarons, Dakarai I. "Effect of Common Standards on Publishers Uncertain." *Education Week*, January 14, 2010.

Achievement Gap Initiative at Harvard University. "How High Schools Become Exemplary 2009 Conference Report." The Achievement Gap Initiative, Harvard University, 2009.

Adams, Marilyn Jager. *Beginning to Read: Thinking and Learning about Print*. The MIT Press, 1994.

Adkins, Sam S. "Ambient Insight Comprehensive Report: The US Market for Self-paced eLearning Products and Services: 2010–2015 Forecast and Analysis." Ambient Insight, 2011.

Altbach, Phillip G., Gail P. Kelly, Hugh G. Petrie, and Lois Weis, eds. *Textbooks in American Society: Politics, Policy, and Pedagogy*. Albany, NY: State University of New York, 1991.

American Alliance for Health, Physical Education, Recreation and Dance. *Moving into the Future: National Standards for Physical Education*. 1997.

American Association for the Advancement of Science. Project 2061. *Benchmarks for Science Literacy*. New York: Oxford University Press, 1993.

American Association of Colleges for Teacher Education. "Teacher Performance Assessment Consortium." AACTE, 2011. http://www.aacte.org/index.php?/Programs/Teacher-Performance-Assessment-Consortium-TPAC/teacher-performance-assessment-consortium.html (accessed 2011).

American Council on the Teaching of Foreign Languages. *Standards for Foreign Language Learning: Preparing for the 21st Century*. 1996.

American Educator. "Common Core Curriculum: An Idea Whose Time Has Come." *American Educator*, Winter 2011.

Arizona Department of Education. "Arizona Academic Standards Science Grade 4." 2009. http://www.azed.gov/standards-practices/science-standard/ (accessed 2011).

Ball, Deborah Loewenberg. "What Mathematical Knowledge Is Needed for Teaching Mathematics?" Secretary's Summit on Mathematics. US Department of Education, 2003.

Ball, Deborah Loewenberg, and David Cohen. "Reform by the Book: What Is—or Might Be—the Role of Curriculum Materials in Teacher Learning and Instructional Reform?" *Educational Researcher* 25 (December 1996).

Bereiter, Carl, and Marlene Scardamalia. *Surpassing Ourselves: An Inquiry into the Nature and Implications of Expertise.* Open Court, 1993.

Bess, Jennifer. "Technology Not Always the Best Teaching Tool." *Centre Daily Times*, March 9, 2011.

Bruner, Jerome. *The Process of Education.* Cambridge, MA: Harvard University Press, 1977.

Bureau of Labor Statistics. "Occupational Outlook Handbook, 2010–11 Edition; Teachers–Kindergarten, Elementary, Middle and Secondary." US Department of Labor. 2010. http://www.bls.gov/oco/ocos318.htm (accessed 2011).

Burger, Edward B., et al. *Holt McDougal Algebra 1.* Holt McDougal Hougton Mifflin Harcourt, 2011.

Carmichael, Sheila Byrd, Martino Gabrielle, Kathleen Porter-Magee, and W. Stephen Wilson. *The State of State Standards—and the Common Core—in 2010.* Thomas B. Fordham Institute, 2010.

Center for Civic Education. *National Standards for Civics and Government.* 1994.

Center for Research in Math and Science Education. "Breaking the Cycle: An International Comparison of U.S. Mathematics Teacher Preparation." Michigan State University, 2010.

Center on Education Policy. *A Public Education Primer: Basic (and Sometimes Surprising) Facts about the U.S. Education System.* Washington, DC: Center on Education Policy, 2006.

———. *How Many Schools and Districts Have Not Made Adequate Yearly Progress? Four-Year Trends.* Center on Education Policy, 2010.

Chall, Jeanne. *The Academic Achievement Challenge: What Really Works in the Classroom?* New York: Guilford Press, 2000.

Clements, Douglas H., and Julie Sarama. *Learning and Teaching Early Math: The Learning Trajectories Approach.* Routledge, 2009a.

———. "Learning Trajectories in Early Mathematics—Sequences of Acquisition and Teaching," 1–7. London, ON: Canadian Language and Literacy Research Network, 2009b.

Coggshal, Jane G., Amber Ott, and Molly Lasanga. "Retaining Teacher Talent: Convergence and Contradictions in Teachers' Perceptions of Policy Reform Ideas." Learning Point Associates and Public Agenda, 2010.

Collins, Allan, and Richard Halverson. *Rethinking Education in the Age of Technology: The Digital Revolution and Schooling in America.* New York: Teachers College Press, 2009.

Committee on Science Learning, Kindergarten Through Eighth Grade. *Taking Science to School.* Edited by Richard A. Duschel, Heidi A. Schweingruber and Andrew W. Shouse. Washington, DC: National Academies Press, 2007.

Common Core State Standards Initiative. "Common Core State Standards for English Language Arts and Literacy in History/Social Studies, Science, and Technical Subjects." 2010a. http://www.corestandards.org/the-standards.

———. "Common Core State Standards Initiative Standards-Setting Considerations." 2010b. http://www.corestandards.org/assets/Considerations.pdf (accessed 2011).

Consortium of National Arts Education Associations. *National Standards for Arts Education: Dance, Music, Theatre, Visual Arts.* 1994.

Corcoran, Tom, Federic A. Mosher, and Aaron Rogat. *Learning Progressions in Science: An Evidence-based Approach to Reform.* Center on Continuous Instructional Improvement, Teacher's College, Columbia University, Consortium for Policy Research in Education, 2009.

Council for Economic Education. *Voluntary National Content Standards in Economics.* 2010.

Council of Chief State School Officers and the National Governors Association. Common Core State Standards Initiative. 2010. http://www.corestandards.org/ (accessed 2011).

Cuban, Larry. *Oversold and Underused: Computers in the Classroom.* Harvard University Press, 2001.

———. "A 'Naked Truth' about Technologies in Schools?" January 6, 2010. http://larrycuban.wordpress.com/2010/01/06/a-naked-truth-about-technologies-in-schools/ (accessed 2011).

———. "Computer Use in a High School (1999–2010): Progress or Regress?" February 18, 2011. http://larrycuban.wordpress.com/2011/02/18/computer-use-in-a-high-school-1999-2010-progress-or-regress/ (accessed 2011).

Danitz, Tiffany. "The Standards Revolution in U.S. Schools." *Phi Delta Kappan* 76, no. 10 (June 1995).

Daro, Phil, Frederic A. Mosher, and Tom Corcoran. *Learning Trajectories in Mathematics: A Foundation for Standards, Curriculum, Assessment, and Instruction.* Consortium for Policy Research in Education, 2011.

Desimone, Laura M. "A Primer on Effective Professional Development." *Kappan,* March 2011.

Dillon, Sam. "4,100 Students Prove 'Small Is Better' Rule Wrong." *New York Times,* September 27, 2010.

Dockterman, David A. *Great Teaching in the One Computer Classroom.* Tom Snyder Productions, 1997.

Dolciani, Mary P., Simon L. Berman, and Julius Freilich. *Modern Algebra: Structure and Method.* Boston: Houghton Mifflin Company, 1965.

Donovan, Carol A., and Laura B. Smolkin. "Supporting Informational Writing in the Elementary Grades." *Reading Teacher* 64, no. 6 (March 2011).

Duncan, Arne. "Arne Duncan, U.S. Secretary of Education, Delivers Remarks at the State Educational Technology Directors Association Education Forum." State Educational Technology Directors Association Education Forum. US Department of Education, 2010.

Eakin, Sybil. "Giants of American Education: Horace Mann." *Technos Quarterly* 9, no. 2 (Summer 2000).

Edelfelt, Roy A., and James D. Raths. *A Brief History of Standards in Teacher Education*. Association of Teacher Educators, 1998.

Educational Research Analysts. "Emphasis on Mastery of Basic Addition, Subtraction, Multiplication and Division Facts in 3rd Grade Math Texts Submitted for 1999 Texas Adoption." Chart. 1999. http://www.textbookreviews.org/ (accessed 2010).

Elliott, David L., ed. *Textbooks and Schooling in the United States (89th Yearbook of the National Society for the Study of Education)*. Chicago: National Society for the Study of Education, 1990.

Engler, Natalie. "Distance Learning in the Digital Age." In *The Digital Classroom: How Technology Is Changing the Way We Teach and Learn*, edited by David T. Gordon. Harvard Education Press, 2000.

Fine, Benjamin. "Education in Review: One-Third Increase in Public School Enrollment Foreseen by New Federal Commissioner." *New York Times*, April 10, 1949.

Finn, Chester E., Jr., Liam Julian, and Michael J. Petrilli. *2006 The State of State Standards*. Washington, DC: Thomas B. Fordham Foundation, 2006.

Finn, Chester E., Jr., and Michael J. Petrilli. "Now What? Imperatives and Options for 'Common Core' Implementation and Governance." Thomas B. Fordham Institute, 2010.

Fletcher, Dan. "Brief History, Standardized Testing." *Time*, December 11, 2009.

Florida Department of Education. "Next Generation Sunshine State Standards." Florida Department of Education. September 2007. http://www.floridastandards .org/Standards/FLStandardSearch.aspx (accessed 2011).

Fulp, Sherri L. "Status of Elementary School Science Teaching." 2000 National Survey of Science and Mathematics Education, 2002.

Gates, Bill. "How Teacher Development Could Revolutionize Schools." *Washington Post*, February 28, 2011.

Geiger, John, interview by Beverlee Jobrack. President, Tracermedia Interactive (August 19, 2010).

Glennan, Thomas K., and Arthur Melmed. "Fostering the Use of Educational Technology: Elements of a National Strategy." The Rand Corporation, 1996.

Goals 3 and 4 Technical Planning Group. "Promises to Keep: Creating High Standards for American Students." 1993.

Goldberg, Amie, Michael Russell, and Abigail Cook. "Meta-Analysis Writing with Computers 1992–2002." Technology and Assessment Study Collaborative, Boston College, 2002.

Gordon, Dan. "Wow! 3D Content Awakens the Classroom." *THE Journal*, October 2010.

Gray, Lucinda, Nina Thomas, Laurie Lewis, and Tice Peter. "Educational Technology in U.S. Public Schools: Fall 2008." IES National Center for Education Statistics, US Department of Education, 2010.

Green, Elizabeth. "Building a Better Teacher." *New York Times Magazine*, March 2, 2010.

Griffin, Sharon. "Teaching Number Sense." *Educational Leadership*, February 2004: 39–42.

Grossman, Pam, and Clarissa Thompson. "Curriculum Materials: Scaffolds for New Teacher Learning?" Center for the Study of Teaching and Policy, University of Washington, 2004.

Grossman, P. L., S. W. Valencia, K. Evans, C. Thompson, S. Martin, and N. Place. "Transitions into Teaching: Learning to Teach Writing in Teacher Education and Beyond." *Journal of Literacy Research* 32 (2000): 631–62.

Gugliotta, Guy. "Up in Arms About the American Experience; History Curriculum Guidelines Play Down Traditional Heroes and Focus on Negatives, Critcs Say." *Washington Post*, October 28, 1994, A.03.

Hakel, Milton D., Judith Anderson Koenig, and Stuart W. Elliott. *Assessing Accomplished Teaching: Advanced-Level Certification Programs*. Washington DC: National Academies Press, 2008.

Hefley, James C. *Textbooks on Trial*. Wheaton, IL: Victor Books, 1976.

Henderson, Edmund. *Learning to Read and Spell: The Child's Knowledge of Word*. Northern Illinois University Press, 1981.

Hoffer, Peter Charles. *The Brave New World: A History of Early America*. Baltimore: Johns Hopkins University Press, 2006.

Houghton Mifflin Harcourt. "About Us." 2010. http://www.hmhco.com/around-the -world.html.

Hunter, Madeline. "Madeline Huner Method." Edutech Wiki, May 2007. http:// edutechwiki.com (accessed February 28, 2010).

IES National Center for Education Statistics. "The Condition of Education Learner Outcomes." US Department of Education Institute of Education Sciences, 2008. http://nces.ed.gov/programs/coe/ (accessed 2011).

International Reading Association and National Council of Teachers of English. *Standards for the English Language Arts*. 1996.

International Society for Technology in Education. *National Educational Technology Standards for Students*. 1998.

Jacobs, Joanne. "It Takes a Vision: How Three States Created Great Academic Standards." In *The State of State Standards, 2006* edited by Chester E. Finn Jr., Liam Julian, and Michael J. Petrilli. Washington, DC: Thomas B. Fordham Foundation, 2006.

Jaquith, Ann, Dan Mindich, Ruth Chung Wi, and Linda Darling-Hammond. *Teacher Professional Learning in the United States: State Policies and Strategies Technical Report*. Learning Forward and the Stanford Center for Opportunity Policy in Education, 2010.

Jefferson, Thomas. *The Works of Thomas Jefferson: Notes on Virginia II, Correspondence 1782–1786*. Edited by Paul Leicester Ford. New York and London: G.P. Putnam's Sons, 1904–1905.

Jewett, Thomas. "Jefferson, Education and the Franchise." *Early America Review*, Winter 1996.

Johnson, L., R. Smith, A. Levine, and K. Haywood. *2010 Horizon Report: K–12 Edition*. Austin, TX: The New Media Consortium, 2010.

Kame'enui, Edward J., and Deborah C. Simmons. *Planning and Evaluation Tool for Effective Schoolwide Reading Programs*. Institute for the Development of Educational Achievement College of Education, University of Oregon, Eugene, 2000.

Kawasaki, Guy. Interview by Big Think. "The Secret to Apple's Success" (March 7, 2011).

King, Jennifer B. "Use of Integrated Learning Systems (ILS) to Enhance the Proficiency of Poor Readers in Middle School." University of South Florida, 2000.

Kleiman, Glenn. "Myths and Realities about Technology in K–12 Schools." In *The Digital Classroom*, edited by David T. Gordon. Cambridge, MA: Harvard Education Letter, 2000.

Legler, Ray. *Alternative Certification: A Review of Theory and Research*. North Central Regional Educational Laboratory, Learning Point Associates, 2002.

Lemov, Doug. *Teach like a Champion*. Jossey-Bass Teacher, 2010.

Levine, Arthur. "Educating School Teachers." The Education Schools Project, 2006.

———. "Don't Give Up on Universities." *Inside Higher ED*, April 26, 2010.

Lewis, Anne C. "An Overview of the Standards Movement." *Phi Delta Kappan*, June 1995.

Loveless, Tom. *The 2008 Brown Center Report on American Education: How Well Are American Students Learning*. Washington, DC: The Brookings Institution, 2008.

———. *The 2009 Brown Center Report on American Education: How Well Are American Students Learning?* Washington, DC: Brookings Institution, 2010.

Lussenhop, Jessica. "Oregon Trail: How Three Minnesotans Forged Its Path." *City Pages News*, January 19, 2011.

Makofsky, Nina. "About Vintage Chalkboards." eHow, 2011. http://www.ehow.com/about_4672284_vintage-chalkboards.html.

Marzano, Robert J. *What Works in Schools: Translating Research into Action*. Alexandria, VA: Association for Supervision and Curriculum Development, 2003.

Marzano, Robert J., and John S. Kendall. "The Fall and Rise of Standards-Based Education." NASBE. September 26, 1997. http://www.mcrel.org/PDF/Standards/5962IR_FallAndRise.pdf (accessed February 13, 2011).

"Mathematically Correct Second Grade Mathematics Review." 2000. http://mathematicallycorrect.com/books2e.htm (accessed 2010).

McCollister, Betty. "A Conspiracy of Good Intentions: America's Textbook Fiasco." *The Humanist*, November–December 1993.

McColskey, Wendy, et al. "Teacher Effectiveness, Student Achievement and National Board Certified Teachers." Prepared for the National Board for Professional Teaching Standards, 2006.

McGraw-Hill Books Catalog. *1956 McGraw-Hill Books*. New York: McGraw-Hill, 1956.

McGraw-Hill Companies. "About Us." 2010. http://www.mcgraw-hill.com/site/about-us.

Metiri Group. "Technology in the Schools: What the Reseach Says." 2006.

MetLife. *The MetLife Survey of The American Teacher: Collaborating for Student Success*. MetLife, 2009.

———. *The MetLife Survey of The American Teacher: Preparing Students for College and Careers*. MetLife, 2010.

Meyer, Dan. "Math Class Needs a Makeover." TED: Ideas Worth Spreading, 2010.

Nagel, David. "Foundations Look to Advance Common Core Curriculum." *THE Journal*, April 27, 2011.

National Academy of Sciences. *National Science Education Standards*. National Research Council, 1996.

National Assessment of Educational Progress. *The Nation's Report Card: NAEP 2008 Trends in Academic Progress*. US Department of Education, 2009.

National Board for Professional Teaching Standards. "The Five Core Propositions." NBPTS. 2011. http://www.nbpts.org/about_us/mission_and_history/the_five_core_propositio.

National Center for Higher Education Management Systems. "Public High School Graduation Rates." 2006. http://www.higheredinfo.org/dbrowser/index.php?sub measure36&year2006&levelnation&modedata&state0 (accessed 2010).

National Center for History in the Schools. *National Standards for History Basic Edition*. National Center for History in the Schools, 1996.

National Commission on Excellence in Education. *A Nation at Risk: The Imperative for Educational Reform*. 1983.

National Council for Geographic Education. *Geography for Life: National Geography Standards*. Washington, DC: National Geographic Society Committee on Research and Exploration, 1994.

National Council of Teachers of Mathematics. *Principles and Standards for School Mathematics*. Reston, VA: National Council of Teachers of Mathematics, 2000.

National Education Goals Panel. *The National Education Goals Report: Building a Nation of Learners*. Washington, DC: National Education Goals Panel, 1991.

National Education Standards Improvement Council. *Promises to Keep: Creating High Standards for American Students*. Washington, DC: National Goals Panel, 1993.

National Institute for Literacy. "Put Reading First." Government Report, 2001.

National Research Council. *National Science Education Standards*. Washington, DC: National Academy Press, 1996.

National Staff Development Council. "NSDC's Standards for Staff Development." Learning Forward, 2001. http://www.learningforward.org/standards/index.cfm (accessed 2011).

NCATE. "Unit Standards in Effect 2008." NCATE, 2008. http://ncate.org/Standards/ NCATEUnitStandards/UnitStandardsinEffect2008/tabid/476/Default.aspx (accessed 2011).

———. "NCATE and TEAC Form New Accrediting Body: The Council for the Accreditation of Educator Preparation (CAEP)." NCATE, October 25, 2010. http://www.ncate.org/Public/Newsroom/NCATENewsPressReleases/tabid/669/ EntryId/121/NCATE-and-TEAC-Form-New-Accrediting-Body-The-Council-for -the-Accreditation-of-Educator-Preparation-CAEP.aspx (accessed 2011).

New Jersey Department of Education. "New Jersey Core Curriculum Content Standards." New Jersey Department of Education, 2004.

New York Times. February 7, 1997, A20.

Ohio State University. "School of Teaching and Learning Master of Education (M.ED.) in Middle Childhood Education." 2011. http://ehe.osu.edu/edtl/academics/ med/mce/.

Olsen, Stefanie. "Educational Video Games Mix Cool with Purpose." *New York Times*, November 1, 2009.

Organisation for Economic Co-operation and Development (OECD). "PISA: The Programme for International Student Assessment 2006." OECD, 2006.

———. "PISA 2009 Results: What Students Know and Can Do: Student Performance in Reading, Mathematics, and Science." OECD, 2010.

Oseas, Andrea. "Introduction: An Invitation to Ask: 'What if . . .?'" In *The Digital Classroom*, edited by David T. Gordon. Cambridge, MA: Harvard Education Letter, 2000.

Paine, Steven L., and Andreas Schleicher. "What the U.S. Can Learn from the World's Most Successful Education Reform Efforts." McGraw-Hill Research Foundation, 2011.

Parker, Kathleen. "A Sprig of Verbena and the Gifts of a Great Teacher." *Washington Post*, April 14, 2010.

Partnership for 21st Century Skills. "Framework for 21st Century Learning." P21 Framework Definitions. 2009. http://www.p21.org/index.php?optioncom_content &taskview&id254&Itemid120 (accessed 2011).

Partnership for 21st Century Skills and AACTE. "21st Century Knowledge and Skills in Educator Preparation." Partnership for 21st Century Skills and AACTE, 2010.

Pashler, Harold, Mark McDaniel, Dough Rohrer, and Robert Bjork. "Learning Syles: Concepts and Evidence." Department of Psychology, University of California, San Diego, 2010.

Pearson Education. "History." 2010. http://www.pearson.com/about-us/our-history/ (accessed 2010).

Pflaum, William D. *The Technology Fix*. Alexandria, VA: Association for Supervision and Curriculum Development, 2004.

Pink, Daniel. *Drive: The Surprising Truth about What Motivates Us*. New York: Riverside Books, 2009.

Progress of Education Reform. *The Progress of Education Reform*. Denver, CO: Education Commission of the States, 1996.

Ravitch, Diane. *National Standards in American Education: A Citizen's Guide*. Washington, DC: Brookings Institution, 1995.

———. *Left Back: A Century of Battles over School Reform*. Touchstone, 2000.

———. "A Brief History of Teacher Professionalism." US Department of Education, 2002. http://www2.ed.gov/admins/tchrqual/learn/preparingteachersconference/ ravitch.html (accessed 2011).

———. *The Language Police: How Pressure Groups Restrict What Students Learn*. Knopf, 2003.

———. "Every State Left Behind." *New York Times*, November 7, 2005.

———. *The Death and Life of the Great American School System*. Basic Books, 2010.

Riener, Cedar. "Learning Styles: What's Being Debunked." *Teacher Magazine*, February 24, 2010.

Saperstein, Martin. Editorial Conference. McGraw-Hill, 2000.

Schmidt, William H., Leland S. Cogan, and Curtis C. McKnight. "Equality of Educational Opportunity: Myth or Reality in U.S. Schooling." *American Educator*, Winter 2011.

Schmoker, Michael J. *How We Can Achieve Unprecedented Improvements in Teaching and Learning*. Alexandria, VA: Association for Supervision and Curriculum Development, 2006.

Scholastic and the Bill & Melinda Gates Foundation. "Primary Sources: America's Teachers on America's Schools." Scholastic and The Bill & Melinda Gates Foundation, 2010.

Secretary's Commission on Achieving Necessary Skills. *What Work Requires of Schools: A SCANS Report for America 2000*. US Department of Labor, 1991.

———. *Learning a Living: A Blueprint for High Performance: A SCANS Report for America 2000*. US Department of Labor, 1992.

Senechal, Diana. "The Spark of Specifics: How a Strong Curriculum Enlivens Classroom and School Culture." *American Educator*, Winter 2011.

Sewall, Gilbert T. "Digital Textbooks: They're Coming, But Will They Be Better?" *Education Week*, April 7, 2010.

Shorto, Russell. "How Christian Were the Founders?" *New York Times Magazine*, February 14, 2010.

Spear-Swerling, Louise, and Robert J. Sternberg. *Off Track: When Poor Readers Become "Learning Disabled."* Boulder, CO: Westview Press, 1996.

Springer, Matthew G., et al. "Teacher Pay for Performance: Experimental Evidence from the Project on Incentives in Teaching." National Center on Performance Incentives, Vanderbilt University, 2010.

Stansbury, Meris. "Study Questions Learning-Style Research." *eSchool News*, January 8, 2010.

Starkey, James D. "Attention, Gates: Here's What Makes a Great Teacher." *Education Week*, February 3, 2010: 24.

Steinberg, Matthew P., Elaine Allensworth, and David W. Johnson. "Student and Teacher Safety in Chicago Public Schools: The Roles of Community Context and School Social Organization." Chicago School Research at the University of Chicago Urban Education Institute, 2011.

Stern, Sheldon M., and Jeremy A. Stern. *The State of State U.S. History Standards 2011*. The Fordham Institute, 2011.

Stigler, James W., and James Hiebert. *The Teaching Gap*. New York: The Free Press, 1999.

Stotsky, Sandra, and Peter Lang. *What's at Stake in the K–12 Standards Wars: A Primer for Educational Policy Makers*. Peter Lang, 2000.

Susanj, Nathan. "Are Laptops Helping Lower Merion Students Learn?" *Ardmore-Merion-Wynnewood Patch*, January 11, 2011.

Szachowicz, Sue. "School of Thought in Brockton, Mass." *Need to Know*. PBS. February 3, 2011.

"Technology Counts: Teachers & Technology." *Education Week* 30 (March 17, 2011): 20.

Texas State Board of Education. "Chapter 111. Texas Essential Knowledge and Skills for Mathematics." Texas Education Agency. August 1, 2006. http://ritter.tea.state.tx.us/rules/tac/chapter111/ch111a.html#111.13 (accessed 2011).

TN.GOV. Tennessee Government Curriculum Standards. 2011. http://www.tn.gov/education/ci/ss/index.shtml (accessed 2011).

Tomlinson, Carol. The Differentiated Classroom: Responding to the Needs of all Learners. Alexandria, VA: Association for Supervision and Curriculum Development, 1999.

Tyson-Bernstein, Harriet. *A Conspiracy of Good Intentions*. Washington, DC: Council for Basic Education, 1988.

US Department of Education. No Child Left Behind. 2002. http://www2.ed.gov/policy/elsec/leg/esea02/index.html (accessed 2011).

———. "Intervention: SRA Real Math Building Blocks PreK." July 23, 2007. http://ies.ed.gov/ncee/wwc/reports/early_ed/sra_prek/index.asp (accessed March 3, 2010).

———. "The Final Report of the National Mathematics Advisory Panel." Government Report, 2008.

———. "A Blueprint for Reform: The Reauthorization of the Elementary and Secondary Education Act." 2010a.

———. "National Education Technology Plan 2010: Transforming American Education Learning Powered by Technology." Office of Educational Technology, 2010b.

US Department of Labor. *Teaching the SCANS Competencies*. US Department of Labor, 1993.

Virginia, State of. "Virginia Constitution." Justia.com Laws and Regulations, 1971. http://law.justia.com/virginia/constitution/constitution.html#8S1.

Weber, Dave. "Tab for New Approach to Teaching Math? $200 Million: Educators Say Paying to Improve Math Education Is Essential, Despite Budget Cuts." *Orlando Sentinel*, February 15, 2010.

WestEd. *Teachers Who Learn, Kids Who Achieve*. WestEd, 2000.

Whitehurst, Grover J. "Research on Teacher Preparation and Professional Development." US Department of Education, 2002. http://www2.ed.gov/admins/tchrqual/learn/preparingteachersconference/whitehurst.html (accessed 2011).

———. "Don't Forget Curriculum." Brown Center Letters on Education #3. Brookings Institution, October 2009. http://www.brookings.edu/papers/2009/1014_curriculum_whitehurst.aspx.

Whiting, David. Interview by Beverlee Jobrack. Vice President, McGraw-Hill (February 12, 2010).

Whitman, David. *The Mad, Mad World of Textbook Adoption*. Washington DC: Thomas B. Fordham Institute, 2004.

Wiggins, Grant, and Jay McTighe. *Understanding by Design*. Alexandria, VA: Association of Supervision and Curriculum Development, 1998.

Wilson, Suzanne M., Robert E. Floden, and Joan Ferrini-Mundy. "Teacher Preparation Research: Current Knowledge, Gaps, and Recommendations." Center for the Study of Teaching and Policy, University of Washington, 2001.

Wiske, Stone. "A New Culture of Teaching for the 21st Century." In *The Digital Classroom*, edited by David T. Gordon. Harvard Education Press, 2000.

Wolpert-Gawron, Heather. "The Bunk of Debunking Learning Styles." *Teacher Magazine*, February 17, 2010.

Index